Law as Engineering

Law as Engineering

Thinking About What Lawyers Do

David Howarth

University of Cambridge, UK

Edward Elgar

Cheltenham, UK • Northampton, MA, USA

Published by
Edward Elgar Publishing Limited
The Lypiatts
15 Lansdown Road
Cheltenham
Glos GL50 2JA
UK

Edward Elgar Publishing, Inc.
William Pratt House
9 Dewey Court
Northampton
Massachusetts 01060
USA

A catalogue record for this book
is available from the British Library

Library of Congress Control Number: 2012947333

This book is available electronically in the ElgarOnline.com
Law Subject Collection, E-ISBN 978 0 85793 378 2

ISBN 978 0 85793 377 5 (cased)

Typeset by Servis Filmsetting Ltd, Stockport, Cheshire
Printed and bound by MPG Books Group, UK

Contents

Preface

This book might be described as an exercise in going too far. Its origins are in a seemingly innocent question raised by Jan Parker, the editor of the journal *Arts and Humanities in Higher Education*, namely, was the study of law in universities a proper topic for her journal – in other words, is law one of the humanities? In the course of trying to answer that question, in a form that turned into an article for the journal,[1] it occurred to me that law had far more in common with a discipline that most people would consider very distant from it, namely engineering. The initial comparison focused on two points: first, the fact that both disciplines were practical rather than theoretical, in the sense that their ultimate purpose was to change the state of the world rather than merely to understand it; and second, the similar relationship both had with other, more theoretical disciplines – that engineering drew upon mathematics and the natural sciences, but could not be reduced to those sciences, and law could draw upon history, linguistics, economics, sociology, psychology and political science (and, within limits, literature), but also could not be reduced to them.

My initial purpose was merely to make a point about these relationships between academic disciplines, and to indicate some of the consequences that might follow for legal research and education. It subsequently became clear, however, that the analogy between law and engineering could be pushed further and further, all the time yielding interesting insights. For example, it yields a surprisingly accurate answer, at least as a first cut, to the question 'what do lawyers do?' Most lawyers, most of the time, are engaged by clients to produce structures – especially contracts, but also statutes and even constitutions – that are intended to produce some desired effect. That is, of course, what engineers do. That insight in turn produces questions about how lawyers and engineers carry out their work, questions about the processes of design. Again the comparison proved useful, uncovering similarities that help in understanding both processes, but also points of difference that not only help in understanding in a different way but also suggest ways in which lawyers might learn from engineers (and perhaps

---

[1] 'Is Law a Humanity (Or Is It More Like Engineering)?' (2004) 3(1) Arts and Humanities in Higher Education 9–28.

vice versa). Furthermore, as this book attempts to show, comparing lawyers to engineers produces insights into how lawyers ought to behave, that is into legal ethics. Those insights come precisely at the point where the factual analogy between law and engineering breaks down, where lawyers do not presently behave as engineers behave, or at least where the two sets of ethical codes diverge. The comparison is apposite enough, however, that it can be used to suggest that lawyers ought to behave in ways which would make it more accurate than it presently is.

Usually, if one pushes an analogy further and further it ceases to be useful. Indeed, it starts to become unhelpful, and begins to look more like a literary device or a conceit than an analytical tool. The famous analogy between society and the human body is that kind of analogy. It might help us to understand that societies depend simultaneously on functional specialisation (just as the head has a different function from the legs, so the Civil Service is doing a job different from that of the railway industry) and on the interdependencies between those functions. Soon, however, the analogy loses its explanatory power and becomes unhelpful, or even irritating. Do we care, for example, what the societal equivalent is of the pancreas or the appendix? The law-as-engineering analogy, I would claim, goes a very long way before becoming useless or irritating. The very fact that we can still draw useful insights even where the comparison is not entirely accurate is an indication that the limits of this particular analogy might lie a long way from its origin.

Scott Boorman, whose help and encouragement with this project have been invaluable, suggests that there is a difference between 'tactical' and 'strategic' analogies – that the former help one to overcome an immediate problem in explanation, classification or communication, but take one no further, whereas the latter identify credible structural similarities between complex phenomena that help to organise what we know about them and so continue to yield insights when pressed further and further. Because a strategic analogy works at a structural level, it will work for many different kinds of example and using many different kinds of evidence. It will even work when the comparison indicates some divergence between the phenomena. Where divergence occurs inside an explanation that otherwise successfully reflects a high degree of overall structural similarity, divergence itself does its own explanatory work: in circumstances where an analogy usually holds, it is inherently interesting why in specific instances, it does not hold. Divergence outside structural similarity, in contrast, is just divergence, with nothing more to offer. My hope for law-as-engineering is that I might have stumbled across such a 'strategic' analogy.

Analogies, of course, have dangers, one of which is the temptation to refuse to recognise that they have broken down. Claiming that a lack of correspondence is merely an instructive divergence might amount to precisely that kind of self-deception. The problem is even greater for the type of analogy developed here, where we are not looking for simple point-to-point correspondences but for the ways in which collections of facts about one thing might be usefully compared to collections of facts about another. The only practical test, however, of whether an analogy has broken down is whether continuing to press it leads to a better understanding or a worse understanding of the subject matter – in other words, is the analogy still revealing more than it is concealing? Ultimately, that question is decided not by those who devise analogies but by those who use them.

Another possible way of characterising a 'strategic' analogy is that it never reaches its ultimate boundary – that every time one pushes it further, a new insight emerges. If that is correct, one could never definitively claim to have found one, because we could never know when the process of pushing the analogy further will cease to be fruitful. All that can be said at any one time is that the limits of an analogy have not yet been reached. If we think of strategic analogies in those terms, I can only say that it will be interesting to see where the limits of law-as-engineering will occur.

There are many other people, apart from Jan Parker and Scott Boorman, to thank for their help and encouragement in this project, too many perhaps to mention by name. I would, however, particularly pick out the members of the faculty of the University of Southampton Law School, who, with great forbearance, allowed me to use one of their annual Gabriele Ganz lectures, in which they might reasonably have expected me to talk from the perspective of a practising politician about the relationship between law and politics, instead to try out some of the ideas that have taken this project from the first article to where it now stands.[2]

I would also thank the various engineers whom I have bothered for information and enlightenment about engineering, and especially Nathan Crilly, whose guidance on engineering design processes helped fill in some large holes in my knowledge. Thanks also to all the lawyers, in particular the practising lawyers, conversations with whom have helped clarify my thinking about many aspects of current legal practice. In particular I would very much thank those who took the trouble to read previous drafts of the manuscript and to provide corrections to my factual mistakes and lively counter-arguments to my conclusions. They include Nicholas Aleksander, of Gibson Dunn, Mike Smyth, formerly of Clifford Chance, and Stephen Laws, formerly First Parliamentary Counsel. As both a lawyer and an

---

[2]   http://www.southampton.ac.uk/law/news/2008/10/23_the_thirteenth_gabrie
le_ganz_public_law_lecture.page.

academic sociologist, Scott Boorman deserves special mention for devoting an enormous amount of his own time to reading an earlier draft and for coming up with numerous suggestions for improvement, only a small number of which are properly acknowledged in the text.

None of the aforementioned is, of course, responsible for the errors that remain, and I am sure that each will disagree with at least some of the conclusions to which I have come.

1. Introduction

How should we characterise what lawyers do? The question has both a sociological component and an evaluative component. As a sociological question it asks what functions lawyers perform – what precisely would be lost if they did not exist? As an evaluative question, it consists of asking what good do lawyers do? Are they worth having, and if so, are some kinds of lawyers more worth having than others?

One of the dangers of inquiries of this kind is that there is a temptation to take the questions in the wrong order, to take the evaluative question first and to ask the sociological question only in the form of asking to what extent the real world meets the standards set by the ideal. For example, one might conceive of the role of lawyers as, in some form or other, to secure justice, and then to ask how far the legal profession provides that form of justice. One example of that procedure sets up an ideal of the 'lawyer-as-hero', the lawyer who fights injustice through the courts, taking on the rich and powerful to win cases for the poor and oppressed,[1] and then points out, unsurprisingly, that heroism is in practice in short supply. At its most extreme, one could follow Tony Kronman and set up an ideal lawyer as a lost figure from the past, in his case the ideal of the 'lawyer-statesman', a lawyer 'possessed of great practical wisdom and exceptional persuasive powers, devoted to the public good but keenly aware of the limitations of human beings and their political arrangements',[2] and then berate the present for not living up to that ideal.

Another danger is to frame both questions in terms of public opinion about lawyers. Lawyers, of course, are not very popular. In the USA, a leading political consultant used to advise his clients '[i]t's almost impossible to go too far in demonizing lawyers.'[3] He also remarked,

---

[1] Marvin Mindes and Alan Acock, 'Trickster, Hero, Helper: A Report on the Lawyer Image' (1982) 7 Law & Social Inquiry 177–233.

[2] *The Lost Lawyer: Failing Ideals of the Legal Profession* (Cambridge, MA: Harvard U.P., 1995) 12.

[3] Luntz Research Companies, *Language of the 21st Century* (Alexandra VA: Luntz Research Companies, 1997) at 128, cited in Marc Galanter, 'In the Winter of Our Discontent: Law, Anti-Law and Social Science' (2006) 2 Annual Review of

A good indicator of the depth of emotion Americans have regarding the current legal system is their utter disdain for the term personal injury lawyer. When asked what comes to mind when they hear the term 'personal injury lawyers,' Americans use words like . . . 'creeps,' 'bottom-feeders, 'overpaid,' and 'evil'.[4]

The USA might be an outlier, but lawyers' reputation is a cause of anxiety to them in many jurisdictions. Market research carried out in 2011 in 15 European countries and in Russia showed that a majority of respondents trusted lawyers 'not very much' or 'not at all'.[5] Admittedly lawyers scored much better than journalists, politicians, trade union leaders, advertisers, footballers, financial advisers, civil servants and car salesmen, and slightly better than international business, bankers and priests, but worse than the police and meteorologists, and much worse than doctors, nurses, teachers, airline pilots, firefighters, and farmers.[6] In England, although public opinion surveys generally find a majority of the public 'very' or 'fairly' satisfied with the way lawyers do their work, their ratings are very much lower than those of the medical professions and teachers.[7] One might characterise lawyers in the way public opinion does and ask what lawyers might do to improve their reputation. But public opinion about lawyers does not necessarily tell us much about what lawyers really do. Few of those offering an opinion will have had recent personal contact with a lawyer,[8] and portrayals of lawyers in the media and in fiction are unlikely accurately to reflect lawyers' work.

A third danger is to start with lawyers' characterisations of themselves. Lawyers have various theories of what they do, from the flattering (lawyer-as-hero), via the more modest (lawyer-as-helper, or limited purpose friend[9]) to the condemnatory (lawyer-as-hired gun, or trickster).[10]

Law and Social Sciences 1–16 at 10, and in Benjamin Barton, *The Law-Judge Bias in the American Legal Process* (Cambridge: Cambridge U.P., 2010) at 139.

[4]   Frank Luntz, *Republican Playbook* Part VIII 'Lawsuit Abuse Reform: A Commonsense Approach' http://www.politicalstrategy.org/archives/001205.php.

[5]   Readers Digest Trusted Brands Survey 2011 http://www.rdtrustedbrands.com/about.shtml.

[6]   Readers Digest Trusted Brands Survey 2011.

[7]   Ipsos Mori 1999–2004 http://www.ipsos-mori.com/researchpublications/researcharchive/14/Opinion-of-Professions-How-Well-Do-They-Do-Their-Jobs.aspx?view=wide.

[8]   We estimate in Chapter 2 that, in Britain, there is, as a maximum, about a 10 per cent chance of an individual using the services of a lawyer in a year on a single occasion, with the actual figure probably being much lower.

[9]   Mindes and Acock (1982) and Edward Dauer and Arthur Leff, 'The Lawyer as Friend' (1977) 86 Yale Law Journal 573–84.

[10]   E.g. Mindes and Acock (1982).

But these characterisations are not so much descriptions of what they do as engagements with evaluations others make, or evaluations lawyers think others make, about them.

In this book, the starting point for the enquiry is broadly sociological. The question we ask is a very simple one. What kind of work are lawyers engaged in? We ask that question both for lawyers who offer their services on the open market and for those who work for the state. We observe (see Chapter 2) that what most of them are doing most of the time is drawing up documents that are intended to have effects desired by their clients. In the private sector those documents might be contracts or company constitutions or wills or conveyances. In the public sector, lawyers might also be producing contracts, but they additionally generate drafts of regulations and statutes.

Most descriptions of law, popular and academic, assume that being a lawyer means being a litigator. It assumes that thinking about law means thinking about cases decided by courts and that the supreme position in the law is that of judge. But most of the time lawyers have nothing to do with courts. One might argue that the documents lawyers draw up anticipate what courts might say about them and that their effects flow because courts will enforce them. But on closer inspection even that claim has to be greatly qualified. Contracts and statutes are often drafted not as instructions to judges about enforcement but as plans for those affected by them to apply directly to themselves. Court enforcement is often seen not as a benefit the document might bring but as a disaster to be avoided. No doubt the possibility that a court might at some point declare a rule used in the document to be invalid is a danger to be taken into account, but even that is not by itself a knock-down argument against using the rule. Rules that are difficult to enforce have their own place in the panoply of rules lawyers might use.

The characterisation of lawyers that best fits what lawyers actually do is not hero, or statesman, or trickster, or hired gun – all of which in some way relate back to litigation – but engineer. Clients come to lawyers, as they come to engineers, with problems that they cannot solve themselves. The service both engineers and lawyers provide is the solving of those problems. But more than that, although both lawyers and engineers might solve clients' problems merely by offering advice and guidance, the central instrument for solving problems that both use is a device of some kind – usually a physical device in the case of engineers and a document in the case of lawyers, although, as we shall see, it is less the physical embodiment of a device that matters as how it alters the system within which it operates.

The lawyer-engineer comparison starts as a mere metaphor, as a literary figure of speech that uses a single point of comparison between otherwise different things to emphasise a particular point about the things being compared, but as one presses the comparison further it soon becomes clear that the analogies between law and engineering go deeper. Those analogies can be used to illuminate otherwise unexplored caves and tunnels of what lawyers do. For example, lawyers, like engineers, face the task of designing new useful devices. What processes do they go through to produce those devices? How does creativity work in each profession? Are there lessons that each might learn from the other? In particular, can lawyers become more innovative and effective as designers of new devices by using the methods of engineers? This books starts to explore these possibilities (see Chapter 3). It deals not only with lawyers in private practice, but also those who work in government, especially those engaged in the design of statutes.

Lawyers and engineers also face common ethical problems. Should they design devices for harmful purposes – for example to do physical or financial harm to others? Even when their own purposes are not malicious, what responsibility do lawyers have if clients use what is made for them to damage others? Can we use the comparison between lawyers and engineers to throw new light on lawyers' ethical responsibilities? In particular, we shall observe that, to a considerable degree, legal ethics takes as its starting point the situation of a litigator (and, in England and the USA, the situation of a litigator in an adversary system), which leaves it with little to say about the ethical problems that face lawyers in their engineering activities. Can we instead ground legal ethics in the problems faced by lawyers with devices to design, using as a starting point the parallel problems that engineers face? We take up this challenge in Chapter 4, where we concentrate on an example that serves to illustrate the nature and scope of the problems lawyers face in their engineering activities. The great Great Crash of 2008 followed an extraordinary expansion of credit that arose from what is essentially a set of legally-engineered financial innovations: securitised mortgages, the recombination of securitised mortgages into collateralised debt obligations, higher levels of recombination of collateralised debt obligations and eventually the invention of instruments that effectively allowed betting on movements in value of the recombined obligations. Some of what happened was fraudulent and deceptive, and lawyers should ask themselves serious questions about their part in such activities, but much of it was not fraudulent but simply dangerous for the market as a whole and ultimately for the wealth and well-being of millions of people. As we shall argue in Chapter 4, ethical standards drawn from litigation look especially irrelevant and inadequate in the circumstances of the Great Crash. Lawyers would do better to look instead to the ethical principles that engineers have developed, largely as a result of various disasters in which engineering errors have been implicated.

The comparison of law and engineering might also have lessons for research and teaching. Legal research, at least for those engaged in it, often seems a peculiarly ill-defined activity. What is it? Who specifically is it for? What is it meant to achieve? Comparisons with research in engineering provide ideas for answering those questions more clearly and distinctly than we now do. As for academic teaching of law, it has long suffered from a crisis of identity. Is it training for the profession? If so, why does it ignore what most of the profession does? If it is not, what is it? What kind of knowledge does it impart? Again, the engineering comparison can provide provocative answers to those questions. These issues are taken up in Chapter 5.

We can also ask how the conventionally dominant activities of litigation and adjudication look when we observe them through the lens of law-as-engineering. In this reversal of the familiar world, elements of legal life that are currently taken for granted, such as the aggressive style of litigators in an adversary system, become odd, strange and questionable. Perhaps more importantly, the role of judges can be re-assessed. Should we see judges as also engaged in engineering? If so, what kind of engineering is it? What are its characteristics and limitations? What aspects of their role might help them or hinder them in carrying out engineering functions? These questions form a subsidiary but important theme of chapters 3 to 5.

In Chapter 6, we attempt an assessment of the benefits and drawbacks of the whole approach. In particular we confront a number of arguments against the law-as-engineering approach, that it is wrong to move the centre of attention of lawyers away from the courts; that seeing law as a form of engineering encourages instrumentalist thinking that promotes private interests and relegates the common good; that law-as-engineering encourages a manipulative view of human relations; and that it breaks any links law might have with justice. The common theme of those objections is that thinking about law as engineering is technocratic and immoral, charges we will contest. We will argue, on the contrary, that seeing law as a form of engineering is the best way to rescue lawyers from the kind of behaviour that contributed to the Great Crash.

PRECURSORS

The comparison between law and engineering is not entirely new, although it has perhaps never been taken quite as seriously or in as much depth as it is here. The comparison has arisen previously in at least three contexts, each of which contributes positively to the conception of law-as-engineering but to each of which objections have been raised that the broader version

espoused here strives to meet. The first context is that of American legal
realism and its successors, such as the Lasswell–McDougal school of law-
as-policy. The second context is that of the transactions-costs economic
analysis of law, especially the work of Ronald Gilson. The third context is
the study of the consequences for legal practice of new technology, a field
led by Richard Susskind.

Roscoe Pound, the Legal Realists and their Successors

Perhaps the earliest suggestion that law should be compared to engineering
came in a series of lectures on legal history delivered in the 1920s by the
American legal polymath Roscoe Pound. Pound devoted his final lecture to
what he called an engineering interpretation of legal history.[11] Pound asked
his listeners to think of jurisprudence as 'a science of social engineering'.[12]
He explained that jurisprudence was 'that part of the whole field [of
social control] which may be achieved by the ordering of human relations
through the action of politically organized society.' Pound returned many
times to the theme of 'social engineering',[13] perhaps explaining the concept
most clearly in *The Ideal Element in Law*:

> [Jurisprudence seen as social engineering] is an organized body of knowledge
> with respect to the means of satisfying human demands and expectations,
> securing interests, giving effect to claims or desires, with the least friction and
> waste, so far as these things can be brought about by the legal order; whereby
> the means of satisfaction may be made to go as far as possible. It is the task of
> the social sciences to make this process . . . continually less wasteful. . . . As one
> of the social sciences jurisprudence has for its field to discover what part of this
> task may be achieved or furthered by the legal order and how.[14]

He stressed the orientation of both engineering and law to action, remark-
ing that engineering 'is a doing of things, not a serving as passive instruments through which mathematical formulas and mechanical laws realize
themselves'.[15]

---

[11]   Roscoe Pound, *Interpretations of Legal History* (Cambridge: Cambridge
U.P., 1923) at 141–65.
[12]   Pound (1923) at 152.
[13]   E.g. Roscoe Pound, *Social Control Through Law* (New Brunswick:
Transaction Publishers, 1997 [originally New Haven, Yale U.P., 1942)) at 64; *An
Introduction to the Philosophy of Law* (New Haven: Yale U.P.; London: Oxford
U.P., 1922) at 47, *The Ideal Element in Law* ([Calcutta]: University of Calcutta,
1958) at 234 and 315.
[14]   Pound (1958) at 234.
[15]   Pound (1923) at 152.

Pound took the analogy seriously, to the extent of making references to the engineering literature of the time.[16] He also made a serious effort to defend law-as-social-engineering from the accusation that it was, in comparison with real engineering, imprecise. He asserted, 'The materials of legal experience are as objective and as valid for scientific treatment no less than those of engineering experience.' He attributed any apparent difference in precision to the fact that legal formulas were all ultimately about what people could not do, so that they were always under pressure from those who wanted to push them further, whereas engineering formulas were about permitting action to take place.[17] Whether or not his explanation is persuasive (and one might think that the human sciences are inherently less precise than the physical) he at least cared enough about the analogy to argue the point.

The engineering analogy (or at least the engineering metaphor) was taken up by Pound's younger contemporaries,[18] several of whom identified themselves, or were identified by others, as the 'realist movement'. It is not entirely clear whether there ever was a 'movement' in the sense of an organised group bound together by a common set of beliefs and aims,[19] but there is little doubt that the 1920s and 1930s saw a reaction against the view, associated with the pioneer of American legal education, Christopher Columbus Langdell, that law schools should concern themselves with law and with nothing else, and, further, against the view that law was to be found largely in the judgments of the appellate courts.[20] That reaction took many forms. One was that lawyers should concern themselves with the social sciences, or even practise social science themselves. A second was that academic lawyers should study not just appellate courts but also first instance courts (and not just what courts said but how they came to say what they said, including their findings of fact). A third was that regulation and statutes were as legitimate objects of study as appellate cases. That third concern, with regulation, both arose from and in its turn encouraged

---

[16]   Pound (1958) at 315.

[17]   Pound (1958) at 315.

[18]   See N.E.H. Hull, *Roscoe Pound and Karl Llewellyn: Searching for an American Jurisprudence* (Chicago: University of Chicago Press, 1997) at 144.

[19]   See e.g. Neil Duxbury, *Patterns of American Jurisprudence* (Oxford: Clarendon Press, 1995) at 69 for the view that realism was more a mood than a movement. Other writers, however, see more coherence in realism – see e.g. Laura Kalman, *Legal Realism at Yale 1927–1960* (Chapel Hill: University of North Carolina Press, 1986) and William Twining, *Karl Llewellyn and the Realist Movement* (London: Weidenfeld and Nicolson, 1973).

[20]   See e.g. Kalman (1986), Hull (1997), Duxbury (1995) and Twining (1973) for numerous examples.

a considerable migration of legal talent into the administration of Franklin D. Roosevelt, especially into the institutions of the New Deal.[21]

Pound disagreed with some of the positions taken by his younger colleagues, or at least what he took to be their positions, especially those that appeared to reduce legal rules to psychology.[22] But what bound him to them was the view that law should be used as an instrument of social and political progress, free from illusions drawn from tradition and myth. Many of the realists were eager to promote social and economic change using the law. Their default setting was that the law was not a product of nature or part of the inevitable order of things, but an artefact produced by humans for their own use. Despite the disagreements between Pound and the realists, Pound would be speaking for many of them when he wrote:

> The engineer is judged by what he does. His work is judged by its adequacy to the purposes for which it is done, not by its conformity to some ideal form of a traditional plan. We are beginning, in contrast with the last century, to think of jurist and judge and law-maker in the same way.[23]

---

[21]   The best example is Jerome Frank, the author of the iconoclastic *Law and the Modern Mind*, who served at the Agricultural Adjustment Administration, Reconstruction Finance Association and the Securities and Exchange Commission. William Douglas wrote an important report on corporate reconstruction and chaired the Securities and Exchange Commission before being raised to the Supreme Court bench. Walton Hamilton served on a large number of advisory boards of regulatory agencies, was a member of the National Industrial Recovery Board and eventually became head of the consumer division of the National Recovery Administration. Herman Oliphant worked for the Farm Credit Administration before becoming chief counsel at Treasury. Thurman Arnold took part in litigation for the administration before becoming head of the Antitrust Division of the Justice Department. Felix Cohen went to the Department of the Interior, where he worked in Indian policy. See e.g. Roy Kreitner, 'Biographing Realist Jurisprudence' (2010) 35 Law & Social Inquiry 765–91 and Robert Gordon, 'Professors and Policymakers' in Anthony Kronman (ed.), *History of the Yale Law School* (New Haven: Yale U.P., 2004). Perhaps most strikingly of all, James Landis was a member of the Federal Trade Commission and the Securities and Exchange Commission, and later, after an intervening period as Dean of the Harvard Law School, returned to Washington to serve as chairman of the Civil Aeronautics Board. See Donald Ritchie, *James M. Landis: Dean of the Regulators* (Cambridge: Harvard U.P., 1980). For the intellectual parallels between legal realism and the New Deal, see generally G. Edward White, 'From Sociological Jurisprudence to Realism: Jurisprudence and Social Change in Early Twentieth-Century America' (1972) 58 Virginia Law Review 999–1028, 1025–28.

[22]   See e.g. White (1972).

[23]   Pound (1923) at 152.

Pound's particular version of law as social engineering was not, however, always well received even by his realist successors. Karl Llewellyn, for example, doubted Pound's assumption that 'social science' could lead society in the direction of an unproblematic consensus around a single conception of progress and thought that Pound had entangled description and evaluation to a degree that threw both into doubt.[24] The New Deal Democrats among the realists would have been acutely aware of the strong political opposition to Roosevelt's administration and the contested nature of the idea of progress. Consequently, realist interest in social science often concentrated less on informing the construction of progressive measures and more on exposing the anti-progressive assumptions of judges and what the realists saw as political conservatism disguising itself as technical law.[25]

In the wider world, the idea of social engineering has fared even worse than Pound's conception. It has come to mean attempts, doomed to end either in failure or in violence, to alter the way whole societies operate, especially to alter the values their members hold. A typical usage is that of the historian Paul Johnson, who applied the term to the massive schemes of social transformation attempted with appalling results by Hitler and Stalin.[26] Stalin himself referred to some of his own plans as 'engineering human souls'. The whole impression is one of treating human beings with contempt, shifting them about, in Johnson's words, like so much concrete, and when they refuse to move, resorting to murder. Perhaps more credible than the choleric Johnson is Karl Popper, whose condemnation of social engineering was limited to 'utopian social engineering', that is any endeavour to engineer whole societies. He was prepared to accept 'piecemeal social engineering', which he thought of as much smaller scale attempts to improve particular aspects of society.[27] But even smaller scale social engineering by government has become a term of reprobation, referring to allegedly over-ambitious forays into altering a society's status structure or its distribution of economic opportunity, or attempts to do so using institutions set up to do something different.[28] Social engineering is also

---

[24] See Hull (1997) at 143.

[25] See e.g. Laura Kalman, *The Strange Career of Legal Liberalism* (New Haven: Yale U.P., 1998) at 13–22.

[26] See Paul Johnson, *A History of the Modern World from 1917 to the 1980s* (London: Weidenfeld and Nicolson, 1983).

[27] Karl Popper, *The Poverty of Historicism* (London: Routledge, 1957) at 58ff.

[28] Examples of all these occur in the UK debate about undergraduate admissions to certain universities. See e.g. Editorial 'Excellent universities, not

associated with manipulation and deceit, with not treating people as rational beings able to make their own decisions on the basis of evidence and argument.[29]

Pound's social engineering conception of law plausibly counts as a precursor to treating what lawyers do as a version of what engineers do, but there are important differences. Pound focused on judges and legislators and the scale of his conception of social engineering was vast, working at the level of whole societies. Law-as-engineering, in contrast, encompasses the work of lawyers in private practice and those working at a much smaller scale – on transactions and on movements of small amounts of property. Pound's was also a heavily value-laden approach, full of reforming zeal and optimism, but also open to attack on moral and political grounds as manipulative and elitist. The comparison of lawyers and engineers we shall be attempting here is not intended to be heavily value-laden. The comparison is intended initially as a description of what lawyers do, rather than an evaluation of it. The description might illuminate potential areas of ethical difficulty for lawyers, as we shall see, and it facilitates evaluation of lawyers' work both individually and collectively, but it carries with it no particular degree of ambition. As for manipulation, although one cannot deny the coercive element in law, there is no a priori reason to think that legal devices are necessarily deceptive. Indeed, one needs to assume that they are not necessarily deceptive to be in a position to criticise those that are.

If one is looking in the same era as Pound for a perspective close to the form of law-as-engineering we take up in this book, one has to turn to the work of Karl Llewellyn himself. One of Llewellyn's constant themes was the importance of the perspective of the private lawyer who makes useful devices for clients, the perspective of the legal 'counsellor' who sees the law in terms of 'what it will do, or what he can get it to do for him:

---

social engineering' Daily Telegraph 20 February 2012 at 21 and Mary Evans, 'The interview X factor: the elusive "potential" that dictates success'. Times Higher Education Supplement, 10 December 2009 at 24 (in the interests of accuracy, however, it should be pointed out that, contrary to the Evans' assertion, the Vice-Chancellor of the University of Cambridge did not use the term 'social engineering' to describe UK higher education policy in a speech in September 2008. She used the phrase 'engines for promoting social justice' (see Press Association, 'University Intake Pressure Condemned' Press Association Regional Newswire – East Anglia, 10 September 2008).

[29] More recently, it has acquired an additional and even more negative connotation, that of frauds carried out on the internet by deceiving people to carry out actions that give away their personal and financial details.

foundation, tool or hazard.'[30] Llewellyn's own personal experience as a young commercial lawyer informed his point of view:

> 'If I were a court', my old chief W. W. Lancaster used to say gently but very firmly, when I had worked out what I thought a neat but novel road through a difficulty – 'If I were a court, Mr. Llewellyn, you would persuade me. But I am not a court; I am counsel for a bank. Surely you can find a way which will not raise these – doubtless untenable–doubts.' That did not mean that Lancaster was unaware of the need and beauty of creative counselling, of finding a good way through which one might have to back by creative advocacy. What it meant was that in the particular matter in hand he felt the risk too great for the return until the possibilities of a safer road had been explored. That was judgment.[31]

Even Llewellyn's much quoted, and much misinterpreted, remark, often taken as the slogan of legal realism, 'What these officials do about disputes is, to my mind, the law itself', is to be understood, as Llewellyn himself later explained,[32] as the law from the point of view of counsellors, rather than from the lofty position of legal philosophers (in Llewellyn's lexicon, 'jurisprudes'). The 'reckonability' he demanded of judges was essentially a degree of certainty in the law that would make it useable by lawyers in the mould of Mr Lancaster.[33]

Llewellyn tended to describe what lawyers do in terms not of engineering but of 'craft',[34] and he emphasised what he called the lawyers' 'situation sense'[35] rather than developing any organised body of knowledge about the processes of legal design. For Llewellyn, lawyering is an activity that involves mainly tacit knowledge, that is know-how that cannot be passed

---

[30] Karl Llewellyn, 'The Modern Approach to Counselling and Advocacy – Especially in Commercial Transactions' (1947) 46 Columbia Law Review 167–195 at 177 and in *Jurisprudence: Realism in Theory and Practise* (Chicago: University of Chicago Press, 1962) at 323–51.

[31] Llewellyn (1947) at 177 note 10. W. W. Lancaster was a partner at the New York firm Shearman and Sterling, where Llewellyn worked for three years before entering academia.

[32] Karl Llewellyn, *The Bramble Bush* (New York: Oceana Publications, 1960) (1960a) at 8–10.

[33] Karl Llewellyn, *The Common Law Tradition: Deciding Appeals* (Boston: Little, Brown, 1960) (1960b) e.g. at 17ff and 200ff.

[34] E.g. 'The Crafts of Law Re-valued' (1942) 15 Rocky Mountain Law Review 1–7, and in Llewellyn (1962) at 316–22. Llewellyn does refer to law as engineering in the context of Pound's work (see Hull (1997) at 144) and in an important passage in *The Bramble Bush*, the 'cozenages of Cepola' passage (at 145), which we will discuss in Chapter 6.

[35] See Llewellyn (1960b) passim.

on by precept alone.[36] But, as we shall see, there was a similar tradition in engineering before conscious efforts were made to replace it with organised knowledge about design. Moreover, Llewellyn's ultimate characterisation of legal realism, as 'an effort at more effective legal technology', [37] directly captures the spirit of law-as-engineering. For these reasons, Llewellyn stands as a very important precursor for the more systematic comparison between law and engineering attempted here.

We should also mention one of legal realism's successors, the Law, Science and Policy (LSP) approach pioneered at Yale by Harold Lasswell and Myres McDougal during and after the Second World War.[38] The Lasswell–McDougal approach has been described as thorough-going legal realism minus legal realism's tendency toward cynicism and plus extra-added American values, or as an attempt to synthesise Pound's value-oriented approach with the more radical realism of his successors. In essence it assumes that lawyers are policy-makers, in the sense of people who take decisions that set the direction of their society for the future, and offers them a comprehensive, systems-based view of society from which to derive their assessment of facts, together with a set of western democratic values from which to derive their decisions.

The LSP approach, especially its use of systems thinking, comes close to the law-as-engineering approach, but there are problems in its view of lawyers as pure policy-makers and of law itself as nothing except 'fundamental policy'. LSP is so firmly focused on finding the best future direction for the whole community that the idea of following rules is subsumed into policy decision, a position that has the perhaps illuminating, but not

---

[36] Cf. Michael Polanyi's concept of tacit knowledge, developed in *Personal Knowledge: Towards a Post Critical Philosophy* (London: Routledge, 1960) and *The Tacit Dimension* (New York: Anchor Books, 1967). Llewellyn did, however, have direct experience of the difficulty of making the tacit explicit. See Karl Llewellyn and E. Adamson Hoebel, *The Cheyenne Way* (Norman, OK: University of Oklahoma Press, 1941) at 40.

[37] Llewellyn (1960a) at 9–10.

[38] See for the development of their thinking, McDougal, 'Fuller v. The American Realists' (1940–41) 50 Yale Law Journal 827–40, Lasswell and McDougal, 'Legal Education and Public Policy: Professional Training in the Public Interest' (1943) 52 Yale Law Journal 203–295, Lasswell, 'The Interrelations of World Organization and Society' (1946) 55 Yale Law Journal 870–88, McDougal, 'Law as a Process of Decision – A Policy-Oriented Approach to Legal Study' (1956) 1 Natural Law Forum 53–72, McDougal, 'Jurisprudence for a Free Society' (1966) 1 Georgia Law Review 1–19, Lasswell and McDougal, 'Jurisprudence in Policy-Oriented Perspective' (1967) 19 University of Florida Law Review 486–513. The work is now represented by the monumental compendium *Jurisprudence for a Free Society: Studies in Law, Science and Policy* (Dordrecht, London: Nijhoff, 1992).

necessarily accurate, corollary that people who in their everyday lives apply the law to themselves should count as policy-makers.[39] More importantly, the boundary in LSP between law and other forms of policy-making is ultimately very difficult to discern. Llewellyn thought that it had disappeared altogether and that Lasswell and McDougal had downgraded the law itself to the level of mere technicality.[40] Reviewing one of Lasswell and McDougal's earliest works, a proposal for educating lawyers as policy-makers (which included training not only in skills such as negotiation but also public relations) he expressed surprise that law students in their programme would spend very little time learning any law or absorbing lawyers' ways of thinking about the law.[41] In their turn, Lasswell and McDougal condemned Llewellyn for worrying too much about the perspective of the private lawyer and not enough about the perspective of the 'scholar looking for enlightenment' or of 'the general community'.[42]

If one starts with what lawyers actually do, Llewellyn has the better of this argument. Most lawyers are not policy-makers and most policy-makers are not lawyers. The role lawyers play in transmitting policy decisions embodied in law to people and organisations in the wider society is important, and there might always be some play in how that happens which requires lawyers to make some choices, but it would be odd for lawyers carrying out that transmitting role to see themselves primarily as regulators of their clients rather than their servants. One can perhaps see a police officer as having some sort of street-level policy-making role, but a lawyer is not in the same position. A lawyer is not primarily an agent of the state, but rather an agent of the client. Moreover, although much public policy ends up in legal form, and lawyers are therefore embedded in the policy process to a degree that is often overlooked, there is much more to public policy than law. There is a good case for educating policy-makers in a systematic way so that they are aware of all the different fields of knowledge and disciplines that might be relevant to policy – which includes not just the social sciences beloved of Pound, the realists and LSP but also the physical sciences and engineering itself – and there is similarly a case for some lawyers both in government service and in private practice to undergo that training themselves so that they can better understand

---

[39] See Lasswell and McDougal (1992) Appendix 5 (reprinting Myres McDougal, 'The Application of Constitutive Prescriptions: An Addendum to Justice Cardozo' (1979) 1 Cardozo Law Review 135–70).

[40] Karl Llewellyn, 'McDougal and Lasswell Plan for Legal Education' (1943) 43 Columbia Law Review 476–85.

[41] Llewellyn (1943).

[42] Lasswell and McDougal (1992) at 39–46.

processes that are relevant to their clients. There is also a good case for including knowledge of the law and of law-making processes in the curriculum of a school of public policy, so that policy-makers understand the law not just as a last minute trap ('The Judge over Your Shoulder' in the words of a celebrated pamphlet prepared for UK civil servants to remind them of the possibility of judicial review[43]) but as a constructive search for legitimate authority. But that does not amount to a case for dissolving the difference between law and policy. The products of the Ecole Nationale d'Administration, for example, who receive instruction in law as part of their rigorous training in the formation of public policy, might well be a policy-making elite of the type envisaged by Lasswell and McDougal, but they are not lawyers.[44]

Equally important, LSP, unlike law-as-engineering, lacks a sense of lawyers making devices for other people to use. LSP concentrates very heavily on official decision-making about disputes – indeed, on judicial decision-making, although that is by its inventor's own choice rather than by necessity – leaving little or no room for the concept of the client or the idea that the client might be an active, indeed dominant, participant in the creative process, rather than merely play the role of an object of regulation.[45] One can equally criticise Llewellyn for focusing on disputes, both in

---

[43]   For the latest edition, see http://www.tsol.gov.uk/Publications/Scheme_Publications/judge.pdf.

[44]   The conflation of lawyers and policy-makers might nevertheless be understandable in the specific circumstances of the USA, especially before the development of schools of government and public policy in the 1960s, because the USA lacks a permanent, policy-relevant higher civil service, either of the strictly neutral British type or of the more flexible French type, and US lawyers have long offered themselves to government as, in Arthur Leff's words, 'freelance bureaucrats' (see Dauer and Leff (1977) at 581) joining the administration when their preferred party comes to office and rejoining their law firms when it leaves.

[45]   One might, at this point, mention some other isolated attempts to apply a systems approach to aspects of the law. One example is Ralph Jones and Kent Joscelyn, 'A Systems Approach to the Analysis of Transportation Law' (1976) 8 Transportation Law Journal 71–89, which treats traffic law as a regulatory subsystem within the transport system. Another is Sheldon Goldman and Thomas Jahnige, 'Systems Analysis and Judicial Systems: Potential and Limitations' (1971) 3(3) Polity 334–59, which might be interpreted as an early attempt to describe the courts in engineering terms. Another attempt to describe law in systems theory terms, perhaps even more general than LSP, can be found in Anthony D'Amato, *Jurisprudence: A Descriptive and Normative Analysis of Law* (Dordrecht: Martinus Nijhoff, 1984), especially chapter 4. D'Amato draws explicitly on the cybernetics tradition of Norbert Wiener, which concentrates on the connections between information and control in systems. The main problem with D'Amato's account is that, although it supplies some of the institutional detail Wiener's work lacked,

the common law and in other contexts,[46] but in Llewellyn's case, the object of the exercise was always 'reckonablility', a concept rooted in the use of the law by Mr Lancaster and his clients.

Law-as-engineering seeks to avoid LSP's problems. It conceives of lawyers not as policy-makers, although they might play a role in policy-making, but as makers of devices for others, a task for which they need above all to understand the law itself.

One other successor of Pound and the realists deserves to be mentioned, but this time one from a context originally distant from the USA. The Polish sociologist of law Adam Podgórecki, building on the earlier work of his compatriot Leo Petrażycki, made an effort to rehabilitate the idea of social engineering, and in doing so came close to comparing lawyers and engineers.[47] Podgórecki's conception of social engineering includes any human attempt to create social effects, including (but not necessarily limited to) deliberate efforts artificially to create new social structure. Podgórecki gives social engineering a new name ('sociotechnics', which he traces back to Karl Mannheim) as part of his strategy to separate out its positive and normative elements, which previous versions of social engineering, especially Pound's, tended to conflate. For Podgórecki, even large scale plans to change social relations are at least potentially beneficial. For him, there is nothing inherently immoral about macro-social engineering any more than meso- or micro-social engineering. It is just that at the macro-scale both the risks and the rewards are greater. Podgórecki reserves condemnation for what he calls 'dark' uses of social engineering, that is to say morally wrong uses of the techniques of social engineering. But he points out that such 'dark' social engineering can operate at small and medium scale, not just at the scale of whole societies.

Both Petrażycki and Podgórecki were interested in law as a means of social engineering, or of sociotechnics, but when they wrote about legal engineering it was mainly at a macro level. Podgórecki's work moved away from specific interest in law just at the point where a combination of legal studies and his interest in meso- or micro-sociotechnics would have yielded

---

very much like Wiener's work, it seems to lack any conception of human agency or creativity. Attempts continue, however, to fill that gap – see e.g. Ralf-Eckhard Türke, *Governance: Systemic Foundation and Framework* (Heidelberg: Springer Physica Verlag, 2008).

[46] Especially in Llewellyn (1960b) and Llewellyn and Hoebel (1941).

[47] Adam Podgórecki,'Sociotechnics: Basic Issues and Concepts' in Adam Podgórecki, Jon Alexander and Rob Shields (eds), *Social Engineering* (Ottawa: Carleton U.P., 1996).

a field very close to law-as-engineering. It is, nevertheless, close enough to law-as-engineering to be seen as a comparable idea.[48]

Finally, we must mention Lon Fuller. Although only a successor to Pound in the loose sense of being a fellow critic of legal positivism, Fuller's overriding concern with the purpose of legal rules, and his enduring interest in lawyers in private commercial practice took him in the direction of law-as-engineering. Fuller preferred the metaphor of the lawyer as architect to that of the lawyer as engineer,[49] but his starting point was precisely the same view of what lawyers do as that taken in this book:

> The lawyer drafts constitutions, treaties, charters, by-laws, statutes, contracts, wills, and deeds. All of these serve to impose forms on men's relations with one another. The lawyer is constantly studying these forms and discovering, by reflective analysis and practical experience, what results flow from particular forms of order. [50]

He also identified a problem in thinking about law that law-as-engineering would recognise:

> One might expect that the major effort of legal philosophy would be directed toward this department of the lawyer's activities. Instead we find it almost entirely neglected. . . . American legal philosophy has been litigation-oriented for many decades.[51]

One important feature of Fuller's approach, however, is that, rather like Pound, though in a more sophisticated way, Fuller seemed to meld the descriptive and the evaluative. He was interested in what he called 'eunomics', 'the science, theory or study of good order and workable

---

[48]   One might also mention work that has some affinity to law-as-engineering because it deploys a broadly sociotechnical approach at levels not limited to the macro, work such as Cass Sunstein's application of behavioural economics to legal policy, although claiming this work as a precursor would be a stretch. Slightly more distant, stressing the needs of both lawyers and clients and coming from a psychological, indeed psychiatric, tradition, is the study of lawyers' activities in preventing conflict and planning the future avoidance of conflict – see e.g. Louis Brown and Edward Dauer, *Planning by Lawyers: Materials on a Nonadversarial Legal Process* (Mineola, NY: Foundation Press, 1978).

[49]   See 'The Lawyer as an Architect of Social Structures' in *The Principles of Social Order: selected essays of Lon L Fuller* (Durham NC: Duke U.P., 1981).

[50]   Lon Fuller, 'American Legal Philosophy at Mid-Century – A Review of Edwin W. Patterson's Jurisprudence, Men and Ideas of the Law' (1953) 6 Journal of Legal Education 457–85, 476–77

[51]   Fuller (1953) at 477.

arrangements'.[52] He rejected what he named 'the doctrine of the infinite pliability of social arrangements', that is 'the view that, given a sufficient agreement on ends or a dictator strong enough to impose his own ends, society can be so arranged as to effectuate (within the limits of its resources) any conceivable combination or hierarchy of ends'.[53] He contended instead that 'There are natural laws of social order'.[54] The implication was that legal arrangements that go with the grain of those natural laws are better conceived than those that do not.

The comparison of law and engineering, as we shall see in Chapters 3 and 4, suggests a different way of approaching the same issue. Fuller's approach rightly emphasises the importance of purpose in the law – the idea that legal constructions have purposes that can be fulfilled or not fulfilled. But there is a difference between purposes not being fulfilled and purposes being fulfilled for a wrongful end. One can separate the possibility of the existence of principles of successful design from the evaluation of what those designs achieve, for good or ill. In Fuller's own terms, the science of workable arrangements is different from the study of good order. Law-as-engineering endeavours to preserve that separation.

Lawyers as Transactions Costs Engineers

The second precursor for the idea of law-as-engineering springs from the law and economics tradition. One of the most influential concepts in the economic analysis of law is that of transactions costs – not conventional costs of production (wages, interest, rent, materials and so on) but rather the costs of putting them together and selling the product in the market. Transactions costs include the costs of searching for other people with whom to contract (including customers, investors and employees), the costs of negotiating and coming to agreement with them, the costs of monitoring them after agreement and during the period of performing their agreements, and any costs of enforcing the agreement. Transactions costs are usually thought of as the friction of the economic world, and like friction, they are often taken to be wasteful and unproductive – to be minimised if at all possible. One problem for lawyers is that their work largely consists of transactions costs – they take part in the negotiation, monitoring and enforcement of deals. It usually makes sense for legal costs to be reduced or, if possible, eliminated. But that raises an interesting puzzle,

---

[52] Fuller (1953) at 477.
[53] Fuller (1953) at 474.
[54] Fuller (1953) at 473.

namely why anyone should hire lawyers in the first place. If transactions costs are wasteful friction, why do businesses volunteer to spend money on them? That question is in turn related to a normative question about whether lawyers can defend themselves against accusations that they add to the costs of doing business for the sole purpose and with the sole effect of generating fees. In other words, are lawyers parasites on business?

The answers to these questions about business and business lawyers are, according to Ronald Gilson, connected. Lawyers might be generators of transactions costs, but their job is to reduce transactions costs overall. In the real world of deals, as opposed to the ideal zero-transactions-cost world of the theorists, transactions costs cannot be eliminated, but they can, by sensible planning, be reduced. Lawyers are, according to Gilson, experts at reducing such costs. Businesses hire them, perfectly rationally, as long as the savings they make to transactions costs overall outweigh their own contribution to them, including their fees. Lawyers are, in this view, transactions costs engineers.[55]

Gilson's original conception has been enriched in several ways. Stephen Schwarcz put forward another explanation of the value of lawyers, namely that they reduce regulatory costs.[56] The main value of legal design from this perspective is to remove regulatory obstacles and risks from the path to where the client wants to go. George Dent broadened the focus further from transactions and regulation to the wider work of business lawyers, including choice of business form and design of corporate governance structures, yielding a perspective he called 'enterprise architecture'.[57] Perhaps the most important advance of all on Gilson's original conception is that of Manuel Utset, who has pointed out that, in some fields, the contribution of lawyers is not confined to the reduction of transactions costs but extends to making products, which places lawyers in the role of production engineers, not just transactions costs engineers.[58] The

---

[55] Ronald Gilson, 'Value Creation by Business Lawyers: Legal Skills and Asset Pricing' (1984) 94 Yale Law Journal 239–313.

[56] Steven Schwarcz, 'Explaining the Value of Transactional Lawyering' (2007) 12 Stanford Journal of Law Business and Finance 486.

[57] George Dent, 'Business Lawyers as Enterprise Architects' (2008–2009) 64 Business Law 279–314. See also John Flood and Eleni Skordaki, 'Structuring Transactions: The Case of Real Estate Finance', in Volkmar Gessner (ed.), *Contractual Certainty in International Trade: Empirical Studies and Theoretical Debates on Institutional Support for Global Economic Exchanges* (Oxford: Hart Publishing, 2009) chapter 6 for the use of the lawyers-as-architects metaphor, in perhaps its most natural habitat, namely real estate finance.

[58] Manuel Utset, 'Producing Information: Initial Public Offerings, Production Costs and the Producing Lawyer' (1995) 74 Oregon Law Review 275–313.

production role is particularly clear where the desired product is itself an object with no existence outside the law, for example shares in a company.[59] Utset has now embarked in precisely the direction this book seeks to go, that of applying engineering concepts to legal problems. He is, for example, applying concepts drawn from the engineering of information systems to problems in the design of companies.[60]

Law-as-engineering can be seen as a generalisation of Gilson's insights. Gilson's purpose is to show that business lawyers add value for their clients (or, to put it more neutrally, that it is rational for businesses to buy non-litigious legal services). His further purpose is to show that that expenditure on business law advice is welfare-enhancing for both sides to a deal, and is not just a transfer from one side to the other. Law-as-engineering as a more general perspective is neutral about these questions of welfare. It is perfectly possible, for example, for lawyers to create and clients willingly to pay for devices whose sole purpose is to capture gains created by others, in other words devices, such as tax avoidance schemes, that are designed for non-productive rent seeking. Lawyers can also create purely distributive devices, such as wills and trusts, which satisfy those who are distributing their resources but which might not allocate resources to their most productive use. The possibility that devices might be social-welfare-enhancing is important not just empirically but also ethically, but it is not itself necessarily an accurate descriptive characterisation of what lawyers make.

Another aspect of lawyers' work that takes law-as-engineering beyond the research project begun by Gilson is government work. No doubt governments might be interested in reducing transactions costs or in maximising their return in the deals in which they themselves engage – in government procurement, for example – but the value created for government by those who draft statutes and regulations is not commercial (though it might have some effect on commercial value) but political. Some theorists might want to reduce the value of public policy to cost-benefit analysis in which the state's own purposes play no part,[61] but even if they are right (which seems unlikely),[62] the way that value is brought into being

---

[59]   Utset (1995).

[60]   Manuel Utset, 'Designing Corporate Governance Regimes' (2012) 15 Journal of Applied Economics ___ (http://ssrn.com/abstract=1810148).

[61]   See e.g. Louis Kaplow and Steven Shavell, *Fairness versus Welfare* (Cambridge, MA: Harvard U.P., 2006).

[62]   See e.g. Michael Dorff, 'Why Welfare Depends on Fairness: A Reply to Kaplow and Shavell' (2002) 75 Southern California Law Review 847. See more generally the arguments in Michael Sandel, *What Money Can't Buy: The Moral Limits of Markets* (London: Allen Lane, 2012).

is through lawyers being hired by the state, not directly by the beneficiaries of the policy concerned.

Lawyers as Knowledge Engineers

The final and most recent precursor for law-as-engineering is the suggestion by Richard Susskind that, because of the advances of information and communications technology, lawyers in the future will find themselves with nothing much to do unless they transform themselves into brokers of legal knowledge and become information engineers.[63] Susskind has observed the rise of information technology in the law. These include expert systems that assist in the application of complex sets of rules and programmes that generate model contract clauses and forms. There are also now programmes that assist lawyers to search documents for relevant facts.[64] Susskind combines that observation with observations about the rise of the internet, and especially the rise of self-help websites that give information helpful for various kinds of legal self-diagnosis and for finding do-it-yourself remedies. He concludes that lawyers are under threat of being replaced by technology – at least their prestige is at risk as they become identified with selling standardised 'products'. Their only future is in very high value bespoke lawyering or in designing expert systems either for the use of the few remaining high value lawyers or for public use. Thus, Susskind warns, lawyers need to become knowledge engineers, people whose job is the integration of human knowledge into computer systems.

Susskind's prognostications are not without difficulties. Legal expert systems do not seem to have advanced at the pace previously predicted and are still perhaps better seen as aids for experts rather than as replacements of experts. More important, even if one could find instructions on the internet about how to carry out various transactions, many people would still think it prudent to have someone else do it, someone who is experienced, who can spot circumstances in which the normal procedures do not work and, perhaps most of all, has professional indemnity insurance if the transaction goes wrong. The detail of Susskind's work, however, is not as important as his underlying conception of lawyers as systematic solvers of problems and producers of desirable results. That conception is entirely compatible with the law-as-engineering and to that extent counts, albeit within a limited range, as one of its precursors.

---

[63] Richard Susskind, *The End of Lawyers? Rethinking the Nature of Legal Services* (Oxford: Oxford U.P., 2008).

[64] See e.g. http://protect.autonomy.com/products/legal/index.htm.

Summary

Looking across the range of precursors of law-as-engineering, we can see a number of themes, all of which have echoes in the past, but which can now to be brought together. First, it is important to unite what lawyers do in the private sector with what they do for government. Conceptions based only on private sector activity (e.g. lawyers as transactions costs engineers) or only on legislation and appellate judgments (e.g. Pound's social engineering) are incomplete, though complementary. Second, it is important to remove litigation and courts from the centre of how we see law and lawyers. Lon Fuller went a long way to achieving that for himself, but his comment that most legal thinking is in thrall to judges and the courts is still largely true today. Third, it is important to separate the descriptive and the evaluative, at least for the purposes of analysis. Lawyers might be engineers, but we can observe not only competent and incompetent engineers but also moral and immoral engineers. Fourth, the relationship between lawyers and clients is very important. Lawyers provide services not in the abstract but for particular people and for particular purposes.

2.   What do lawyers do?

The popular image of lawyers is all about litigation. The vast majority of fictional lawyers centre their lives on the courts, either as advocates or as judges. One researcher has noted that 'Out of the 40 [TV] series on law produced in Britain from 1950 onwards there are only three lawyer-focused series where the courtroom is not fundamental to the series'.[1] From Portia to Judge John Deed, being a lawyer means having a role in court. That image is partly explained by the obvious attractions of the criminal law as drama, both for producers of fiction and of news programmes, and it is noticeable that countries with different kinds of criminal procedure tend to produce legal drama that concentrates on other parts of the process. In France, for example, drama tends to emphasise not the trial but the investigation, and the central legal figure is often the *juge d'instruction*.[2] But even there, lawyers are typically involved in conflict and contention. Outside the criminal law, television viewers' most likely legal encounters are still litigious – news items about civil trials or applications for judicial review, or advertisements encouraging them to take part in personal injury litigation. Even the UK government's advice to young people thinking about a legal career as a solicitor, not even as a barrister or trial lawyer, refers repeatedly to 'representing' clients in 'court', preparing papers for 'court', researching 'cases', being 'persuasive' and being able to work on 'several cases at once'.[3] The few hints that lawyers might do anything else seem only to point to a life of painstaking drudgery

---

[1]   Paul Robson, 'Lawyers and the Legal System on TV: the British Experience' (2006) 2 International Journal of Law in Context 333–62, at 33. One exception to the rule that lawyers in popular culture work exclusively in litigation and advocacy, however, is the work of Louis Auchincloss, where characters appear from the author's own milieu of the Wall Street law firms, lawyers who are more interested in trusts and estates than courtrooms – see William Domnarski, 'Trouble in Paradise: Wall Street Lawyers and the Fiction of Louis Auchincloss' (1987) 12 Journal of Contemporary Law 243–59 – but even Auchincloss wrote *The Embezzler* (1966), about white collar crime.

[2]   Examples include 'Engrenages', 'Boulevard du palais', 'Alice Nevers: Le juge est une femme', and 'les Cordier, juge et flic'.

[3]   https://nationalcareersservice.direct.gov.uk/advice/planning/jobprofiles/Pages/solicitor.aspx.

– young people are warned that they will need 'the ability to absorb and analyse large amounts of information' and 'a high level of accuracy and attention to detail', though a young reader might take even those qualities as relevant to litigation.

The emphasis on litigation reaches into legal education, at least in the English-speaking world. In universities, law students learn mainly about what judges have said or done about disputes. Judges are the central characters in lecture courses on law even more than they are in fiction. Meanwhile, those who teach law devote most of their research to compiling, commenting on, analysing or criticising the output of those same judges. A quick look through the footnotes to most English-language academic legal articles will reveal that the raw material most academics work from most of the time is the output of the courts. Moreover, legal theory, especially post-Ronald Dworkin, seems obsessed with 'judges' and 'courts'. Legal theory has not only long been dismissive of legislation, as Jeremy Waldron has extensively analysed,[4] but it is also dismissive, with very few exceptions, of any uses of the law outside the courtroom.

But, as most academic lawyers realise when they encounter their former students years after graduation, in the real world of legal practice, most lawyers never go anywhere near a court or even a law report, and would treat the prospect of doing so with distaste or even dread. According to data in the possession of the Law Society of England and Wales, of the 115,475 practising solicitors in 2010, only 10,942 said that they worked in the criminal courts and 21,937 said that they offered general litigation services.[5] Litigation is even more of a minority activity for major firms. In 2011, Clifford Chance listed only 345 of its 2625 lawyers, as involved in litigation and dispute resolution, and Linklaters categorised as litigators a mere 43 of its 488 worldwide partners.[6] Even if one assumes that the overwhelming majority of barristers in private practice (of whom there are about 12,000) are litigators, the picture that emerges is that, by a large margin, the majority of lawyers carry out work that is very different from the public image of the profession.

What is it, then, that lawyers do? The answer is that they mostly facilitate transactions or deals. The same Law Society data reveal that in 2010, 20,696 solicitors said that they practised in the field of 'business affairs',

---

[4]   Jeremy Waldron, *The Dignity of Legislation*, (Cambridge: Cambridge U.P., 1999).

[5]   See Law Society Research, 'Factsheet: Categories of work undertaken by solicitors 2010'. 16,681 also said that they offered 'commercial litigation', but the two figures are not cumulative, since solicitors could say that they offered both.

[6]   Calculated from information available on these firms' websites.

20,176 were in 'commercial property', 17,828 in 'conveyancing, residential', 13,685 in 'wills and probate', 8327 in 'corporate finance' and 7713 in 'mergers and acquisitions', all of which are essentially about facilitating transactions. There is some evidence for an increase in litigious work within commercial law in the late part of the 20th century, especially international arbitrations and other forms of alternative dispute resolution,[7] and we are certainly no longer in the world in which solicitors thought that litigation was either so insignificant or so undignified that their litigation departments were run not by partners, or even by lawyers, but by managing clerks.[8] But litigation is not what most lawyers do most of the time. Even family law (13,633 solicitors in 2010), which seems inherently conflictual and court-based, not only contains some areas of activity better characterised as regulatory rather than contentious (for example adoption), but also is experiencing an increasing emphasis on non-court-based resolution of disputes by agreement (for example family mediation – claimed as a separate specialism by 810 solicitors in 2010, about the same number who claimed to specialise in defamation).

The major firms are even more oriented to deals than the profession as a whole. Allen and Overy, for example, lists 431 of its 2179 lawyers as practising 'finance' and 359 'mergers and acquisitions' – in both cases two and a half times the average for the profession as a whole. Even fields of activity that at first sight seem to be entirely concerned with conflict turn out on further inspection to contain a large element of facilitation. 'Employment', for example, (12,591 England and Wales solicitors in 2010) looks like contentious work – unfair dismissal claims, discrimination cases and so on – but the major London firms' descriptions of the field paint a very different picture. Linklaters, for example, gives pride of place in its website's account of its employment law practice not to contentious work, but to transactions work mainly concerned with structuring incentives for employees.[9] Some of those incentives will, no doubt, involve encouraging employees to leave after a merger or acquisition, but much of the work revolves around encouraging them not to leave, around creating and smoothing the transfer of employee benefits. Allen and Overy's website, for example, claims, 'Our

───────────────────

[7]   John Flood, 'Megalawyering in the Global Order: the Cultural, Social and Economic Transformation of Global Legal Practice' (1996) 3 International Journal of the Legal Profession 169–214, 185–86.

[8]   Laurie Dennett, *Slaughter and May: A Century in the City* (Cambridge: Granta, 1989) 223.

[9]   http://www.linklaters.com/WhatWeDo/Practices/EmployeeIncentives/Pages/Index.aspx?WT.sp=Primary.

lawyers are experts in all the legal aspects of implementing and structuring share plans and pension schemes'.[10]

In the United States, the picture is perhaps not as starkly non-litigious, but it is not as court-based as the public image of lawyers would imply. Martindale-Hubbell, the leading US directory of lawyers, lists 1,202,871 US lawyers. For reasons related to, for example, state regulation of advertising by lawyers, some of them offer little or no information about their areas of practice, and the system of self-description is not entirely systematic. But of those who do offer information about their areas of practice, 59,685 list themselves as practising 'criminal law', and 84,177 claim to be litigators of various types, whereas 79,691 say that they practice corporate law and 98,898 'business law', of whom only around a fifth offer 'business litigation' as a sub-discipline.

Turning to a jurisdiction outside the common law world, a comparable situation seems to obtain in France. If one looks only at the profession of *avocat*, and so ignores the separate, and mostly transactional, profession of *notaire*, one again finds that criminal law in particular, and perhaps litigation in general are far from representative of what lawyers do. As of 2011, there were 53,744 *avocats* in France.[11] The number claiming a specialisation was only 11,216 (and, for reasons not yet explained, the proportion claiming a specialisation seems to have been going down over the past decade), but of those who do, the overwhelming majority are in business law. As the Ministry of Justice comments, 'Les avocats se spécialisent massivement dans les secteurs du droit intéressant la vie économique et sociale. En effet, plus de six mentions sur dix recouvrent des spécialités du droit pour lesquelles le conseil aux entreprises est développé.'[12] Only 5 per cent of *avocats* claiming to have a specialism said that it was in criminal law (*droit pénal*).[13]

---

[10] Allen and Overy, *Start at the Top* (n.d. http://www.wheretowork.com/allenovery/A&OBrochure.pdf).

[11] These figures come from the Ministère de la Justices et des Libertés (http://www.justice.gouv.fr/budget-et-statistiques-10054/etudes-statistiques-10058/statistiques-sur-la-profession-davocat-2011-23319.html) and L'Observatoire du Conseil National des Barreaux, *Avocats: évolutions et tendances de la profession, Année 2011* (Paris: CNB, 2011).

[12] See http://www.justice.gouv.fr/budget-et-statistiques-10054/etudes-statistiques-10058/statistiques-sur-la-profession-davocat-2011-23319.html [Translation: 'Lawyers [*avocats*] specialise massively in the law about economic and social life. In fact, more than six out of ten instances refer to the fields of specialisation for which the role of business lawyer developed.'].

[13] L'Observatoire du Conseil National des Barreaux, *Avocats: évolutions et tendances de la profession, Année 2011* (Paris: CNB, 2011) p. 45. It is worth

This real world of lawyers rarely breaks into public consciousness. Only one British TV drama series even came close to reflecting it. 'Trust' was set in a City law firm. Its plots often involved business deals and litigation made only an occasional appearance. Sadly, perhaps precisely because it contradicted the popular stereotype, it lasted only six episodes. But what about real world contacts between lawyers and the public? If the public built their view of lawyers from personal experience, as opposed to media portrayals, would the situation be different? Public contact with lawyers is largely limited to a small number of situations: in essence, house purchase, crime, personal injury, wills, probate and divorce. The number of such contacts is far from negligible: about one million residential properties in England and Wales change hands each year;[14] around one million criminal offences, not including traffic offences, are prosecuted each year – although the number of discrete criminal defendants is lower;[15] about 900,000 personal injury cases a year are registered with the Compensation Recovery Unit;[16] lawyers write about 250,000 wills a year;[17] about 150,000 estates a year are granted probate with the assistance of lawyers; [18] and between 100,000 and 150,000 couples divorce each year.[19] But even at its highest, the proportion of the population that comes directly into contact with lawyers each year in these ways seems unlikely much to exceed 10 per cent. To the extent that the groups overlap (for example where residential

---

noting, however, that the French figures seem to arise from a survey that required respondents to indicate only one specialism (the column thus sums to 100 per cent), whereas in the England and Wales and US surveys, respondents could choose more than one area of specialisation.

[14] See HM Land Registry, House Price Index February 2012, p. 12. Volumes exceeded 1.4 million per year in 2006–7, fell to under half a million in 2009 and subsequently returned to about 650,000 in 2012.

[15] See Ministry of Justice, Criminal justice statistics: Quarterly Update http://www.justice.gov.uk/statistics/criminal-justice/criminal-justice-statistics.

[16] See Department for Work and Pensions, Compensation Recovery Unit Performance Data (http://www.dwp.gov.uk/other-specialists/compensation-recovery-unit/performance-and-statistics/performance-statistics/).

[17] In a survey commissioned by the Law Society, just under half the adult population claimed to have made a will, although at least a third of that business had been lost to non-legally qualified will-writers, (see Law Society, *Investigation into Will Writing Call for Evidence by the Legal Services Board: Response by the Law Society of England and Wales* (London: Law Society, December 2010) Annex A), all of which implies, assuming that on average we live 60 years as adults, an annual rate of about 250,000.

[18] See Probate Service http://www.justice.gov.uk/guidance/courts-and-tribunals/courts/probate/about.htm.

[19] Office of National Statistics, *Statistical Bulletin: Divorces in England and Wales 2009* (London, TSO, 17 Feb 2011).

property sales arise from death or divorce) the real figure will be lower. Personal contacts reflect the actual balance of legal work between the facilitation of transactions and litigation better than media portrayals, but even they distort the reality of the balance of lawyers' work. Even if we count probate and divorce as transactional (because they are usually not contested, although some aspects, such as custody of children do give rise to disputes) and assume that both sides are legally represented in property transactions, we find 1.9 million litigious contacts per year as against 2.6 million non-litigious contacts, which looks rather more litigious than the lawyers' specialisation data for the same jurisdiction. The explanation of the difference, of course, is business and commerce, where lawyers carry out their transactional work.[20] But even the numbers of people who come across lawyers in this their natural habitat is small. Most businesses will see lawyers rarely. It might be difficult for the 1000 companies listed on the London Stock Exchange, and perhaps for the further 1000 listed on the AIM, to go a whole year without taking legal advice, but, at least in Britain, small and even medium-sized businesses tend to rely more on accountants for advice than on lawyers.[21] As for commercial transactions, even medium-sized firms might use contract terms put together from trade association standard forms or patched together from the forms used by others. It is difficult to avoid the conclusion that much of what lawyers do is invisible to the public.

Misunderstanding of what lawyers do appears even in political debate.

---

[20]   Estimating the size of the gap is difficult, but Heinz et al. found that, at least in Chicago, the 'corporate sector consumed more than twice the amount of Chicago lawyers' time devoted to personal and small-business client work in 1995 (64 percent versus 29 percent)' (John Heinz, Robert Nelson, Rebecca Sandefur and Edward Laumann, *Urban Lawyers: The New Social Structure of the Bar* (Chicago: University of Chicago Press, 2005) at 43. In the 1970s the preponderance of corporate work was already present but at a lower level (see John Heinz and Edward Laumann, *Chicago Lawyers: The Social Structure of the Bar* (New York: Russell Sage, 1982) at 42).

[21]   See e.g. Robert Bennett and Paul Robson, 'The Use of External Business Advice by SMEs in Britain' (1999) 11 Entrepreneurship & Regional Development 155–80 (finding that more than 80 per cent of SMEs turn to accountants for advice, as opposed to about 50 per cent for lawyers, that accountants are far more likely to be the sole source of advice for SMEs than lawyers and that the use of lawyers is at its lowest among the very smallest firms). The British government's annual survey of small businesses asks whether respondents have sought external advice in the previous year and if so, from whom. It usually finds that about 40 per cent of SMEs have sought advice from accountants, as opposed to 10 per cent from lawyers. See e.g. IFF Research, *BIS Small Business Survey 2010* (London: HMSO, April 2011) at 64.

Perhaps misled by the fact that the vast bulk of public subsidy for legal services is spent on litigation, whether criminal or civil, politicians often assume that all lawyers are litigators.[22] In the House of Commons, for example, when the wording of a bill is unclear, thus opening up the possibility of challenge in the courts, it is often alleged that lawyers will 'have a field day'.[23] Members of Parliament, no doubt in common with many of their constituents, subscribe to Bentham's view that 'the power of the lawyer is in the uncertainty of the law' and that lawyers 'wish . . . to see all waters troubled.'[24] As we shall see, in reality, legal uncertainty and troubled waters are far from conducive to legal practice.

TRANSACTIONAL LAWYERS

What then is the reality of what lawyers do? The place to start is with the tens of thousands of lawyers in commercial practice. As a City of London lawyer told a researcher in the 1990s, 'We are here to facilitate business . . . Business people want solutions, and that's what lawyers are here to

---

[22] Parliamentarians might also have been misled by the balance between barristers (mostly litigators) and solicitors (mostly not) among MPs. In the 21st century, the balance in the House between the two branches of the profession has been roughly even, even though in reality there are nearly ten times more solicitors than barristers. In the 20th century barristers outnumbered solicitors, often to an enormous extent. See also pp. 207–8 in this volume.

[23] E.g. HC Debates 9 Feb 1996: Column 621 (Peter Atkinson), 1 Mar 1996: Column 1139 (Andrew Robathan), 28 Jan 2002: Column 103 (John McDonnell), 8 Feb 2001: Column 1128 (Eric Forth), 16 Jul 2004: Column 1680 (surprisingly uttered by a lawyer, Andrew Dismore), 9 Nov 2005: Column 411 (Lembit Opik), 31 Jan 2006: Column 211 (another lawyer, Dominic Grieve, later Attorney-General), 16 Apr 2007: Column 72 (David Blunkett), 3 Nov 2009: Column 794 (Mike Penning), HC Standing Committee A on the Greater London Authority Bill, 4 Feb 1999 (Mike Gapes), HC Standing Committee B on the Freedom of Information Bill, 25 January 2000 (Harry Greenway), HC 3rd Standing Committee on Delegated Legislation on the Draft Part-time Workers (Prevention of Less Favourable Treatment) Regulations, 18 May 2000 [ca. 11 am] (Alan Johnson), HC Special Standing Committee on the Adoption and Children Bill, 27 November 2001 [ca. 4.45pm] (Tim Loughton). Lawyers almost uniquely benefit from 'field days', but occasionally the beneficiary is the press – e.g. HC Deb 2 March 1994: Column 1047 (David Evans), 22 Jan 2009: Column 933 (Alan Duncan).

[24] Jeremy Bentham, Letter to James Mackintosh (1808), *Works* (J. Bowring ed., Edinburgh, 1838–43) vol 10, ch XVI. There is, however, another interpretation of how lawyers' power arises from uncertainty, but it is an interpretation that also produces responsibility. We take up this theme in Chapter 4.

provide.'[25] The type of facilitation varies with the type of business. SMEs will normally require solutions that work locally with their immediate suppliers, employees and customers. But at the top end of the scale in terms of value, where business has become global, legal solutions need to work globally, and law firms compete to provide services that cross jurisdictional boundaries. Michael Bray, a senior lawyer at Clifford Chance, told Richard Susskind in an interview published in 2002:

> It's an integrated global product where you will get the benefit of the team which is working across jurisdictions, and across different legal systems, which will be solution oriented, commercially minded, filter the law, and deliver the client ultimately a product which is what the client wants, something which is really going to help them.[26]

Facilitation also varies with the point in the business's process at which lawyers are asked to provide solutions. For example, a traditional role of transactions lawyers – but one that now seems faintly out of date – is to review contractual documents that their clients have themselves already negotiated, or which have been presented to them by the other side of the deal.[27] The lawyer's principal job at that stage is to understand what the client thinks the deal is, and to see whether the documents deliver that deal. If there are gaps in the agreement or clauses the client seems not to have understood, the lawyer's role is to suggest amendments for the client to take to the other side. This 'let me see the contract' role can be useful but it has limitations. If the document is fundamentally unsatisfactory, perhaps involving a serious lack of enforceability, the lawyers' intervention might result in costly delays in the negotiations. Indeed, this kind of lawyering can look not so much like problem-solving as problem-discovery, and clients have been known to feel that their lawyers are over-cautious and not prepared to take a 'business' view. On the other hand, lawyers'

---

[25] Jane Lewis with Jill Keegan, *Defining Legal Business: Understanding the Work of the Largest Law Firms* (London: Law Society, 1997) at 10.

[26] Richard Susskind, *The Susskind Interviews: Legal Experts in Changing Times* (London: Sweet and Maxwell, 2005). It is interesting that Susskind's choice of interviewees also betrays a bias in favour of litigation. Of Susskind's 18 interviewees, only two are transactions lawyers (Michael Bray and Tony Williams). Six are judges (all former barristers), three Lord Chancellors (all previously barristers), one an Attorney-General (a barrister), two practising barristers and one a former barrister and MP. The balance is made up of two academics – one in jurisprudence, the other in political science – and a civil servant.

[27] See e.g. John Flood, 'Doing Business: The Management of Uncertainty in Lawyers' Work' (1991) 25 Law and Society Review 41–71 at 64.

conversations often feature the sheer recklessness of clients whose understanding of their legal position was hopelessly inadequate.

More clearly useful to clients is the task of solving problems before
they arise and incorporating those solutions into their agreements during
the course of the negotiation. The tendency in the US has been to bring
lawyers into the process earlier than, for example, in England, for example,
so that US lawyers have tended to play a larger role as negotiators rather
than as merely advisers to negotiators,[28] and largely as a consequence have
sometimes seemed more entrepreneurial than their English counterparts,
who correspondingly have sometimes appeared more technical, but in
both places lawyers now habitually play a part in framing the deal as it
develops.[29]

Part of what lawyers do is translation – taking the clients' business
agreements as the starting point and translating them into legal form[30]
– but lawyers also take part in shaping the substantive deals themselves.
Their role often takes the form of 'conflict-blocking', that is anticipating
conflicts between their client and someone else – for instance the other
side of the deal or a regulator – and offering ideas for how that conflict
might be avoided or resolved.[31] For example, one side to a deal might be
uncertain about something the other side knows about, and does not want
merely to accept the other side's word for it. The solution might be for the
risk to be shared by the side in the better position to know the relevant
fact to warrant its truth but for the remedy if the situation turns out to be
otherwise to be limited to a specific sum.[32] A variation is where the other
side to the deal wants to reduce its level of uncertainty (for example asking
for security for a loan) but the client is worried that the other side might
act opportunistically. The lawyer therefore negotiates a dispute resolution
device that reduces the other side's uncertainty but which retains the confidence of the client.[33] In other instances, the lawyer might spot risks based
on future scenarios neither the client nor the other side might have thought
of, risks that the agreement can anticipate and share. For example, neither
party might have thought about who would carry the cost of a third party

---

[28]   For US lawyers' as negotiators, see Flood (1991).
[29]   Flood (1996) at 192–93. The degree to which UK lawyers can offer business
advice is to some degree limited by the law on financial intermediaries. See e.g. Part
XX of the Financial Services and Markets Act 2000.
[30]   Tina Stark, 'Thinking Like a Deal Lawyer' (2004) 54 Journal of Legal
Education 223.
[31]   Stephen Nathanson, *What Lawyers Do* (London: Sweet and Maxwell, 1997).
[32]   Nathanson (1997) at 122.
[33]   See Flood (1991) at 57ff.

supplier not being able to deliver on time, or about what happens if the regulatory environment changes.

Lawyers use their knowledge of the law to anticipate and block conflict, but it would be a mistake to think that all of their activity is built around anticipating what courts would do about the provisions of the documents they draft, or indeed that the only readers of the documents they expect are judges. Very few contracts become subject to court proceedings (in one study US lawyers thought 2 per cent,[34] but that must be an over-estimate). Transactions lawyers tend to think of contracts as setting out a map of the parties' relationship for use by the parties themselves, so that the intended readership of the documents they draft can include the parties themselves and not just other lawyers.[35] Although keeping the parties out of court is also an important function, there is some evidence that lawyers think of the mapping function as more important.[36] One example is the framework contract put together to govern the building of Terminal 5 at Heathrow Airport, the operation of which was studied by Simon Deakin and Aristea Koukiadaki.[37] The Terminal 5 contract included extensive provisions about labour matters that were probably not legally enforceable in English law. They were included because the point of the contract documentation was not so much to guide a court about what the parties intended but to guide the parties in the way they implemented the contract. That function included the labour aspects of the deal regardless of whether they could be enforced. In effect, the contract was written as a comprehensive code of the deal for the parties.

A shorter-term part of the conflict-blocking task is what might be

---

[34] Steven Schwarcz, 'Explaining the Value of Transactional Lawyering' (2007) 12 Stanford Journal of Law, Business & Finance 486–535. The median value was 1 per cent, suggesting that the 2 per cent mean results from a few outliers.

[35] This point that there are multiple audiences for legal documents and that those audiences include lay people often arises in the pedagogic literature on legal drafting (for example, Lenné Eidson Espenschied, *Contract Drafting: Powerful Prose in Transactional Practice* (Chicago: American Bar Association Publishing, 2010) 27–28, and so perhaps it represents more an ideal to be achieved than current practice, but at least transactions lawyers recognise the possibility.

[36] Schwarcz (2007) found that, although an overwhelming majority of lawyers considered that their function was both 'setting forth a roadmap for the parties to follow in their ongoing relationship' and 'protecting your client from future litigation', no respondents at all thought that their function was exclusively the latter. Interestingly, although the number of respondents was very low, clients put more emphasis on avoiding litigation.

[37] See Simon Deakin and Aristea Koukiadaki, 'Governance Processes, Labour–Management Partnership and Employee Voice in the Construction of Heathrow Terminal 5' (2009) 38 Industrial Law Journal 365–89.

termed 'regulatory smoothing'. This is the job of ensuring that the deal
will not fall foul of action by regulatory agencies or become commercially
unattractive because of the costs of regulatory compliance or taxation.[38] It
is in this area that the transactions lawyer's job comes closest to that of the
advocate, since often the task will not be confined to designing compliant
structures but might also include persuading regulators that the proposed
structures are indeed compliant.

All these types of advice require the lawyer to understand the client's
business (and for many transactions lawyers the test of a good lawyer is as
much how much he or she understands the client's business as how much
he or she understands the law).[39] They also require a sense of proportion
and of their own limitations. As David Caruth, one of the few City lawyers
ever to publish a memoir put it, in the end the client 'knows the business
and, except in a peripheral way, you do not'.[40] Lawyers with good imagina-
tions can generate very large numbers of possible scenarios that, in principle, might be provided for in the agreement, but to deal with a scenario eats
up time and effort and causes delay. The issue is how likely the scenario is
to happen and, if it did happen, how important or difficult to deal with it
would be. It might be interesting to ask what might happen if a director of
one the parties is incapacitated by a sudden illness while passing through
the airspace of Vanuatu, but holding up negotiations to agree a specific
solution to that question would not be worth it. Delivering commercial
value to a client requires an appreciation for what is now fashionably called
the client's 'appetite for risk' as much as understanding the law related to
the client's goals.

In any particular deal or transaction, there might be a few or many
points where conflict might usefully be anticipated and blocked, but as
deals become more complex the potential number of problems grows
correspondingly. In addition, large numbers of potential techniques for
dealing with such problems have been identified.[41] The result is that
lawyers tend to work on deals in teams, not as individuals. In the US, law
firms, particularly Cravath, developed a method of training their associates in which deals would be broken down into their constituent parts,
each under the control of a specialist, a method that came to define the
approach of the whole firm to its transactional work.[42] The reality of

---

[38]   See e.g. Schwarcz (2007).
[39]   Lewis with Keegan (1997).
[40]   David Caruth, *A Life of Three Strands: A City Lawyer's Memoir* (London:
Avon Books, 1998).
[41]   See Nathanson (1997) at 100–129 for a number of practical examples.
[42]   See   John   Flood,   'Resurgent   Professionalism?   Partnership   and

negotiation and drafting is often more messy and disorganised than the Cravath method would suggest,[43] especially in the US, where, as a broad generalisation, it is more common than in England for clients to be treated as 'belonging' to particular lawyers as opposed to belonging to the firm as a whole,[44] but the process is distinctly social and organisational rather than individual.

Law firms often develop their own standard methods for use in appropriate circumstances, including standard draft clauses for contracts or even standard whole agreements, which they refine over the years and use again and again. David Caruth described the process, as it existed long before the development of word-processing:

> I well remember the first steel contract that I was involved with for Davey [an engineering company] – this was Skopje in Yugoslavia – and the document we ultimately produced I used as a bible until the day I retired very nearly 30 years later. Of course some of the language was out of date but a great deal of it – let's just take as an example the force majeure clause – was still relevant and appropriate. A little bit of tinkering here and there and you had what you really needed for most suitable similar transactions.[45]

Individual lawyers used to collect their own standard documents, their 'precedents' in the course of their career. As law firms grew, however, the firms themselves started to collect precedents and to gather them together in their libraries for use across the firm. Indeed, a potential for conflict developed between individual lawyers and firms about ownership of precedents.[46] As firms grew yet bigger and started to recognise a division of labour between lawyers who dealt directly with clients and lawyers who worked in the background on tasks such as research ('professional support lawyers'),[47] they put increasing effort, using information technology, into

---

Professionalism in Global Law Firms' in D. Muzio and S. Ackroyd (eds), *Redirections in the Study of Expert Labour* (Basingstoke: Palgrave, 2007).

[43]   See Flood (1991).

[44]   I am grateful to Nicholas Aleksander for this point, and for the thought that it might be possible to test hypotheses about whether firms treated clients as belonging to the firm or to individual lawyers by asking them about their attitude towards partners taking sabbaticals!

[45]   Caruth (1998) at 38–9.

[46]   Caruth (1998) at 38.

[47]   Ann Donakey, 'It's Who You Know ... PSLs, Knowledge Brokers and Firm-wide Innovation' (2005) 7 Managing Partner 9. The use of PSLs combined with sophisticated precedent and model document systems seems especially advanced in London, and has produced a law firm structure characterised by a high ratio of associates to partners, at least when compared, for example, to

capturing and recording not just the documents but also the experience generated by the deals in which the firm was involved.[48] These electronic archives constitute much of the capital that law firms now possess.[49]

It has also become possible for firms to innovate without linking the innovation to specific clients or specific matters the firm is currently dealing with. Law firms have always created innovations for the benefit of specific clients and some have gone on to market those innovations to other clients. The best documented such innovation is the invention of the 'poison pill' defence against takeover bids by the US firm Wachtell Lipton.[50] But it has now become possible to develop the innovations first and to find the clients later – in other words for law firms to offer not just a service but a product.[51]

New York. The model is very cost-effective, but it has serious disadvantages for young lawyers, who might find themselves highly specialised – indeed specialised in what economists would recognise as highly firm-specific methods – but without anywhere to go in their careers.

[48] David Jabbari, 'Know it all: The New KM Strategy at Allen & Overy' (2006) 9 Inside Knowledge 8, David Orozco, 'Legal Knowledge as an Intellectual Property Management Resource' (2010) 47 American Business Law Journal 687–726.

[49] Many transactions, of course, use market standard forms, which are open to alteration, but which benefit from, or suffer from, a form of network externality, in which there are considerable advantages associated with using a form easily recognised by others. Indeed, a research project has grown up around such lawyer-designed standard form contracts, a project which is interested in why contracts seem to change more slowly than pure economic rationality might suggest. See e.g. Stephen Choi and Mitu Gulati, 'The Evolution of Boilerplate Contracts: Evidence from the Sovereign Debt Market' New York University School of Law, Law and Economics Research Paper Series: Research Paper No. 05-17 (2005), Mark Weidemaier and Mitu Gulati, 'How Markets Work: The Lawyer's Version' (2012) (http://works.bepress.com/mark_weidemaier/7), Mitu Gulati and Robert Scott, 'The Three and a Half Minute Transaction: Boilerplate and the Limits of Contract Design' Columbia Law and Economics Working Paper No. 407 (2011). In addition to the network externality point, a possible further avenue for research is to think about the social processes that now produce and alter these standard documents within law firms. If the process for changing a document involves many people, all of whom are very busy, it is not perhaps surprising that they change slowly. It might be worth asking whether law firms who have dedicated professional support lawyers with the authority to make changes to standard documents achieve greater flexibility than those who lack such a role.

[50] Michael Powell, 'Professional Innovation: Corporate Lawyers and Private Lawmaking' (1993) 18 Law & Social Inquiry 423–52.

[51] Richard Susskind, *The End of Lawyers? Rethinking the Nature of Legal Services* (Oxford: Oxford U.P., 2008) e.g. at 38ff. There are, however, limits to the 'product' model, as enumerated by the late Larry Ribstein in his paper 'The Death of Big Law' [2010] (3) Wisconsin Law Review 749–815– at 778ff.

The idea of lawyers as creators and marketers of innovation might sound odd in some ears. The standard picture of a lawyer is someone hidebound by the past, constantly referring to its authority and warning that, in effect, nothing should ever be done for the first time. There might even be reasons for lawyers to hide the fact that they innovate. Some researchers, for example, speculate that lawyers in the sovereign bond market found it convenient to play down the extent to which they were innovating because they were acting on behalf of issuers and did not particularly want buyers to know that important clauses had been changed.[52] But innovation is inherent in problem-solving and problem-solving is what most lawyers are paid to do. As David Caruth put it, clients [do] 'not want to hear from a lawyer and, if [they do, they look] for solutions not insurmountable problems.'[53]

Innovation can also be driven more conventionally by new developments in what clients want to do. For example, lawyers in the 1990s were faced with the task of drafting new types of commercial agreement about website development. Initially they borrowed clauses about intellectual property, confidentiality and payment terms from earlier agreements designed for software development agreements and then adjusted them to the new form of deal. Ten years later, the terms generated for website development were in turn used as a basis for agreements about internet service access.[54]

Software has developed to take on many of the deal lawyer's drafting tasks,[55] prompting speculation that lawyers might find themselves replaced by computers and that law firms should turn themselves into publishing houses concentrating on the generation of up-to-date documentation.[56] So far, however, there is little sign of the disappearance of commercial lawyers. A number of factors make the task of fully automating the work of transactions lawyers very difficult: the requirements of

---

[52] Mark Weidemaier and Mitu Gulati, 'How Markets Work: The Lawyer's Version' (2011).

[53] Caruth. at 68–69.

[54] See e.g. Lenné Eidson Espenschied, *Contract Drafting: Powerful Prose in Transactional Practice* (Chicago: American Bar Association Publishing, 2010) at 25.

[55] E.g. HotDocs (http://www.hotdocs.com), D3 and its successors (www.microsystems.com), DealBuilder (www.businessintegrity.com), and Exari (www.exari.com). For the most general account of legal document software, see Marc Lauritsen and Thomas Gordon, 'Toward a General Theory of Document Modeling', Proceedings of the 12th International Conference on Artificial Intelligence and Law (2009).

[56] Susskind (2008) chapter 8.

business change in unpredictable ways; both the law and the regulatory environment can change not just in content but in degree of predictability; and many of the tasks lawyers take on to make deals work concern the requirements of human beings rather than systems of rules.[57] The cost of automation is itself considerable, especially if one includes training costs, and might not be justified except for the most common and straightforward transactions. But most of all, legal transactional work requires a constant willingness to innovate – not necessarily actual innovation but a preparedness to abandon an established method and look for a new one. Judging when innovation is required and possessing the creativity to innovate successfully when it is required are not yet tasks that machines can do. One might speculate that the systemisation and automation of legal documentation, instead of losing lawyers their jobs, might be allowing lawyers to concentrate more on the substance of their advice. If anything, automation, by increasing thinking time and reducing the need for drudge work, puts an even higher premium on the critical and creative aspects of transactional lawyering.

Lawyers are not the only sources of transactional innovation. Indeed, David Caruth marks as a turning point in the City of London an incident in which the third draft of a takeover document, drafted not by a law firm but by a merchant bank lands on the desk of the bidder's lawyer before the lawyer even knew that the client was making a bid. (Caruth's conclusion was that he should move from his firm to work as an in-house lawyer for a bank – on the assumption that although the bank had produced the document, it was not bankers who had written it, but their own lawyers, and so if he wanted to be in the thick of the interesting action, that is where he should be – another explanation, however, might be that the increasing regulation of takeovers through the City Code was leading to a standardisation of documents to the extent that even bankers could draft them). Furthermore, law firms vary in the extent to which they see themselves as in direct competition with those other sources of innovation – banks, accountants, venture capitalists. For example, they vary in the extent to which they want to commit themselves to business advice rather

---

[57] Tony Williams, one of Richard Susskind's interviewees in 2002, recounted the tasks he was involved in as the head of Clifford Chance's Moscow office as follows: 'A range of things, from, say somebody like Merrill Lynch setting up in Moscow; or a big joint venture between Atlantic Richfield . . . and Luk Oil. . . . To explore for and exploit oil in Russia; including anything those clients want including getting their flats in Moscow or their work permits' – Susskind (2005) at 18.

than purely legal advice.[58] Very few would want to go as far as the law firms of Silicon Valley who compete directly with venture capitalists and banks to the extent of, in effect, investing their own money in the companies they advise.[59] But law firms do have some enduring advantages over those other sources of innovation and advice, advantages that arise from the requirements of their regulatory smoothing role and from understanding what happens legally if the parties fail to specify their own solution to problems.

OUTSIDE THE MAGIC CIRCLE

One objection to the picture painted here of lawyers as innovatory facilitators of business might be that it applies only to the elite firms of New York and London, or perhaps those firms plus a few outlier firms in areas of exceptionally high economic growth, such as Silicon Valley, and that outside that magical world, transactions lawyers do little more than drudge work. But here is an account from Stephen Nathanson of a private client lawyer engaging in the allegedly routine matter of advising a client about a will that challenges that notion.[60]

> I have a client with quite a bit of money and not much to do. She comes into the office often to update her will. She is a widow with three daughters, two of whom are married with children. The unmarried, youngest one is a big disappointment to her mother. She has a history of minor psychiatric problems but refuses to get psychiatric counselling at the university where she is a student.
>
> The last time my client wanted a will updated, her instructions were to cut the youngest daughter out of the will completely. I asked her why she wanted to do this. We had a long discussion and she explained in detail what a disappointment her youngest child was, how she was unwilling to help herself and take responsibility for her life.
>
> I advised against disinheriting her. I explained that when someone who has a

---

[58] Lewis with Keegan (1997). Note also the limitations British firms face about financial advice under Part XX of the Financial Services and Markets Act 2000.

[59] Mark Suchman, 'Dealmakers and Counselors: Law Firms as Intermediaries in the Development of Silicon Valley', in Martin Kenney, *Understanding Silicon Valley: the Anatomy of an Entrepreneurial Region* (Palo Alto: Stanford U.P., 2000) esp. at 91ff (Silicon Valley law firms accepting stock in lieu of fees). See also Mark Suchman and Mia Cahill, 'The Hired Gun as Facilitator: Lawyers and the Suppression of Business Disputes in Silicon Valley' (1996) 21 Law and Social Inquiry 679–712 and Lisa Bernstein, 'The Silicon Valley Lawyer as Transactions Cost Engineer' (1995) 74 Oregon Law Review 239–55.

[60] Nathanson (1997) at 108–9.

will dies, and a child feels unhappy about the provisions, she can apply to court for a will variation. The court has a discretion to give her something from the estate. So I told her to provide a small amount in the will for that daughter and prepare a letter to me explaining her reasons for providing that amount. If her letter showed good judgment and the amount provided was large enough, the daughter would be less likely to sue later on.

I also told her that if she cut her daughter out completely, she risked having the estate eaten up by legal costs in the event of a contested claim being made, to say nothing of the animosity that would be created between the sisters.

Alternatively, I said, she could distribute *inter vivos* gifts to the children now . . . or set up a trust with them as beneficiaries. I also suggested she see a counsellor to see if she could improve her relationship with her daughter. But she did not like any of my suggestions. She wanted to punish her daughter. She told me, 'You're missing the point! I want her to *know* she's being left out! The money will do more harm than good. If she knows the money is coming, she won't do anything to help herself.'

It was at this point that a light bulb went on over my head. I said: 'You want her to know you feel like cutting her out, right? Well then write her a letter telling her that and the reasons why. If it's satisfaction you want you'll have plenty of it because you'll be able to see her reaction while you're still *alive*. Then you let me do your will and include provisions for her in it. After you're gone, that will probably give her such a pleasant surprise, she won't bring action against the estate. The estate will be saved thousands in legal costs.'

To my relief, my client liked the idea. Her maternal instinct to try to help her daughter overrode her desire to teach her a lesson.

So we went ahead with it. She wrote a letter to her daughter that I had to amend before it went out. It was too angry and direct. Of course, it was what one might expect an angry mother to write. But it could be misconstrued by a third party such as a judge. So I softened the language, transforming accusations into reasoned protests. In the letter, mum was able to express her hurt and disappointment and ask the daughter to pull up her boot straps. Mum also mentioned the inheritance and her fear that it would be squandered in an irresponsible way by the daughter.

We then discussed how to benefit the daughter in the will. After some discussion, I was able to get her to agree to provide quite generously for the daughter, although not nearly as generously as for the other two daughters. The provision for the youngest daughter was subject to a corporate-managed trust with strict conditions. The other two daughters were to receive their interests in the estate with no conditions. I drafted the will and she executed it.

This account contains much of what one needs to know about lawyers' work. Even in drafting wills, lawyers require understanding of what their clients want combined with an ability to anticipate and avoid the problems their clients will encounter if they blindly pursue what they want. The work is fundamentally about solving problems, which requires understanding the problem from the client's point of view (as illustrated by Nathanson's lawyer's 'light-bulb' moment), and it involves considerable creativity. The lawyer's first ideas, a standard piece of advice about leaving a legacy large enough to discourage a costly dispute and making provision while alive rather than when dead, did not solve the problem because they failed to fulfil the client's desire to shock the daughter into action. The lawyer could not solve the problem before seeing the problem from the client's point of view. The lawyer's second idea, however, separating out communicating with the daughter from specifying the contents of the will, solves both the client's problem and the difficulties identified by the lawyer about the client's solution.

The story also illustrates the subtle interaction between what the client wants and what the lawyer thinks it is wise for the client to want, an interaction that expresses itself in the interplay between the lawyer-client conversation about the definition of the problem and their conversation about the identification of solutions. The lawyer realises that the client has not been entirely honest about what she wants, or at least has not arrived at an adequate level of self-awareness about what she wants. She wants to punish the daughter, but she does not really want to exclude her completely. Notice also how the lawyer transformed what for the client was a single unified problem and solution into four separate but linked problems and two separate but linked solutions. For the client the problem was that offering the prospect of money to her disappointing daughter would make her behave even more badly, and the solution was to cut the daughter out of the will. For the lawyer the problems were that the client was disappointed with her daughter and wanted the daughter to know that; that the client did not want the prospect of money from her estate to undermine any motivation the daughter might have to improve herself; that the client did not really want her daughter to get nothing at all (the light-bulb); and that if the client cut her daughter out of the will completely, there would be a very costly dispute that would leave the family financially and emotionally worse off (the problem the lawyer saw but not the client). Hence the twin solutions to write a letter to the daughter saying she will get nothing (solves problems one and two), but in reality to leave her something (solves problem three and, with luck, problem four). Here as elsewhere, lawyering can involve leading clients into thinking differently about what their problems are in the first place before offering solutions, not just solving the problem as presented by the client.[61]

Note further that the lawyer uses both a knowledge of the law in theory (that children can challenge wills and that it matters whether it can be shown that the testator was making a conscious decision based on sound

---

[61] See also Louis Brown and Edward Dauer, *Planning by Lawyers: Cases and Materials* (Mineola: Foundation Press, 1978) at 271.

reasoning) and in practice, that the language of the client's draft of the letter was likely to be understood in an unhelpful way by a judge. But that the lawyer's motivation throughout was not winning lawsuits but avoiding them.

LAWYERS IN THE PUBLIC SERVICE

It is now time to introduce another part of the legal profession. About 5 per cent of lawyers in England and Wales work directly in the public service, including 2000 lawyers in the Government Legal Service and about 4000 in local authorities.[62] The profile of their work is in many ways similar to in-house lawyers of large commercial organisations. As a lawyer who works directly for a National Health Service trust told the Law Society Gazette:[63]

> NHS lawyers' terms of reference are increasingly varied, and include: representing trusts at public enquiries; dealing with complaints; Freedom of Information Act requests and data protection issues; commercial property work; landlord and tenant disputes; EU procurement regulations; employment law; shared-service agreements; joint ventures; and commercial contract work.

The aspects of the work that are specific to the public sector are largely matters of conflict-blocking and regulatory smoothing (freedom

---

[62]   For the UK Government Legal Service, see http://www.gls.gov.uk/. For the estimate of 4000 lawyers in local government, see http://www.lawcareers.net/information/alternativecareers/LocalGovernment.aspx. Comparative figures are difficult to find for the US, but the US Department of Justice alone claims to employ more than 10,000 lawyers (http://www.justice.gov/oarm/). Comparable figures for France are difficult to find since the French government for many years did not count as a separate category of civil servant those who deal with 'affaires juridiques', a category that now includes the jobs of 'cadre juridique', 'consultant juridique' and 'assistant juridique', but, for example, in 2009, in the Interior Ministry, 10 per cent of civil servants came into that category (see http://www.unsa-interieur-ats.fr/media/up/action_sociale/BILAN_SOCIAL_SG_2009.pdf). In the statistics published by French local government, little distinction is made between administrative generalists and lawyers (itself an indication of the importance of lawyers), but the overall figure is some 95,000 (see Observatoire de l'emploi, des métiers et des competences de la fonction publique territorial, Tendances de l'emploi territorial: Note de conjuncture, N° 15 (March 2011) (http://www.observatoire.cnfpt.fr/documents/032011/290311111445v7v8927NoteConjoncture.pdf).
[63]   Jonathan Rayner, 'Solicitor wants forum for "isolated" NHS lawyers' Law Society Gazette, 27 January 2011.

of information, EU procurement rules). Very little is litigation-related (landlord and tenant disputes and some employment law). The aspect of NHS legal work that might have occurred first to an outsider – medical negligence litigation – does not feature at all. That work is assigned to a specific organisation, the NHS Litigation Authority, and contracted out by them to private firms.[64]

Lawyers in local government have a similar range of tasks, especially in the employment and property fields, but with two additional elements. Local authorities act as regulators in their own right, and need to understand both their powers and their obligations, and they spend public money on a wide variety of functions, so they need to understand the limits of their legal authorisation to spend. The first question a local authority lawyer needs to ask when asked to advise about a proposed new council policy is 'do we have legal authority to do this?'[65]

Lawyers in national government again have the same range of transactional tasks, and the same authorisation questions arising from regulation and expenditure as local government lawyers. But because central government has greater access to the power to make new law than local government, if the answer to the question 'do we have authority to do this?' comes back 'no', central government lawyers can more easily ask a further question, namely 'If we don't have the necessary authority, how do we get it?' The answer to the further question might range from the relatively straightforward (e.g. we can make secondary legislation) via the relatively easy in normal circumstances (we can propose a new statute), to the difficult (e.g. we need a change in EU law) or the very difficult (e.g. we need to persuade every other signatory to agree to an amendment to the European Convention on Human Rights).

Central government lawyers also have the task, sometimes itself a consequence of identifying a gap in the government's authority to act, of translating policy into law. The process involves understanding what policy-makers want to achieve and constructing an effective means of delivering what they want to achieve. As Stephen Laws, First Parliamentary Counsel (the head of the UK government department charged with drafting legislation), has pointed out, that process is full of possible

---

[64]   See the NHSLA Framework document (2002) (http://www.nhsla.com/NR/rdonlyres/D872241A-43E3-492B-8F74-32FB0586608F/0/Frameworkdocument.pdf) and its annual reports.

[65]   See e.g. John Tradewell, 'The Power to do anything . . .' in Mirza Ahmad (ed.), *A Passion for Leadership & Going Beyond Austerity* (ACSeS, 2011) (http://www.acses.org.uk/public_file/filename/45/A_Passion_for_Leadership___Going_Beyond_Austerity.pdf) p. 67 at 68 (the default setting is 'can we do this?').

misunderstandings, what he calls 'missing the policy-maker's point', mis-understandings that have to be corrected by an iterative process of drafting and comment. [66] For example, as Laws lays out, those drafting legislation sometimes too readily assume that the point of legislation is to change the behaviour of members of the public, when in fact it might have other, perfectly legitimate, aims such as altering a decision-making structure, authorising expenditure or prioritising resources, all of which might ulti-mately change behaviour but whose immediate point is to allocate the power to decide whether or how to use public resources. Sometimes, the potential for misunderstanding is more political than policy-based, for example when legislative lawyers advise that to achieve the government's required ends only minimal legislation is necessary, but ministers want a comprehensive restatement of the law because comprehensive restatements are easier to explain, or merely look more impressive. There are also other policy aims, only hinted at by Laws when he refers to 'signalling', that are perhaps not immediately comprehensible to lawyers, but that are increas-ingly important to politicians. One example is 'signalling' to the elector-ate the government's particular claims to virtue on a particular topic by entrenching policy priorities in statute, and incidentally making political difficulties for any future governments that might want to change course. Examples include the Child Poverty Act 2010 (creating statutory targets for reducing child poverty), the Children, Schools and Families Bill 2010 (which, as originally drafted, would have created parental 'guarantees' in education that were apparently never intended to be legally binding), and the Fiscal Responsibility Act 2010 (declaring that it is illegal for the budget deficit not to fall year on year). Legislative lawyers need to understand

---

[66]   Stephen Laws, 'Giving Effect to Policy in Legislation: How to Avoid Missing the Point' (2011) 32 Statute Law Review 1–16. The appellation 'Parliamentary Counsel' is a classic linguistic false friend (or perhaps a classic example of British eccentricity), for it refers to the government's legal adviser for parliamentary business (it was originally called 'Parliamentary Counsel to the Treasury') and not to any official of Parliament. Indeed it is an important rule of the British system of government that mere Members of Parliament have no access to the expertise of Parliamentary Counsel unless the government decides to allow them access. (In fact, even government departments are not allowed to use Parliamentary Counsel unless authorised by the Parliamentary Business and Legislation Committee of the Cabinet, the committee of ministers that controls the government's legislative programme in parliament.) Individual members of parliament have to do their own research and drafting, assisted in the final stages by the staff of Parliament, particularly the Clerk of Legislation and her assistants. Oddly, most of the relevant Parliamentary staff seem not to have been trained as lawyers, although they develop considerable expertise.

these political motives as well, bizarre as they might seem. In the well-worn, if cynical, phrase of Lord Thring, the original UK Parliamentary Counsel, 'Bills are made to pass no less than . . . razors . . . were made to sell'.[67] The important point about bills from the point of view of legislative lawyers is that they should achieve the ends the government envisages for them, rather than the ends an outsider might imagine for them.

Difficulties arise, however, not only because lawyers fail to grasp policy-makers' purposes but also because policy-makers are not clear about their purposes in the first place. For example, a proposed provision might catch activities beyond those policy-makers were thinking about, might grant powers that might be used for unintended purposes, might undermine existing allocations of authority or might even violate international treaties. Incoherence of these types might remain hidden until the process of attempting to draft the legislation starts in earnest.[68] In addition, Edward Page has tracked the process by which UK parliamentary counsel analyse policy proposals for their underlying logic and internal coherence, on the theory that proposals that make no internal sense cannot be turned into comprehensible statutes.[69] In its guidance about its services, the Office of Parliamentary Counsel warns other government departments that they can expect 'cautious detachment' about policy.[70] The process of challenge may reveal not only difficult drafting problems but also inconsistencies or gaps in policy-makers' thinking.

In the same way that Nathanson's will lawyer realised that the mother was not being entirely honest, or lacked self-awareness, about what she wanted for her daughter, the Office of Parliamentary Counsel realises that government departments might not always be entirely honest about their

---

[67]   Henry Thring, 'The Simplification of the Law' (Jan 1874) 136 (271) The Quarterly Review 55–74 at 66. The reference is to an 18th century lyric in which the purchaser of some exceedingly cheap razors complains to the seller that they do not shave, to which the seller replies that they were not made to shave 'but to sell'. See George Engel, '"Bills are made to pass as razors are made to sell": practical constraints in the preparation of legislation' (1983) 4 Statute Law Review 7–23 at 9. The whole of Thring's article is still worth reading today, not just for its views on law reform but also for its still pertinent observations on politicians' attitudes towards legislation.

[68]   See Laws (2011) at 8.

[69]   Edward Page, 'Their Word is Law: Parliamentary Counsel and Creative Policy Analysis' [2009] Public Law 790–811.

[70]   See Office of Parliamentary Counsel, *A Summary of Working with Parliamentary Counsel* (London: Cabinet Office, 2011) (hereinafter OPC (2011a)) at 4 (http://www.cabinetoffice.gov.uk/sites/default/files/resources/WWPC_WEB_GUIDE_SUMMARY_6_DEC_2011.pdf).

policy intentions, or at least might not be aware of the extent to which policy intentions have been fudged in the process of development. The Office's guidance repeatedly stresses the importance of departments being 'frank' with counsel and hints that one of the reasons drafting might need several iterations (at least three rounds, it warns)[71] is to ensure that all of the department's objectives are in the open.

It is to facilitate the process of challenge that the Office of Parliamentary Counsel insists, with very few exceptions, on what at first sight seems an eccentric practice that departments should send them not draft clauses but simply a narrative that lays out the effects the department wants.[72] Counsel need to think through the various options open to them in turning the brief into a statute and want to avoid being pinned down into a single option produced by departmental lawyers who might not have thought through the wider implications.

Outsiders might assume that the intended readership of statutes is the judiciary, since statutes represent, in a sense, the legislature's attempts to instruct the courts. Most of the time legislation is applied without anyone going near a court. It is applied not just by public officials but by business managers trying to comply with employment law, public health law, health and safety at work law, company law, tax law and so on, and by individuals, especially those engaged in regulated professions. Many people, in other words, need to apply the law to themselves.[73] Another set of target readers are, of course, lawyers, who play an important role in transmitting legal requirements, both specific and general, to their clients.[74] In addition, there are other professional advisers, such as architects, planning consultants and accountants, who might not be legally qualified but who in practice offer guidance on the law within their specialisms. These are all potential readers and appliers of statutes. Significantly, the Office of Parliamentary

---

[71] See OPC (2011a) at 7.

[72] See OPC (2011a) at 9.

[73] How 'self-application' of the law works is a matter of interest to sociologists (see e.g. Donald Black, *The Social Structure of Right and Wrong* (San Diego: Academic Press, 1993) 65ff) and legal theorists (see e.g. James Maxeiner, 'Legal Indeterminancy Made in America: U.S. Legal Methods and the Rule of Law' (2006–2007) 41 Valparaiso University Law Review 517–89 at 523–24). One does not have to believe, however, that without self-application no legal system or even no society would not survive – which may or may not be true – to appreciate why legislative lawyers might think that designing statutes so that they could be applied without resort to a judge might be desirable.

[74] See e.g. Gillian Hadfield, 'Don't forget the lawyers: The role of lawyers in promoting the rule of law in (emerging) market democracies' (2006–2007) 56 DePaul Law Review 401–21.

Counsel in its guidance on drafting techniques gives pride of place as its first set of readers to those who will apply statutes without going near a court.[75]

Laws is also clear that the courts are not the only readership for statutes, and might not even be the principal readership. Statutes aimed at guiding regulators are directed at those regulators and statutes concerned with managing public resources are directed at the managers of those resources. Courts might at some stage have to interpret such statutes, but, Laws hopes, when that necessity arises (and it is a formal goal of the Office of Parliamentary Counsel that they draft with the intention of minimising the risk of litigation),[76] they will see that statutes designed to address complex policy problems should not be interpreted as if they were intended to create simple rights and duties. That is, the courts are not the principal target readership for these statutes and he hopes that the judges understand that.

In the US, the formal arrangements for legislative drafting are different – ultimately reflecting constitutional differences about the separation of powers – but the functions of legislative lawyers are fundamentally the same as in the UK.[77] One senior counsel of the House of Representatives Office of Legislative Counsel described the job as 'taking the idea of any Member or committee of the House of Representatives requesting the services of the Office and transforming it into legislative language or, as one of my clients used to say, "the magic words"'.[78] The same interaction with policy issues exists in the USA as elsewhere. Congressional counsel

---

[75] Office of Parliamentary Counsel, *Drafting Guidance* (London: Cabinet Office, 2011) (hereinafter OPC (2011b)) at 2 (http://www.cabinetoffice.gov.uk/sites/default/files/resources/Office_of_the_Parliamentary_Counsel_revised_guidance_16_12_11.pdf).

[76] See OPC (2011a) at 2.

[77] See e.g. M. Douglass Bellis, 'Drafting in the US Congress' (2001) 22 Statute Law Review 38–44. Legislative drafting in the US is a function of the legislative branch, not, as in the UK, of the executive branch, being located in the Offices of Legislative Counsel in the two Houses. The distinctively American eccentricity of the arrangements is perhaps that it began very late – the start of the 20th century – and for several years was run as a private charity, before gaining official status in the House of Representatives only in 1919. More broadly the relationship between a country's constitution and its arrangements for drafting legislation would be a topic of research worth pursuing. For an account of the French system, which involves an institution so far unknown in the US or the UK, namely the Council of State, see John Bell, 'What Is the Function of the Conseil d'Etat in the Preparation of Legislation?' (2000) 49 International and Comparative Law Quarterly 661.

[78] Sandra Strokoff, 'How Our Laws Are Made: A Ghost Writer's View' http://www.house.gov/legcoun/strokoff.shtml#footnote1 (expanded version of the

are not allowed to insert their own views about members' policies into
their drafting, but their interaction with members can reveal ways in which
those policies need further thought.[79] It is important, legislative counsel
remind themselves in their own style guide, to 'find out what the client
really wants to do', to 'analyze the legal and other problems in doing that'
and to find solutions that 'will be administrable and enforceable' and will
'keep hassles and litigation to a minimum'.[80] Furthermore, US legislative
counsel understand that the intended principal audience for a statute or an
amendment might vary and that legislators might want to get a message
across to '(A) The world, (B) The American people, (C) Fellow legislators,
(D) Legislative staff, (E) Administrators, (F) Courts, (G) Constituents, (H)
The media, (I) Others'.[81]

The biggest difference between the US and the UK is that, whereas
British legislative lawyers work in theory to a single client – the department
sponsoring the bill – their American counterparts work to the individual
members of Congress, all of whom might have their own policy objectives.
The result is that US legislative lawyers might find themselves drafting the
same piece of legislation from many different points of view. One effect of
that plurality is high potential for loss of policy coherence. As one House
of Representatives legislative counsel remarked:[82]

> Our responsibility is to reflect the ideas of Members of Congress accurately in
> legislative language. That isn't to say that we can't affect policy by pointing out
> the consequences or meanings of the printed word. Trying to close loopholes
> before they open is a constant challenge. It is easy to overlook the consequences
> of the simplest word.

But another effect of plurality is that it provides US legislative lawyers
with an additional function, namely informal mediation. Although legislative counsel maintain a strict relationship of confidentiality with each
member, they cannot help but notice that sometimes members from

---

same article in (Summer 1996) 59(2) The Philadelphia Lawyer, Philadelphia Bar
Association Quarterly Magazine).
[79]   See Strokoff (1996).
[80]   *House Legislative Counsel's Manual on Drafting Style* (1995) (http://www.
house.gov/legcoun/pdf/draftstyle.pdf) at 1. It adds as a final aim to 'convince the
client that the drafter is the best to come down the pike since Solomon', which
might also be taken as a goal of the Office of Parliamentary Counsel.
[81]   *House Legislative Counsel's Manual on Drafting Style* (1995) at 4. Two
decades later, one might question the proposed order – the media might now come
first.
[82]   Bellis (2001) at 41.

different political traditions have basically similar ideas, but are prevented from seeing so by the political language they want to use. By translating various political slogans into the same neutral legal language, legislative counsel can effectively uncover a consensus where none was previously suspected.[83]

One interesting twist of the US House of Representatives system is that inexperienced lawyers are allowed to practise on amendments that have little or no chance of being passed, a practice that has the perhaps unexpected result that the most junior lawyers in the office are usually assigned the task of drafting proposed amendments to the US Constitution.[84]

Another difference between the organisation of the Office of Parliamentary Counsel and the House Office of Legislative Counsel, though not perhaps as great as sometimes reported, is that the Office of Parliamentary Counsel is somewhat less specialised than its US counterpart. House legislative counsel are allocated work within fairly narrow specialisms, within which they tend to stay, although, as one of them remarked:[85]

[B]ecause of the relatively small number of attorneys handling anything that comes in the door, we use the term 'specialist' loosely. I, for example, am responsible for legislation involving trade with other countries, exports from the United States, controlling the proliferation of arms and weapons of mass destruction, all forms of intellectual property, and matters affecting the Federal courts and civil actions, and I share responsibility with other attorneys on all other matters affecting international relations.

In contrast, in the Office of Parliamentary Counsel, teams are allocated, at least as a first cut, to all the legislative work generated by two or three whole departments of state.[86] The leaders of the teams are expected to switch the group of departments they face every five years (that is, each new Parliament) and team members move teams more frequently than that – previously perhaps as frequently as every year but now less frequently than that. Although the Office of Parliamentary Counsel does not operate, as some researchers have reported, according to a version of the

---

[83]   Bellis (2001) at 42–43.
[84]   See Strokoff (1996).
[85]   See Strokoff (1996).
[86]   I am very grateful to Stephen Laws for the information laid out here. The system described is as he left it when he retired as First Parliamentary Counsel, but it seems to have been continued by his successor. See House of Commons, Political and Constitutional Reform Committee, Evidence Session 14 June 2012 (to be published as HC 74-ii) at questions 56 and 57.

'cab-rank' principle, according to which barristers take on the next client to come through the door, [87] it takes the view that the undoubted benefits of specialisation need to be balanced against other requirements, such as flexibility, staff development and, perhaps most important, the maintenance of a degree of objectivity and distance from the departmental point of view.

TRANSACTIONS LAWYERS AND LEGISLATIVE LAWYERS COMPARED

Academic lawyers sometimes make strong distinctions between 'private' law and 'public' law, but legislative drafters and transactions lawyers, despite working on very different subject matter, share important characteristics. Both make a product they want to deliver to their client in a form that will achieve what the client wants to achieve. Both use processes of conflict-blocking, of anticipating future problems and resolving them in conjunction with the client. Both require insight into the client's view of the world. There are also parallel issues for lawyers about their role. Most strikingly, just as transactions lawyers have to think about the extent to which they should give business advice, not just legal advice, legislative lawyers have to think about the extent to which they should become involved in giving what is effectively policy advice.

There is also a parallel about the intended readership of both kinds of lawyers' products. The assumption that both contracts and statutes are written only for future courts to read turns out to be inaccurate. Although both transactions lawyers and legislative lawyers need to think about how their words might be interpreted by judges, they also think about how others might use them to regulate themselves.

One area in which transactions lawyers and legislative lawyers seem to differ, at least in the UK, is in their attitude to precedents and model documents. As we have seen, the collection and cataloguing of relevant precedents is of immense importance to transactions lawyers. It is their stock in trade, and forms the basis of designing standard documentation for future transactions. UK legislative lawyers, however, at least in the Office of Parliamentary Counsel, seem deliberately to shy away from precedents and pride themselves on treating each legislative proposal as new and requiring its own analysis and drafting.[88] But the difference is not as

---

[87]   See Page (2009) at 797.
[88]   Laws (2011) at 6.

great as first appears. Transactions lawyers, or at least the good ones, do not re-use their precedents and models blindly, but instead seek to adapt them to new circumstances, and for their part, legislative lawyers, although wary of boiler-plate and stock phrases, maintain their own stock of standard techniques and ways of thinking, which they seek to pass on to their successors, or sometimes consciously to change.

WHAT DO LAWYERS DO?

Lawyers, whether in the private or public sector, spend most of their time translating the desires of their clients into legal form and trying to keep their clients out of trouble. To achieve good results, they need to understand what their clients want, and the context within which they want it. They also need to understand the difficulties characteristically encountered by their clients, both legal and in life. They rarely, if ever, set foot in a courtroom,[89] and although their thoughts might occasionally wander to speculation about how judges might interpret the documents they create, they are just as likely to focus on how their clients, or other lawyers, might use them.

The characteristics of legal work are far from the combination of courtroom drama and overwhelming paperwork portrayed by the media and government careers advice. The qualities lawyers need most are not histrionics or pedantry but controlled imagination and creativity: imagination to comprehend problems both from their client's point of view and from the point of view of the law, and creativity in solving those problems. That is not to say that all lawyers possess the qualities of imagination and creativity. Many will not. But understanding what lawyers do has implications for what should count as good lawyering and what should count as an aptitude for law.

But what is the nature of the service lawyers provide? What good does it do for their clients? We have seen that lawyers facilitate transactions, help people to interact with the state, design plans of action in which the state

---

[89] Nor does setting foot in courtrooms do them any good in their careers – it is alleged, for example, that only one litigator has ever become the Senior Partner of a Magic Circle firm. Indeed, one can glean from the histories of the City law firms that litigation was, even well into the second half of the twentieth century, a low status activity managed not by solicitors themselves but by clerks. One solicitor remarks, 'It's all about class of course. Chaps never litigated, and the litigation practices of the City of London were in many cases begun by the one-time batmen who had served under the partner officers during WW2.'

is not likely to intervene, and draft statutes. That seems a very disparate set of functions. How can it be that a single profession is interested in them all? Is there anything that binds them together? It is to that question which we now turn.

3. Law as engineering

What is the service that lawyers offer their clients? Lawyers themselves tend to think in terms of 'advice'. Clients want to achieve something – restructure a debt, float a company, securitise assets, buy a house, provide for relatives after they die, or bring in a new government policy – and lawyers advise them about how to do it. But 'advice' does not fully capture what lawyers offer. Clients do not write contracts or leases or statutes on the advice of lawyers. Lawyers write them. Indeed, contracts, leases and statutes are often difficult for clients to understand without assistance. Their importance lies, for clients, in what they accomplish, not in their inner workings. Lawyers' advice comes in the form of informing clients about what it is possible or not possible to achieve (or possible or not possible to achieve easily). It is about the risks attached to the various courses of action lawyers can facilitate, not about how that facilitation works.

A better way of characterising the situation is that lawyers make things for their clients. Clients want things that help them to achieve their ends, and are interested in their effects and risks, but they are not particularly interested in the detail of how they work. Clients, from banks to governments, want to change their circumstances and want to put in place arrangements that bring about those changes, but specifically how those arrangements work is left to lawyers. Lawyers maintain a stock of standard techniques and precedents that help them achieve ends that clients repeatedly want, but they also on occasion develop new techniques, or new combinations of techniques, to meet new requirements or new circumstances. Even standard-looking jobs are potentially different from the norm and providing a good service often involves choosing existing techniques very carefully to suit the precise requirements of the client.

The job lawyers do, from corporate finance to legislative drafting, of making things for clients is arguably the most important, and it is probably the most frequent, job they have. But it is a job that is poorly understood outside the world of law firms and government. It is difficult from the outside even to see it as a single type of activity. As information technology radically changes economic relationships and different lawyers come to serve very different clients, some people ask whether there is any sense in which lawyers are still members of the same profession.[1]

There is, however, a way of explaining what lawyers offer that both grasps and unifies much of what they do. It is to see their job in terms of a much more easily grasped type of job, a job that also involves making things for clients. That job is that of the engineer.

ENGINEERS

Just as there are many kinds of lawyer, there are many kinds of engineer. In historical terms, it is more than arguable that modern engineering began in the military,[2] but by the end of the 18th century, civil engineering, which is to say not military engineering, was developing as a profession. As the 19th century progressed, civil engineering further specialised and formalised – spinning off first mechanical engineers and naval engineers (curiously known as 'naval architects', to distinguish those who design ships from those who carry out other engineering tasks at sea) and later mining, electrical and chemical engineers. Specialisation continued throughout the following century and continues to this day. Many dozens of specialisms have developed with their own professional bodies and journals. Some specialisms are based on the type of object produced. Examples include building bridges, roads or power stations, manufacturing chemicals, making industrial machinery, aircraft, communications systems or medical equipment, devising new silicon chips and developing nano-machines that work at molecular level. Other specialisms are based on the type of effects the engineers are concerned with, for example safety, security, resilience, or sustainability. Others still are based on particular stages of engineering, such as design or materials, or on particular work methods, for example control engineering or concurrent engineering (organising many types of work in

---

[1]   E.g. H.W. Arthurs, 'A Lot of Knowledge is a Dangerous Thing: Will the Legal Profession Survive the Knowledge Explosion?' (1995) 18 Dalhousie Law Journal 295–309, Herbert Kritzer, 'The Professions Are Dead, Long Live the Professions: Legal Practice in a Post-professional World' (1999) 33 Law & Society Review 713–59, Andrew Francis, *Law at the Edge: Emergent and Divergent Models of Legal Professionalism* (Farnham: Ashgate, 2011) at 3ff.

[2]   E.g. Michael Davis, *Thinking Like an Engineer: Studies in the Ethics of a Profession* (Oxford: Oxford U.P., 1998) 9–11. Another point of view is that the origins of engineering are in water and sewerage – think, for example, about the aqueducts and the cloaca maxima of Rome. (Or in both – Scott Boorman points out that the Roman engineer Frontinus wrote a treatise on stratagems and a treatise on aqueducts!).

parallel). These different types of classification can cross-cut to produce sub-specialisms, such as the design of nuclear power station safety systems or the sustainability of the materials used to make aircraft. Occasionally debate breaks out about whether a new offshoot is genuinely 'engineering' or something else (for example there was for a time a fierce debate about the status of software engineering),[3] and engineers, especially in Britain, have often been concerned about the use of the term for other types of job, especially non-graduate technical trades.[4]

All engineers, however, have in common a commitment to one central activity – making useful things. The Institution of Civil Engineers' Royal Charter refers, rather grandly, to engineering as 'the art of directing the great sources of power in Nature for the use and convenience of man', a phrase usually attributed to Thomas Tredgold, an early writer of engineering textbooks. The philosopher Michael Davis, after long observation of engineers, offered a rather more straightforward statement that engineering is 'the practical study of how to make people and things work better together'.[5] In other words, engineering is about the creation of artefacts that get jobs done.

The central point of these ways of characterising engineering is that engineers are committed not just to understanding the world but to changing it. This is the central feature of engineering that distinguishes it from science. For scientists understanding nature is important whether or not it leads to 'directing [its] great sources of power'. For engineers, understanding is a means to an end, the end of making useful things. Another way of expressing the difference between engineering and science is that engineering creates new objects that nature would not have produced by itself. Engineering is inherently concerned with the 'artificial', in the literal sense of making things by skill, but also in the extended sense of 'unnatural'.[6] As a leading engineering textbook says 'Scientists try to understand nature. Engineers try to make things that do not exist in nature.'[7]

The difference between engineering and science operates not just in the abstract but in how engineers and scientists think about themselves. Davis

---

3   See e.g. Davis (1998) chapter 3.

4   See e.g. Helen Marshall, Lynne McClymont and Lucy Joyce, *Public Attitudes to and Perceptions of Engineering and Engineers* (London: Royal Academy of Engineering, 2007).

5   Davis (1998) at ix.

6   See Herbert Simon, *Sciences of the Artificial* (Cambridge, MA: MIT Press, 1996) at 4–5.

7   Y.C. Fung and P. Tong, *Classical and Computational Solid Mechanics* (Singapore: World Scientific, 2001) at 1.

carried out a series of informal surveys of mixed groups of scientists and engineers who were working together in the same institution, sometimes on the same projects. He asked them whether they would rather invent something useful or discover new knowledge. Scientists overwhelmingly preferred discovering new knowledge. Engineers even more overwhelmingly preferred inventing something useful.[8] Engineers use science but engineers are not scientists. More importantly, scientists are not engineers.

Engineers are not even 'applied' scientists, in the sense of those who merely take advances in theoretical knowledge and apply them to practical problems. Engineers do 'apply' science some of the time, for example using the results of scientific investigations into the properties of materials when considering which materials to use, and scientific advances can prompt engineering advances, for example the discovery of a new material might prompt engineers to find a use for it. The relationship between engineering and science, however, is not simple. For one thing, since engineers are interested in making objects that work, it is often a sensible approach for them not to search out new materials and processes but to look for new ways of using old ones. For another, it is mistake to believe that the intellectual movement is always from science to engineering. The contrary movement is also important. Engineers frequently find that they have reached the limits of scientific knowledge about what they are working with. That might happen in at least two ways. First, engineers deal with complex interactions between different processes, whereas scientists, to understand those processes clearly, will often have radically isolated them. For engineering purposes, it is important not just to understand how processes and materials behave in an abstract or experimental world but how they behave in the manifold complexity of the real world. Second, engineers can reach the limits of science for the more fundamental reason that scientists have simply not studied or have not succeeded in understanding the processes or materials the engineer would like to use. The needs of engineers to know more about a particular field or a specific question can in this way often set science's agenda. For example, in a classic study, Walter Vincenti demonstrated that advances in the engineering of aircraft wings preceded scientific understanding of how airfoils work and engineers' questions about them prompted subsequent scientific progress.[9] Herbert Simon's

---

[8] Davis (1998) at 15–16.

[9] Walter Vincenti, *What do Engineers Know and how do they Know it?* (Baltimore: Johns Hopkins U.P., 1990) chapter 2. One might go even further and point out that the methods and thought processes of scientists who make scientific breakthroughs look far more like those of engineers making new inventions than those implied by the classic hypothetico-deductive method, and that therefore

conclusion was perhaps even more radical, that it is in the act of designing new useful things that we come to understand the world.[10]

But more than that, many engineers claim that engineering is not merely applied science because it generates its own forms of knowledge, knowledge about 'how to make people and things work better together'. In particular, they claim that it generates knowledge about engineering itself. They insist, with Vincenti, that engineering knowledge is not just 'know-how', a set of unspoken practices, but knowledge that can be stated clearly, tested and transmitted. Herbert Simon came to the same conclusion, and indeed insisted that knowledge about the process of design unifies a large number of disciplines, starting with engineering but going beyond it to include human behaviour in fields such as town planning.[11] Simon saw that what unified these fields was that they were concerned with human beings creating something new, and that one could engage in organised study of how that creation happened, and of how created objects behave, a 'science of the artificial'. That science would, unlike the science of nature, automatically incorporate human purposes and forethought.[12]

For a time controversy surrounded whether the process of creating new useful objects, or 'design' in its most general and least aesthetic sense, should be taught to engineers. Herbert Simon described how, as academic engineers redefined themselves as fully part of the university rather than as instructors at trade schools, design almost fell out of the curriculum of engineering degree courses.[13] Design was too often thought of as 'intellectually soft, intuitive, informal, and cookbooky' rather than, as appeared proper for a real university discipline, 'intellectually tough, analytic, formalizable, and teachable'.[14] Even the pioneers of its re-establishment in the university curriculum, such as the Cambridge engineer Gordon Glegg, sometimes sounded reticent about their own efforts. 'At first sight the idea of any rules or principles being superimposed on the creative mind seems most likely to hinder than to help,' Glegg wrote in 1969, before, however, continuing, 'but this is really quite untrue in practice. Disciplined thinking focuses inspiration rather than blinkers it.'[15] Largely thanks to figures such as Simon, Vincenti and Glegg, the systematic study of creation, the

---

science is applied engineering rather than the other way round. See Subrate Dasgupta, *Technology and Creativity* (Oxford: Oxford U.P., 1996).

[10] Simon (1996) at 164.
[11] Simon (1996) at 138.
[12] Simon (1996) at 138.
[13] Simon (1996) at 111.
[14] Simon (1996) at 112.
[15] Gordon Glegg, *The Design of Design* (Cambridge: Cambridge U.P., 1969) 1.

study of engineering design, now forms a central part of both engineering teaching and engineering research, forming a link between engineers in all specialisms.

TECHNICAL OBJECTS

The exact division of labour between engineers and other people who are concerned with the creation of objects, such as artists and architects, is not always clear. One view is that engineers are concerned with all aspects of objects except the aesthetic. Some engineers would claim, however, that they are also concerned with the aesthetic and that the difference lies only in the priority they give it compared to the other functions of the object. Another, related, view is that engineers differ from architects in their attention to mathematics and sciences, their concern with all the functions of an object and their organisational abilities.[16]

A more general way of answering the question of what engineers do as opposed to other creators of objects is that engineers make 'technical' objects, physical objects that fulfil 'technical' functions.[17] By 'technical', engineers originally tended to mean that the object changed the physical world either by converting energy from one form to another (machines) or matter from one state to another (apparatus).[18] But engineers extended their scope of activity to include the processing of information and so now include within 'technical' anything (or at least any physical process) that changes the informational state of the world (that is, 'devices').

THE PROCESS OF ENGINEERING DESIGN

Engineers normally now describe the design process as they often describe much else, in terms of systems.[19] Systems analysis can be used for many purposes, but its anchoring in engineering, in the task of changing the state of the world and not just understanding it better, is important. Systems

---

[16]	Davis (1998) at 12.
[17]	Pieter Vermaas, Pieter Kroes, Ibo van de Poel, Maarten Franssen and Wybo Houkes, *A Philosophy of Technology: From Technical Artefacts to Sociotechnical Systems* (Morgan and Claypool, 2011) at 21.
[18]	Gerhard Pahl, Wolfgang Beitz, Jörg Feldhusen and Karl-Heinrich Grote (Ken Wallace and Lucienne Blessing, translators), *Engineering Design: A Systematic Approach* 3rd edition (London: Springer, 2007) at 30.
[19]	See e.g Pahl et al. (2007) at 29.

consist of inputs, outputs and a process that connects the two. They connect to other systems by providing an input for those other systems or by taking their output as an input. One can conceive of systems as a network of inputs and outputs or as a hierarchy in which each system provides inputs for higher levels of the overall system (super-systems) and is made up of components that provide it with inputs (sub-systems). The boundaries between systems or between systems and their super-systems and sub-systems are more an analytical matter than a physical one, since they can often be drawn in different places for different purposes, but engineers tend to choose as boundaries the places at which the flows of inputs and outputs are at their minimum.[20] Useful objects are themselves systems, but they also form parts of bigger systems, some of which they are intended to change. They can also be broken down into sub-systems, each with their own inputs, processes and outputs. Designing a useful object requires understanding at each of these levels and of the relationships between them.

The process of design can be described in general terms as 'the specification of measurable goals, objectives and constraints for the design; the conceptualization and parametrization of alternative candidate designs that meet or surpass specifications; the analysis and ranking of design alternatives; and, finally, the selection, implementation and testing of the most preferred alternative.'[21] Although there is no universal theory of how the process best works, and there are competing views about each step, engineers claim that enough is known about what works and what does not work that the process itself can be researched and taught.

Specification

The process itself starts with a clarification of what difference the eventual artefact is required to produce. The design needs to solve a problem the client actually has, not some other problem. Extended interaction with the client is usually necessary to elicit a clearly defined and measurable brief. Engineers are taught that clients very rarely have a precise view of what they want and indeed might have self-contradictory views, away from which they will often need to be drawn.[22] Eliciting all of the client's objectives is particularly important, since hidden agendas make success or

---

[20] Pahl et al. (2007) at 28. See also e.g. Lars Skyttner, *General Systems Theory: Ideas and Applications* (Singapore: World Scientific, 2001) at 60.
[21] Andrew Sage and William Rouse, *Handbook of Systems Engineering and Management* (London: John Wiley, 2011) at 508, Pahl et al. (2007) at 51–53
[22] Sage and Rouse (2011) at 509–10. Cf Pahl et al. (2007) at 53.

failure a kind of reputational lottery. It is also important, where the client has multiple goals, to elicit the relationships between those goals – their hierarchical arrangement or the acceptable trade-offs between them.[23]

The constraints within which the project has to work also have to be clarified and listed as exhaustively as possible. Many of the constraints for a project will also appear as goals or objectives – for example cost constraints will appear as objectives about maximum costs, timescale constraints will appear as objectives about timing and so on. But there are also constraints the client might not have in mind. One such constraint is the issue of physical feasibility. The engineer knows to check, where the client might not, that the intended effect is not impossible, either because, crudely, it would violate known physical laws, or because, although not physically impossible, it requires some other problem to have been solved that has not yet been solved. In Glegg's phrase, the former relates to whether the project is 'intrinsically impossible', the latter to whether it is 'relatively impossible'.[24] Another important constraint that might not appear in the client's set of objectives is safety. Regulatory safety standards, for example, operate as an important constraint.

Another set of constraints (or objectives) that might be incorporated right from the start concern the manufacture of the object once it is designed. The traditional approach to design assumed that design and manufacture were different problems, and that after it had been devised the designed object could just be 'thrown over the wall' to manufacturers. But that approach led to obvious problems both in terms of feasibility and cost of manufacturing the object. A solution is to build in constraints and objectives about manufacturing right from the start, so that the whole process of design is integrated and so less prone to failure and having to start again. Indeed, the same approach can be extended to build in other sources of later potential difficulty such as marketing and consumer experience, all of which can be tackled concurrently with design and manufacturing problems.[25] The use of these concurrent methods often requires the creation of multi-disciplinary teams, with engineers working with experts in other fields.

---

[23] Sage and Rouse (2011) at 510–11. Expressing these relationships quantitatively can be complex. See e.g. Nadia Nedjah and Luiza De Macedo Mourelle, *Real-World Multi-Objective System Engineering* (Hauppauge, NY: Nova, 2005).

[24] Glegg (1969) at 5.

[25] Sage and Rouse (2011) at 523–27.

Analysis of the Problem

For problems of any complexity, engineers will often attempt to break down the problem as presented by the client and supplemented by the engineer into a comprehensive set of sub-problems. One method is to look for a set of sub-problems that cover the whole of the main problem but which are as far as possible independent of one another, a procedure sometimes called the method of factorisation.[26] Other methods are less concerned with comprehensive coverage but stress the identification of those sub-problems most relevant to finding solutions. For example, the method of 'backward steps' starts with the goal and traces backwards all the steps that could lead to it, a procedure which should generate a tree of sub-problems that have to be solved before one can arrive at the goal. Or one could start with an initial or a previously suggested solution and move forward towards the goal until the solution fails, the method of forward steps.[27]

An important aspect of the way that many engineers think about problems is that they attempt to abstract away from them before turning to concrete solutions. They do this mainly to make sure that they are not looking for the solution in the wrong place, but there is also an idea that abstraction helps by distracting the engineer as far as possible from focussing on specific solutions, so opening up the range of solutions eventually considered ('solution neutrality' as it is sometimes called).[28] In particular they look at the problem functionally, in terms of the effects the relevant systems and sub-systems have on states of energy, material or information, so that they can ask what the desired effect is in more abstract and systematic terms.[29] For example, in traffic engineering the solution to an accident problem might not lie in the layout of the road in the immediate vicinity of the accidents but in the mix of traffic entering the area or the configuration of the public transport network that generates that mix. If engineers concentrated only on what effects different interventions at the accident site might have, as opposed to looking at what the transport system does more generally, they might miss the point that a better solution for the accident problem might be some form of traffic regulation or management or the extension of a public transport network. Of course, analysis of this type might reveal that the better solutions exist at levels of the system so far above that at which the engineer is asked to intervene

---

[26] Pahl et al. (2007) at 58, 61.
[27] See Pahl et al. (2007) at 58 for these and other methods.
[28] Pahl et al. (2007) at 78.
[29] See Pahl et al. (2007) 31ff, chapter 6.

and at which neither the engineer nor the client has the means to act effectively. For example, it might be more effective to ban certain types of vehicle completely (for example four-by-fours with bull-bars) than to engage in any kind of traffic management, but the client might have no way of bringing about such a ban. In such cases, questions arise about the limits of 'engineering'. Are these issues for engineers at all? Is there a level of a sociotechnical system above which engineers have no relevant expertise? But even if there is such a limit, engineers are still interested in how the whole system works and need to understand it if their interventions at other levels are to be effective.

Generation of Options

The process then moves on to looking for options for solutions. Engineers emphasise that it is usually a mistake to move to detailed design of the first plausible solution that comes to mind. There is an important initial step of generating as many plausible ideas as possible, which can then be sorted and assessed.[30] If the characteristics of the problems and sub-problems have been exhaustively specified, it should be possible to draw up a general classification of the choices to be made, which in turn can be used to generate a comprehensive set of possible solutions that recombine the different choices. For example, there might be a set of choices about the configuration of the object and a set of choices about the materials that might be used. Each configuration combined with each material constitutes an option. This is the method of 'systematic variation', often treated as an ideal procedure in the literature,[31] but not always possible. Indeed it is possible that full systemisation itself might not be optimal because it might interfere with the creation of radically new departures.

Other methods for generating possible solutions include analysis of existing solutions and systematically varying their elements, analysis of analogous natural systems, and more intuitive methods such as brainstorming and Delphi methods.[32] Indeed, different strategies might suit different circumstances. Where the goal is to do something that has already been done, but to do it better, the strategy might more naturally involve starting with existing solutions, breaking them down into their sub-systems

---

[30] E.g. Sage and Rouse (2011) at 513–14, Pahl et al. (2007) at 77ff.
[31] E.g. in Pahl et al. (2007), but see, for criticism of treating systematic variation as the ideal method, D. Motte, 'A Review of the Fundamentals of Systematic Engineering Design Process Models' International Design Conference, Dubrovnik, Croatia, 2006.
[32] Sage and Rouse (2011) at 513–14, Pahl et al. (2007) at 82ff.

and then looking for variations on those sub-systems, a method that fits the forward steps method of analysing the problem. Where the goal is to do something new, it is more natural to start with the goal and think about the conditions for bringing it about, more in line with the method of backward steps. [33]

Another variable in how engineers deal with complex problems that have been divided up into sub-problems is the order in which the sub-problems are solved. In the 'process-oriented' approach, the sub-problems are solved in parallel, so that issues of compatibility between the sub-solutions can be tackled as the designers go along. In the 'problem-oriented' approach, the sub-problems are solved in series, following a single guiding principle of solution, with compatibility issues tackled by adjustment as the series is completed. Research on design process styles suggests that inexperienced designers (or designers inexperienced in the kind of problem) tend towards the process variant, whereas experienced designers tend towards the problem variant.[34] But the trend towards incorporating more objectives and constraints from the start, to be resolved concurrently, seems to imply a parallel approach.[35]

Although engineers are usually encouraged to separate as far as possible the process of identifying problems and the process identifying solutions, in practice the two processes interact. The process of generating solutions often suggests new ways of thinking about the problem. In particular, it can lead to further thinking about the functions to be served and about the nature of the whole system, especially at levels above that of the problem as originally described. The result can be a kind of co-evolution between problem and solution, in which the stopping point is convergence rather than a solution to the problem as originally stated.[36] Problems can arise, however, where the degree of drift turns out to be unacceptable to the client and no obvious process of convergence seems available. These problems can suffer from a third kind of impossibility, the impossibility of framing the problem so that it has a satisfactory solution.[37]

---

[33] Note that engineers are often more interested in sufficient conditions than necessary ones. Simon (1996) at 124.

[34] Pahl et al. (2007) at 55.

[35] Sage and Rouse (2011) at 523.

[36] See e.g. Mary Lou Maher and Josiah Poon, 'Modeling Design Exploration as Co-evolution' (1996) 11(3) Microcomputers in Civil Engineering 195–209, Kees Dorst and Nigel Cross, 'Creativity in the Design Process: Co-evolution of Problem–Solution' (2001) 22(5) Design Studies 425–37.

[37] These problems, especially if combined with other elements such as not being able to test prototypes (see below) and no time being available to learn from experience, are often called 'wicked problems', though the epithet is extremely

Assessment of Options

Once solutions have been identified in principle, as options that combine certain functional characteristics, they need to be firmed up into concepts that can be assessed. This is a step which 'almost invariably involves considerable effort'.[38] Solutions need eventually to be specified in a form that can be made and inserted as a sub-system in the system in which the desired effects are intended. That means something like a description of a set of parts and instructions for putting them together.[39]

The next stage is the assessment of options, which involves asking whether the solutions meet, or exceed the standards set at the goal and objective setting stage. Since the development of computer-assisted design systems, which allow rapid re-calculation of how an option would perform, each option will go through an iterative process of adjustment and re-assessment.[40] That process can be conceived as one of optimisation, which is to say aimed at making the option as good as it possibly can be across the various constraints or objectives, or as one of satisficing, which is to say improving each option until it is 'good enough' in terms of the specified objectives, goals and constraints.[41]

Part of the process of assessing designs consists of identifying obstacles that stand in the way of the designs' bringing about the desired states of affairs or their risks of bringing about undesired states.[42] If there are no obstacles in the way of a solution and no risks, the engineer can move

---

unfortunate. See Horst Rittel and Melvin Webber, 'Dilemmas in a General Theory of Planning' (1969) 4 Policy Sciences 155–69, which has generated a voluminous literature across several disciplines. Much of the literature seems merely to express the bafflement technical experts appear almost invariably to experience whenever they encounter politics. The capriciousness of democratic electorates and the consequent necessity for democratic leaders to follow contradictory goals seem to take many experts (but especially town planners) by surprise. A better subject for study might be to ask why that happens and how the education of technical experts might change so that they are not surprised by the obvious.

[38]   Pahl et al. (2007) at 190.

[39]   Sage and Rouse (2011) at 515, Cf Pahl et al. (2007) at 190ff.

[40]   Before the development of CAD systems, the cost of assessing multiple options many times over would have been an important consideration. See e.g. Simon (1996) at 125, citing Marvin Manheim, *Hierarchical Structure: A Model of Design and Planning Processes* (Cambridge, MA: MIT Press, 1966) as the first attempt at incorporating design costs into the design process. The cost of each iteration is no longer so significant, but the time taken overall for assessment still is.

[41]   Sage and Rouse (2011) at 515–16. Simon, who is credited with coining the word 'satisficing', advocates it as a method: See Simon (1996) at 120–23.

[42]   It is important to keep the analysis of risks and obstacles separate from the

immediately to breaking down the option in a set of tasks to be performed to bring the option into being. But where obstacles and risks remain, designers will look for ways of dealing with them.

Those obstacles and risks often flow from or are exacerbated by uncertainties about how the various systems and sub-systems will behave in different conditions. Of particular importance here is the distinction systems engineers make between 'closed' systems and 'open' systems. In a closed system, nothing apart from a specified input is taken to cross the boundary into the system and nothing apart from a specified output is taken to cross the boundary out of it.[43] In open systems, however, the boundary between the system and the system's environment is crossed by more than just the specified inputs and outputs. Open systems are thus constantly interacting with their environment. The introduction of openness to the analysis brings in both an extra dimension of realism but also an extra layer of uncertainty. Closed systems are, however, rare in the natural world and engineers are sometimes warned that if their analysis depends on the presence of a closed system they should re-examine their assumptions.[44]

Just as boundaries between systems are difficult to draw, the boundary between a system and its environment is not always clear, and is more a matter of analytical choice than something forced by reality. Engineers often opt for placing outside the system anything they cannot control.[45] More broadly, the function the system is thought of as serving often plays a decisive role.[46]

There are other important sources of uncertainty. [47] One such source is complexity, in the sense that a system contains a high number of elements and there is high number of possible interactions between those elements, to the extent that the system becomes difficult to describe.[48] Treating a

---

specification of task itself. See Pahl et al. (2007) at 46. Otherwise, the task might be mis-specified as minimising the obstacles rather than achieving the goals.

[43] E.g. Karl-Heinrich Grote, Erik K. Antonsson, *Springer Handbook of Mechanical Engineering,* Volume 10 (New York: Springer, 2009) at 224.

[44] Gregory S. Parnell, Patrick J. Driscoll and Dale L. Henderson, *Decision Making in Systems Engineering and Management* (Hoboken, NJ: John Wiley, 2010) at 36.

[45] Joseph R. Laracy, 'Addressing System Boundary Issues in Complex Socio-Technical Systems' (2007) 2(19) Systems Research Forum 19–26 at 21.

[46] M. M. Ottens, 'The Limitations of Systems Engineering' in Ibo van de Poel, David Goldberg, Michael Davis, (eds) *Philosophy and Engineering: An Emerging Agenda* (London: Springer, 2010).

[47] See William Wulf, 'Engineering Ethics and Society' (2004) 28 Technology in Society 385–90.

[48] Technically, this is 'structural complexity'. See e.g. Olivier de Weck, Daniel

Law as engineering

system as open will often itself introduce complexity. In addition, complexity can obscure the relationships between different levels of the system and can give rise to the problem of 'emergence', a situation in which a system appears not to be explicable at all in terms of the states of its sub-systems and seems explicable only by events at its own level (a classic example is the idea that consciousness is an emergent property because it is not explicable in terms of brain chemistry).[49] Uncertainty can also arise from chaotic effects, namely where the long-term behaviour of the system is very sensitive to its initial conditions, so that even though the process that takes one from the initial conditions to the end result is capable of being modelled with exactitude, inability to observe those initial conditions precisely enough makes accurate prediction of future states of the system very difficult.[50] A third source of uncertainty, especially important if the system includes computing, are discreteness effects, which arise because, unlike in the physical world where small changes in input are usually associated with small changes in output, in the world of computing a change of a single '0' to a '1' can have very large effects.[51]

Only when the options have been assessed should the candidates be collected and systematically compared and ranked. The schema for establishing the ranking order should refer back to the goals, objectives and constraints. In co-evolution processes, there might have been some implied drift in goals and objectives, and one task of the designer is to check whether the drift is acceptable. Occasionally it might be possible to identify a single design that is best in all respects, but usually the ranking has to be treated as problem of making a decision with multiple objectives under uncertainty.[52]

Roos and Christopher Roos, *Engineering Systems* (Cambridge, MA: MIT Press, 2011) at 185.

[49] Wulf (2004) at 387. Wulf's discussion concerns what has been termed 'weak' emergence (see Mark Bedau, 'Weak Emergence' (1997) 11 Philosophical Perspectives 375–99, and 'Downward Causation and the Autonomy of Weak Emergence' (2002) 6(1) Principia 5–50), in which the states of lower levels of the system are accepted as causing the states of higher levels but it is not possible, either in the current state of knowledge or, more radically, ever, to understand how that causation happens, rather than the more controversial 'strong' emergence, in which even in principle one could not explain the properties of a higher level of the system in terms of the states of lower levels.

[50] Wulf (2004) at 387.

[51] Wulf (2004) at 387.

[52] Sage and Rouse (2011) at 516.

Prototype Testing

The next step is to turn the highest ranking option, or if cost allows, the highest ranking options, into prototypes for testing.[53] The process of testing, whether under laboratory conditions or in the field, can lead to further adjustments and improvements (albeit ones that are expensive to incorporate). In the worst case, testing might reveal fatal errors in the design, which will send the process one or more steps back towards the beginning. In the best case, testing confirms the previous calculations and allows the engineers to move with confidence to installation or manufacture.

Sometimes, however, it is not feasible or financially justifiable to test a prototype. For example, if the project is large scale, expensive and one-off, testing might be equivalent in cost and difficult to carrying out the whole project.[54] In that case, the only option is to monitor carefully the process of fabrication, adjusting if possible as new information becomes available.

GENERAL PRINCIPLES OF SUCCESSFUL DESIGN

There have been a great number of attempts to pull together general lessons that might be drawn from the experiences of designers, both successful and unsuccessful, although no universally agreed set of principles for successful design can be said yet to have emerged.[55] There are, however, some obvious points, such as that the client's requirements need to be defined precisely, preferably in quantitative terms, [56] and that the chances of success (though also costs) increase if one builds in more than one way of reaching the desired outcome, that is if the system includes elements of redundancy. But some more specific principles have developed within particular types of engineering that turn out to be good candidates for wider application. For example, the integration of manufacturability into the process of design has yielded a number of generally agreed principles for that kind of process, such as that it is better to minimise the number of parts, to design in modules that can be used for different purposes and that can fit with other components using standard interfaces, and to sub-modularise

---

[53] Sage and Rouse (2011) at 517.

[54] Sage and Rouse (2011) at 517.

[55] See generally, Richard Buchanan, 'Thinking about Design: An Historical Perspective' in Antonie Meijers (ed.), *Philosophy of Technology and Engineering Science* (Oxford: Elsevier, 2009) 409–53.

[56] Glegg (1969) at 8–17, but see Simon (1996) at 145–46.

by standardising components and developing parts that can be used in different ways.[57]

HUMANS IN ENGINEERING SYSTEMS

Engineering is conventionally thought of as concerned with things rather than people, but the extension of engineering from the conversion of energy and states of matter into concern with information has produced a profound change. Although engineering started its analysis of information with the transfer of information from one technical object to another ('signals'), it soon became clear that in many cases the most important system providing input and receiving output was a human being, who in turn might receive input ('messages', perhaps, rather than 'signals')[58] from other human beings. The whole system was not just technical, but sociotechnical. To design devices within sociotechnical systems, engineers have found themselves travelling beyond the physical sciences and beginning to consider the organised study of human behaviour, originally mainly through physiology and cognitive psychology, but now increasingly through economics, sociology and anthropology.[59]

Moreover, in engineers' studies of the design process, the system under study itself is mainly human. It consists of people, and organisations of people, setting and resolving problems. Admittedly, the use of computers in design has revolutionised the scale and speed of the calculations engineers can make, allowing large numbers of detailed simulations to be run. Expert systems can design out the possibility of many errors and can even make suggestions for design improvements. But the device that decides whether a problem has been solved, or at least that the search for a better

---

[57]   Sage and Rouse (2011) at 527. The authors suggest that these principles are close to the axioms of design proposed by Suh, namely to maintain the independence of functional requirements and minimise the information content of the design. See e.g. Suh Nam-Pyo, *The Principles of Design* (Oxford: Oxford U.P., 1990).

[58]   Pahl et al. (2007) at 29.

[59]   See e.g. Gavriel Salvendy (ed.), *Handbook of Human Factors Engineering and Ergonomics* 4th edition (Hoboken, NJ: John Wiley, 2012) 57–383. For sociotechnical systems generally, see Vermaas et al. (2011). Mention might also be made of the tradition of cybernetics – the study of the interaction between control and information – which has from time to time been applied to social systems, with varying degrees of success. For a recent work that develops the tradition see Ralf-Eckhard Türke, *Governance: Systemic Foundation and Framework* (Heidelberg: Springer Physica Verlag, 2008).

solution should stop, even with the aid of the most powerful computers, is ultimately a human being.

Above all, engineers recognise, indeed celebrate, the fact that what they do is creative, and therefore to an added extent unpredictable. But that does not preclude their gathering information and formulating theories about the conditions that might favour or inhibit creativity. They think about, for example, the trade-off between allowing time for ideas to incubate and the risk that allowing time for ideas to develop also means interruptions and diversions that can be disruptive.[60] They are interested in techniques for enhancing creativity, such as alternating between concentration and relaxation.[61] There is also a debate about whether computer-aided design inhibits or encourages creativity.[62] Even creativity, they think, or at least they hope, can to some extent be engineered.

LAWYERS AS ENGINEERS

It should now be apparent that transactional and legislative lawyers have a great deal in common with engineers, perhaps not in the way the professions of engineering and law are organised or in their history, or even in their self-image, but in their basic tasks. Like engineers, transactional and legislative lawyers want to make something useful that works for their clients. They are presented with problems to solve, an undesired current state of affairs, and a desired future state of affairs, with obstacles and risks lying between the two. Lawyers' work consists of getting their clients from one to the other. If there are no obstacles, getting there becomes merely a matter of carrying out a series of tasks, such as filling in the right forms. If there are obstacles, however, lawyers have problems to solve just as engineers do.

Unlike the objects created by engineers, lawyers' objects are embodied not in metal or concrete or plastic, but in relationships between people, and they are designed in words rather than in drawings. The forces they harness

---

[60]   E.g. Pahl et al. (2007) at 54–55.

[61]   See Glegg (1969) at 19. Glegg describes work on the circumstances in which leading thinkers found their key idea. The results were that several ideas occurred to their progenitors while they were in bed, while they were travelling, while they were out walking or even 'sitting in front of the fire'. One great idea even occurred 'at a state dinner'(!)

[62]   E.g. Thomas Kappel and Albert Rubenstein, 'Creativity in Design: The Contribution of Information Technology' (1999) 46(2) IEEE Transactions on Engineering Management 132–43.

are not natural but human, and that includes, although it is by no means limited to, the coercive power of the state.[63] But that is not a decisive objection to the comparison. Contracts, companies, conveyances, wills, trusts, regulations, statutes and constitutions, all useful objects designed and created by lawyers, are, in engineering terms, devices, objects whose effects are in the realm of information rather than in the realms of energy or matter. On the whole, their inputs come from humans and their outputs are received by humans, and so the information flows are 'messages' rather than 'signals', and we can concede that the knowledge most useful for designing them, knowledge about humans rather than physics or chemistry, might not be as exact as that generated by the natural sciences. But it is knowledge nevertheless, knowledge that engineers themselves increasingly use in the design of their own devices. The intention of those who use knowledge about human behaviour to design devices is precisely the same in the two fields – to create change in the world outside the device.

It also helps to understand lawyers' activities in the same way as engineers understand their own activities, in systems terms. The legal object to be created is itself a system – and can be analysed into sub-systems – but if it is to be a solution to a problem in the world, the most important facts about it are facts about its effects in other systems outside of itself. Legal devices are designed to have effects, and to understand those effects requires understanding systems beyond the device itself. In particular, it requires understanding the conditions under which people follow, or fail to follow, legal rules. [64] Legal devices that ignore those conditions are unlikely to work.

---

[63]   Those forces include acceptance of the authority of law, including moral commitment to good order regardless of personal preferences, the co-ordinating effects of convention and the uncertainty reducing effects of planning. See next note for references to the psychology and sociology of acting in consonance with the law.

[64]   Important studies in this field include Tom Tyler, *Why People Obey the Law* 2nd edition (Princeton, NJ: Princeton U.P., 2006), which reports empirical work that brings out the role of legitimacy and procedural fairness, and not coercion or the threat of coercion, in bringing about behaviour consonant with the law (a finding, it should be said, with important implications for commercial law, and not just for criminal law), and Per-Olof Wikstrom, Dietrich Oberwittler, Kyle Treiber and Beth Hardie, *Breaking the Rules: The Social and Situational Dynamics of Young People's Urban Crime* (Oxford: Oxford U.P., 2012), which finds that for some people law-breaking is simply inconceivable – it is not even an option for them – and that for many others moral considerations make law-breaking highly unlikely. Deterrence is thus only relevant to a specific section of the population. In commercial contexts, another important factor is the way agreements constitute plans that guide conduct by reducing uncertainty about how others will behave.

Legal theorists sometimes talk in a way that implies that the only systems that matter beyond the device are other legal objects. For example, they sometimes talk as if the only system a legal device is ever designed to affect is the system of legal decision – the courts. They take the lawyers' habit of asking 'how would a court interpret this?' and turn it into a principle of the separateness of the law, sealing the law off from systems outside it. But from a client's point of view the idea of the separation of the law from life is perplexing. The point of the device is to create desirable effects or to prevent undesirable effects beyond itself, in how humans behave, whether in a commercial deal or inside the political structure or in some regulated aspect of human lives. It is true that the effects might happen indirectly – that the device's effects on human relations outside the law might happen not as a result of the device itself but of the actions of another system – of which the courts would be an example – of a system that uses the device designed by the client's lawyers as an input. But even then, the client is interested not in the internal workings of that other system (which might as well be a black-box from the client's point of view) but in that other system's effects, both on others and on the client. The effects might also be partly indirect, via the interpretation of the legal device by other lawyers without the intervention of courts. But at some point, the effects will reach the world outside the law, and clients would be surprised and disappointed if their lawyers had no interest in those effects.

Nevertheless, some lawyers do attempt to control the extent of their responsibility in a way that limits their job to changing the law itself. They attempt to leave responsibility for whether the law itself has any effect to their clients. In system terms, they accept responsibility only for one system level up, and not beyond. The clearest example of 'only one level up' is the Office of Parliamentary Counsel. In its account of its services for government departments, it warns:[65]

> [T]he essential thing to remember is that Bills, or rather the Acts they become, can achieve only one thing and, as such, can therefore have only one objective – to change the law.

The Office of Parliamentary Counsel goes on to list the ways in which the law can be changed, conceding, for example, that it can change

---

Other conditions include clarity in communication and not demanding the impossible, cf. Lon Fuller, *The Morality of Law* (New Haven: Yale U.P., 1969) chapter 2.

[65] Office of Parliamentary Counsel, *Working with Parliamentary Counsel* (London: Cabinet Office, 2011) (hereinafter OPC (2011c)) at 27 (http://www. cabinetoffice.gov.uk/sites/default/files/resources/WWPC_6_Dec_2011.pdf).

penalties or rewards, but it pointedly fails to discuss whether changes in incentives will have any effect on anyone's behaviour, and goes on to point out that aims for legislation such as hopes that it will change social attitudes, are contingent on other matters, including the extent of respect for the law in society generally.

A similar 'only one level up' conception of the role of lawyers would occur in the transactional context if lawyers saw their job as merely changing the legal rights, duties, powers and immunities of the parties, and leaving to their clients any assessment of whether those changes would generate particular forms of behaviour. But 'only one level up' thinking would be surprising in that context. Unless clients are very experienced (other lawyers, for example), they expect their lawyers to know about the normal effects of what they draft, and not just in the extremely unlikely scenario of a court case, but in practice in the world. If their lawyer's experience is that a certain type of contractual clause is invariably objected to (or even ignored) by certain types of counterparty, the client would expect the lawyer to say so. More broadly, transactions lawyers are usually looking to secure desirable effects in the world, not just in the law. Nathanson's will lawyer, for example, was concerned not just to produce the right legal effects for the client, but also the right emotional effects.

Even in the legislative context, the attitude of the Office of Parliamentary Counsel might reflect an attempt to delineate a division of labour with the lawyers working directly for its departmental clients than a general view that lawyers have no need to think beyond the next level up. The Office of Parliamentary Counsel stresses that it cannot be expert in policy matters beyond its expertise in analysis for consistency and coherence, but it nevertheless requires the departmental lawyers to brief it on the factual and political background to the legislation, which in turn requires the departmental lawyers at least to have sight of documentation in the possession of other departmental officials about how the current law works in practice and what is hoped for, in practical terms, from the new law.[66]

But just as there seems to be a limit to what counts as an engineering problem, lawyers would probably not accept responsibility for the failure of projects that came about, as they would see it, in ways unrelated to legal work. They might concede, for example, that the client might reasonably hold them responsible for an outbreak of litigation, but claim that they are not responsible for the physical failure of a product (for which they might blame an engineer). Legal devices have inherent limitations, they might

---

[66]   OPC (2011c) at 36–37.

argue, the risks of which can only be mitigated but not eliminated, so that risks beyond legal control are inherently not legal matters. But just as it is not easy to delineate precisely what counts as a 'technical object' for the purpose of engineering, it is not easy to put precise limits on the 'legal'. In engineering, the concept of the technical expanded when engineers took on changing informational states in addition to changing energy flows and states of matter. There might not be an entirely clear break either in engineering or law. But at least the engineering analogy gives lawyers a way of thinking about the question that they should find fruitful, namely what is it precisely that we undertake to transform?[67]

Thinking about legal devices in systems terms also helps to understand the relationships between direct and indirect effects and the risks lawyers are dealing with in designing devices. The direct effects of the device are achieved through the self-application of rules, so that risks of non-performance arise not only from intentional defiance of the rules but from failure to understand them (a situation with a parallel for engineers at the interface between machines and humans). One might speculate that the more distant a self-applier is from the process of design the more likely it is that the self-applier will not understand the rules the device uses. That would mean, for example, that there will be a lower risk of failure to understand rules in contracts, in the designing of which the parties take part, than in statutes, in the design of which most of its targets are not involved at all. As the *Drafting Guidance* of the Office of Parliamentary Counsel points out to legislative drafters:[68]

> Your reader does not know what your message is until you deliver it. This contrasts with the position of a party to a commercial agreement, who presumably knows, at least in general terms, what the agreement says.

On the same principle, there might also be more risk of misunderstanding a contract by parts of an organisation not involved in the process of negotiation than in those that were involved.

Indirect effects, via other interpretive or enforcement systems, introduce a new risk of misunderstanding rules. Courts, because they are not involved in drafting either contracts or statutes, are particularly risky. That risk, alongside the relative costs involved, explains the preference of many

---

[67] We return to this issue in Chapter 4, in the context of legal ethics.

[68] Office of Parliamentary Counsel, *Drafting Guidance* (London: Cabinet Office, 2011) (http://www.cabinetoffice.gov.uk/sites/default/files/resources/Off ice_of_the_Parliamentary_Counsel_revised_guidance_16_12_11.pdf) (hereinafter OPC (2011b)) at 3.

commercial contracts for dispute resolution mechanisms closer to the deal itself, such as mediation. Indeed, standard dispute resolution clauses tend to provide a process that moves only slowly away from people with intimate knowledge of the deal, for example mediation has to be exhausted before the dispute is escalated to arbitration, and arbitration starts with each side appointing its own member of the tribunal. A similar preference in government produces giving enforcement powers to administrative agencies and dispute resolution roles to administrative tribunals.

Indirect effects also risk conflict with direct effects, since there is no guarantee that the outputs of these other systems will be consistent with self-appliers' own interpretation of the rules. Conventional legal analysis tends to assume that judicial interpretation of a statute will automatically bring self-application of that statute into line with itself, but simple systems analysis immediately brings that assumption into doubt, and shows why, for example, legislative lawyers are right to treat judicial interpretation as a threat rather than as an opportunity for stabilisation.

The possibility of semi-indirect effects, where self-application occurs through intermediaries such as lawyers, introduces a further set of inputs and outputs. If the intermediaries have been close to the process of designing the rules, one might expect them to be a stabilising influence, but if not, they add another layer of complexity and potential conflict.[69]

The same analysis brings out the trade-off lawyers face in legislative and contractual drafting between using language that will be clear to lawyers and language that will be clear to negotiators (or legislators) and self-appliers. As the Office of Parliamentary Ccounsel's *Drafting Guidance* points out:[70]

> The Act must be capable of being used effectively from day to day, but it must also produce the right result if tested in court. And a Bill's first readers, before it

---

[69]   Another interesting field of study suggested by this analysis is of guidance and commentaries on statutes designed for use by self-appliers or by administrators who lack legal expertise. One question to ask about them is whether they generate convergence in interpretation or divergence. If they are used by some interpreters but not by others, the extra layer of complexity might itself give rise to diverging interpretations. But if they are used instead of the statute and are easier to understand than the statute, one might expect convergence (though not necessarily in the direction the statute itself might have seemed to indicate, as the author can testify from his own experience as the chair of a tribunal dealing with appeals against denial of housing benefits, in which it was not uncommon for officials working from the guidance but not the statutory text to arrive at decisions that were clear, but also clearly wrong).

[70]   OPC (2011b) at 2.

is even passed, will be Ministers and members of the two Houses of Parliament, as well as lobby groups and other interested parties. What one set of readers finds easy may be quite difficult for another set, or may not be understood by them in the way the writer intended. These competing interests need to be balanced and given due weight in what we write. The weight to be given to different competing interests may be different from Bill to Bill.

One lesson for legislative lawyers of the various problems this application of systems analysis has highlighted might be that a process of legislative design that excludes future users of the statute might be defective. Inclusion of judges, at least openly, in the process of drafting new statutes might be difficult, given the objection that judges should not pronounce on the meaning of statutes about which they might be called to adjudicate in the future (an objection that has resulted in the exclusion of Supreme Court judges from the legislative House of Lords), but bringing in self-appliers or, perhaps more plausibly, intermediaries such as lawyers, might improve the effectiveness of the process.

THE PROCESS OF LEGAL DESIGN

What we have suggested so far amounts to saying that law is one of the design disciplines. Herbert Simon identified it as such, alongside business, education, architecture, town planning and medicine.[71] Some fine arts might count as design disciplines – especially painting and sculpture, but also music.[72] One might also add the discipline of public policy. The design disciplines each have their own unique concerns but what unifies them is the process of design itself. One might therefore usefully compare law with any of them, but the comparison with engineering is particularly instructive for a number of reasons. First, lawyers, like engineers, but unlike architects, artists and town planners, have only a limited interest in the aesthetic. One sometimes hears lawyers describe a legal device as 'elegant', but their meaning is close to the engineering ideal of using as few elements as possible to construct a solution. Second, like engineers, but unlike most types of medical professionals, lawyers provide a service for clients whose requirements need to be ascertained before the objectives of the project can be set (plastic surgeons might be an exception, and perhaps

---

[71]   Simon (1996) at 111.
[72]   Richard Buchanan, 'Thinking about Design: An Historical Perspective', in Antonie Meijers (ed.), *Philosophy of Technology and Engineering Science* (Oxford: Elsevier, 2009) 409–53. See also Simon (1996) at e.g. 136 and 188.

some kinds of psychiatrist). Third, unlike many business consultants, but like engineers, lawyers possess specific technical skills their clients lack. Fourthly, like engineers but unlike public policy professionals and town planners, lawyers' clients are not overwhelmingly organs of the state or those who control or would like to control organs of the state. Lawyers and engineers work in both the public and the private sectors. And finally, and perhaps most importantly, engineering has perhaps the most developed and systematic set of ideas about how design works and so there is more with which to compare.

The process of designing legal devices has striking parallels with the engineering design process – although it is fair to say that engineers have been far more reflective and precise about that process than lawyers.

Specification of Objectives

The clearest parallels are at the start of the process, where transactions lawyers and legislative lawyers both stress, as do engineers, the importance of obtaining a clear brief from their clients about what the objectives of the project are. As the Office of Parliamentary Counsel comments laconically: 'An attempt to draft for a policy that is uncertain is likely to produce a draft that is unclear'.[73] There are further parallels in the way both lawyers and engineers realise that clients might not be entirely consistent or honest about their goals, so that part of the task of producing a clear brief is an extended interaction between lawyer and client the goal of which is to clarify what the client wants and to establish clear priorities between competing objectives. Another parallel is the lawyer's identification of constraints that the client might not have grasped, for example mandatory legal rules about wills, contracts or company constitutions that limit how solutions might work.

Glegg's distinction between the 'intrinsically impossible' and the 'relatively impossible' also well describes the difference between a legal problem in which the client wants to do something self-contradictory (e.g. wanting to distribute more than 100 per cent of the profits of a deal, or profits in excess of a company's reserves, or leaving the whole of an estate to more than one person, or, in the legislative field, wanting to set up an autonomous body but to keep control of it),[74] and one in which the client wants

---

[73]   OPC (2011c) at 21 note 15.

[74]   It is sometimes alleged that the policy intention of the Labour government of 1997 for devolution to Scotland and Wales was indeed to create relatively autonomous bodies but to design the electoral system so that the Labour Party

to do something the authority for which does not yet exist and which can only be obtained if someone beyond the client's control acquiesces (e.g. for a UK legislative lawyer where a change in EU law or an international treaty is required, or for a transactions lawyer where any legislative change is required).

One difference between lawyers and engineers appears to be the extent to which the goals and objectives of legal devices are measurable. In engineering measurability is thought to be all important, but lawyers seem not to be overly concerned about it. Lawyers may say that what they deal with is not easily quantifiable, but there are many well-known management techniques for setting targets about essentially qualitative matters. Measurable criteria of success or failure could be devised for many legal projects – whether the company functioned as intended, for example, or the contract was carried out, or the will transferred the testator's property as intended. The problem might instead be cultural, or simply that it has not occurred to clients to quantify what they want.

Another difference is that when lawyers design deals, as opposed to when they design devices such as wills and companies for use by the client alone, the objectives of their client have to combine in some way with the objectives of the other party or parties to the deal, who might want to use their own lawyers in a process of negotiation. Engineering, in contrast, is usually conceived of as a game against nature, rather than one in which there are competing human objectives. The difference, however, is rather less than might first appear. Engineers often have to engage in negotiation, especially in the context of concurrent engineering, in which different objectives will be in play simultaneously.[75] Moreover engineers sometimes work in teams that cross organisational boundaries, and frequently face the problem of ascertaining and clarifying the joint objectives of those organisations.[76] Lawyers might not naturally see themselves as part of a team that encompasses the lawyers of the other parties to a deal, but much negotiation does in reality consist of searching for joint objectives that might make the deal worth making for all sides, and if negotiations fail, it is often because no coherent set of joint objectives could be specified. Furthermore, many of the standard legal 'unblocking' techniques – for

---

would stay in control. If so, it has spectacularly failed in relation to Scotland with election of SNP governments, most notably an SNP majority government in 2011.

[75] See Sage and Rouse (2011) at 403–9 for discussion of negotiation in engineering design.

[76] For an early survey and two case studies, see Margaret Bruce, Fiona Leverick and Dale Littler, 'Complexities of Collaborative Product Development' (1995) 15(9) Technovation 535–52. Similar issues arise in supply chain engineering.

example adjusting the price in exchange for warranties, or inserting right of first refusal or first offer clauses – work because all the lawyers understand them as ways of reconciling the parties' different objectives. In effect, the lawyers work together to solve problems that left to themselves the parties would not solve.

Identification of Problems

If we turn to the mapping of problems, the full closeness of the analogy between engineering design and legal design returns. The Office of Parliamentary Counsel seems particularly committed to the idea of solution-neutrality, to insisting that it must analyse the government's policy problem unencumbered by suggestions from departments about how to draft the legislation. Indeed, it is striking how much the Office of Parliamentary Counsel's working practices resemble those of an office of consulting engineers. For example, although they have a number of standard techniques, they try to avoid standardised solutions, on the ground that over-standardisation inhibits clear analysis of problems.

As for methods of breaking down the problem, Office of Parliamentary Counsel's analysis of policy problems has affinities with the backward steps method, that is asking oneself what conditions would have to be fulfilled for the problem to count as solved and then asking what conditions would have to be fulfilled before those conditions were in their turn fulfilled and so on. In contrast, by emphasising the uniqueness of each problem, the Office of Parliamentary Counsel seems to discourage the method of forwards steps, that is taking an existing solution to some other problem and running it forwards until it fails. It is also conceivable, at least from the way sub-problems are sometimes assigned to separate teams or separate team members, that the Office of Parliamentary Counsel edges towards a version of the method of factorisation, in which problems are broken down into a comprehensive set of sub-problems.[77]

The same set of analytical tools is available to transactions lawyers, although direct evidence of the methods they use is sparse. Caruth's steel contract and the story of the development of e-commerce contracts seem to suggest the popularity of the forward steps process, but the Cravath method suggests a backward steps procedure or even factorisation. If one were looking for parallels with engineering, one would expect the forward steps method to be used only where the problem was fairly familiar and the

---

[77] Edward Page, 'Their Word is Law: Parliamentary Counsel and Creative Policy Analysis' [2009] Public Law 790 at 799.

presenting issue one of marginal improvement. For problems where more innovation was required or expected, one would expect the backward steps method, or even factorisation. The evidence, however, such as we have it at present, seems to suggest that transactions lawyers use the forward steps method in both types of situation.[78] Considerations of costs and of client familiarity with the resulting device appear to be important reasons for the popularity of its use.

Generation of Solution Options

There is also little information available about lawyers' generation of solution options. The creative nature of legal problem solving is clear, and some lawyers have reflected, albeit less formally than engineers, on the conditions for encouraging or inhibiting creativity. Caruth, for example, describes the benefits of taking breaks and decries the modern obsession with putting in long hours of hard work as opposed to allowing ideas to form in the back of the mind. But beyond that, the process seems rather haphazard, at least if compared to the engineering ideal of systematic variation, or even with the less comprehensive but still disciplined methods of varying the elements of existing solutions or looking for solutions to each sub-problem generated by the backwards steps process.

The Office of Parliamentary Counsel is nevertheless aware of the need to generate ideas. That is another reason for its dislike of instructions from departments in the form of draft clauses, which it sees as closing down options, and why it discourages the over-use of precedents. At the same time, however, its 'only one level up' approach must limit the range of possible solutions. In the transactional field, Nathanson's will lawyer tries out two standard solutions with the client and, finding them unsatisfactory, improvises a third. John Flood's studies of business lawyers at work concentrate on the process of negotiation rather than drafting,[79] but his subjects also seem largely to be generating options as they go along. One possible explanation is that the process of negotiation itself, in which several parties will have their own lawyers, will naturally generate a number of options, but the process is hardly systematic and the chances seem considerable that the lawyers will between them miss a solution that would have worked better for all parties.

---

[78] The predominance of the method of forward steps was confirmed in conversations between the author and practising commercial lawyers. Systematic research on the question would, however, be interesting.

[79] E.g. John Flood, 'Doing Business: The Management of Uncertainty in Lawyers' Work' (1991) 25 Law and Society Review 41

Another way of looking at what law firms do, however, especially the production and storage of precedents and gradual adjustment of model documents to cover new situations, combined with occasional inspiration, is that firms are participating in a form of solution-problem co-evolution. For example, the process by which standard contracts were produced for various e-commerce purposes seems to fit the co-evolution model.[80] The transfer of contract clauses from an earlier problem, particularly from software development to website development, seems to have started a process of discovery in which new problems or sub-problems emerge and are then solved by later versions. The overall problem becomes better defined and better understood as the process of solution continues.[81]

The multi-party nature of contract design might limit the number of options generated in another way. Researchers into contracting behaviour have noticed that standard contract terms tend to be 'sticky', that they continue to be used long after the interests of the parties that produced them have changed.[82] In one striking example, rents in domestic leases in Israel continued to be quoted in US dollars, and not in local currency, long after the economic conditions that justified such a practice had disappeared.[83] It appears that the reasons for stickiness were threefold. First, there is the cost to lawyers of generating and thinking through a new way of doing things when the old way, though not optimal, still worked. Second, there was a problem of interoperability, that if all the other apartments in a block were valued in dollars, to value one in another currency, even the local currency, might mean that future decisions by the landlord or by the tenants collectively might have different consequences for different tenants, and thus might make for trouble. Third, there was a problem of signalling, that if one party suggested changing the currency, it would trigger anxiety in the

---

[80]   See e.g. Lenné Eidson Espenschied, *Contract Drafting: Powerful Prose in Transactional Practice* (Chicago: American Bar Association Publishing, 2010) at 25. A number of other possible examples of the process seem to exist. Nicholas Aleksander points, for example, to the collection of standard agreements published by the Loan Market Association (see http://www.lma.eu.com/pages.aspx?p=206) as a candidate for explanation along these lines.

[81]   One might also ask whether different ways of organising law firms assist the process. The 'London' model of relatively fewer partners, very many more professional support lawyers and an emphasis on the interests of the firm rather than on individual partners, seems better suited to generate options systematically than the more individualised 'New York' model.

[82]   Omri Ben-Shahar and John Pottow, 'On the Stickiness of Default Rules' (2006) 33 Florida State University Law Review 651–82

[83]   Doron Teichman, 'Old Habits are Hard to Change: A Case Study of Israeli Real Estate Contracts' (2010) 44 Law and Society Review 299–330.

others that the balance of advantage between the parties was being altered in some unknown way. Keeping to known solutions reduces uncertainty.

Another example of contract stickiness concerns what happened in 2000 to the drafting of sovereign bonds. In that year, in an unexpected interpretation of terms standard in sovereign bonds drafted in New York, a court ruled that there was a way around clauses that required unanimous consent by bondholders for the terms of the bond to be changed in any significant way.[84] One might have expected rapid redrafting in subsequent bond issues of the clauses that allowed the unanimous consent rule to be evaded. In fact, nothing happened at all for several years – bonds continued to be drafted as before – and then, rapidly, they were changed to reflect the entirely different standard used in London, under which terms could be changed by collective action of the bondholders short of unanimity. The same three factors were in play – the cost of redesign for the lawyers, the problems of losing standardisation and the fact that attempts at change would act as a signal that would induce all the parties to assess their exposure to risk, which would delay agreement.

All three effects – the time needed to prepare new clauses, interoperability and signalling – discourage the generation of options. They create a situation in which the method of forward steps is dominant. Problem identification starts with existing solutions and works forward until those existing solutions look like failing. Even at that stage, new options are often generated out of other existing solutions, as in the sovereign bond story, where lawyers turned to the 'London' draft rather than start from scratch.

Another point to note, perhaps one also linked with the costs of option generation, is that the sovereign bond story seems to include an element of co-evolution between problem and solution. Just after the 2000 court decision, one might have conceived of the problem as how to return to a position in which bondholder unanimity was required. But if one sees the court decision not as definitively changing both the law and the behaviour of sovereigns, but as increasing the uncertainty surrounding both, the problem becomes how to return to a satisfactory degree of certainty in the way bonds work – in other words, the functional definition of the problem went one level up, from the functions of clauses within the 'New York' bond to the functions of bonds in general. At the higher functional level, it is not difficult to see why a bond with a controlled collective action clause, though inherently higher in uncertainty than one with an

---

[84] Stephen Choi and Mitu Gulati, 'Innovation in Boilerplate Contracts: An Empirical Examination of Sovereign Bonds' (2004) 53 Emory Law Journal 929–96.

unimpaired unanimity clause, might offer more certainty than one subject to capricious interpretations by judges.

Assessment of Options

If we turn, however, to the assessment of options, lawyers seem to be more organised and self-conscious. Legislative lawyers in particular expend much effort in thinking through the possible consequences of drafts.[85] Their main analytical technique is to generate permutations of circumstances and ask how the draft bill would cope with them.[86] They are acutely aware of the uncertainties that arise from complexity, in the same sense as used in engineering that the number of elements in the law and the number of interactions between them makes the system difficult to describe and even more difficult to predict. One might even observe problems of 'emergence' – that levels of the system have to be treated as if they were not explicable in terms of lower levels. Indeed 'the law' itself might be seen as such an emergent property. Moreover, although one might not expect legal problems to be much affected by chaotic effects, which is essentially a problem of observability, there is a clear link between legal structures and the problem of discreteness, the problem that very small differences in wording can produce enormous differences in consequences (a single 'may' in place of a 'must', for example).

The 'only one level up' approach of Office of Parliamentary Counsel legislative lawyers can be seen as an effort at reducing the degree of uncertainty they face. They are saying that they only purport to assess options for their effect on the law, not for the effect of the law on any system outside itself. They are not denying that the law has outputs that affect the world, but they are saying that those outputs do whatever they do. [87] Office of Parliamentary Counsel lawyers also tend to pay little attention to

---

[85]   Page (2009) 805–8.

[86]   See e.g. OPC (2011c) at 18. The same technique appears to be used in France. See John Bell, 'What Is the Function of the Conseil d'Etat in the Preparation of Legislation?' (2000) 49 International and Comparative Law Quarterly 661—72 at 666. *Working with Parliamentary Counsel* does, however, attempt to wean the Office of Parliamentary Counsel off the view that covering all the logical permutations is more important than furthering the policy of statute through clarity and ease of use.

[87]   In fairness, one should see Stephen Laws' article (Stephen Laws, 'Giving Effect to Policy in Legislation: How to Avoid Missing the Point' (2011) 32 Statute Law Review 1) as a tentative move beyond that approach, at least in the sense of emphasising that statutes might have purposes other than behaviour change and that such purposes are relevant to what drafters do.

the effect the proposed legislation might have indirectly on the law through changing behaviour, again leaving such questions to departments. It is possible, for example, that a statute aimed at changing behaviour might also change what counts as 'reasonable' conduct within the law (think of environmental standards). The Office of Parliamentary Counsel's approach largely excludes any such effects. The combined effect is that the Office of Parliamentary Counsel has set up a 'closed system' analysis of the options. Only specified inputs and outputs count in the analysis and other effects, to and from the environment that surrounds the system, are excluded. The environment, for these purposes, appears to be defined, in a way engineers would find normal, as anything beyond the power of the Office of Parliamentary Counsel to influence, which means most political, economic and social events.

The benefit of closed system analysis is that, within its own terms, it produces greater precision, albeit at the cost of realism. It can also be treated as a special case of an open system analysis of the same situation, and so there is some sense in saying that if a device fails on the basis of assuming a closed system, it is hardly likely to succeed if one relaxes that assumption. That might justify the Office of Parliamentary Counsel's claim that even its more limited analysis of a policy proposal for its coherence and consistency can have broader benefits for the policy process.[88] But engineers are warned against analysis that assumes that systems are closed for good reasons. The unintended inputs and outputs that cross to and from the system and its environment can have very large consequences for performance. The result is that Office of Parliamentary Counsel might be able to identify some legislative proposals that cannot work, but it will let through, and indeed draft up, other equally unworkable proposals where the problems come from such broader inputs and outputs. As we have seen, Office of Parliamentary Counsel seems to assign to departmental lawyers the task of carrying out any open system analysis, but that division of labour and expertise looks, from an engineering point of view, to be a vulnerable point in the process.[89]

Transactions lawyers put similar efforts into assessing solution options

---

[88] OPC (2011c) at 18.

[89] A further point of comparison might be the French system, in which the Conseil d'État, in exercising its scrutiny role over legislation certainly goes beyond effects on the law alone and considers matters such as administrative workability and possible evasion or avoidance. See Bell (2000). Whether this amounts to a fully open-system analysis is unclear, but some researchers see the Conseil as capable of developing its own policy positions. See e.g. Margherita Rendel, *The Administrative Functions of the French Conseil d'Etat* (London: Weidenfeld and Nicolson, 1970).

by thinking through their possible consequences. A survey of US transactions lawyers found that nearly 80 per cent considered that they were
responsible to a 'great' or 'significant' extent for 'anticipating, and drafting
to protect your client against, possible future events that could change your
client's business incentives' and 50 per cent considered themselves responsible to the same extent 'for anticipating, and drafting to protect your
client against, possible future events that could change the business incentives of other transaction parties'.[90] The acceptance by commercial lawyers
of responsibility for anticipating events that might affect their clients' business incentives is important in another way. It reveals that at least these
lawyers are thinking about the effectiveness of what they are constructing
at more than 'one level up'. Success is not just success in changing in the
micro-legal environment surrounding the parties but the success of the deal
itself, in terms the client would recognise. As a consequence, transactions
lawyers seem more willing than legislative lawyers to treat the system they
are operating in as open.

The uncertainties involved for transactions lawyers in assessing risks
at system levels beyond the law are considerable, which might explain
the reluctance of some lawyers to go as far as others in giving business
advice.[91] Assessment of business consequences is just as subject to problems of complexity and discreteness as those faced by legislative lawyers.
In addition, because they concern psychological, social and economic
conditions, they might also be subject to chaotic effects. On the other
hand, transactions lawyers usually operate at a much smaller scale than
the societal, macro-scale faced by legislators. If we assume that lawyers of
all kinds have a limit to their capacity to process information, it might be
that the reason legislative lawyers attempt to draw a line around the law
itself is not that their capacity is less than that of transactions lawyers but
merely that the sheer volume of law they are dealing with leaves no room
for anything else.

Another problem lawyers report in option assessment is that they are
not sure how far to go in generating future contingencies. They fear that

---

[90] See Steven Schwarcz, 'Explaining the Value of Transactional Lawyering'
(2007) 12 Stanford Journal of Law, Business & Finance 486. The difference between
the two is interesting. It might be that lawyers think they have less opportunity to
understand the incentives facing the other parties to the deal, or it might be that
they think it is sufficient to draft in such a way that their own client is protected
against any such changes.

[91] Some of those risks are legal, for example the restrictions imposed by Part
XX of the Financial Markets and Services Act 2000 and the possibility that a
disappointed client might be litigious.

by inventing, testing and then adjusting for more and more future scenarios, they might be unnecessarily frustrating their clients and causing
them avoidable cost. The Office of Parliamentary Counsel attempts a
pre-emptive strike when it advises departments that '[because] Counsel in
OPC are occupationally disposed to be literal-minded and cautious about
unspoken assumptions, the commentary provided by the OPC team may
be quite detailed'.[92] Transactions lawyers are also bothered about whether
they might be going too far in providing against future contingencies. One
wrote on her blog:[93]

> Recently I was in a meeting with a group of attorneys reviewing two proposed
> addenda to a contract. One was very detailed – contained definitions, covered
> all possible contingencies and outcomes. Its sheer length and complexity made
> it more difficult to follow. The second was much shorter thus easier to under-
> stand and addressed only the most likely complications. A spirited discussion
> ensued.

Boiled down, at issue was which document of the two better served its
purpose, which, in a transactional setting is presumably to accomplish the
parties' contractual goals or to provide a smooth exit if achieving those
ultimate goals is not possible. Can a well-intentioned effort to provide,
to the extent possible, all permutations and contingencies be too much
information? Can the sheer volume and density of the detail cloud the very
information you seek to provide?

In engineering terms, what is happening here is that lawyers are engaging in a recognisable process of refining options in the course of assessing
them, but they have developed no clear stopping rule for that process.
Since they are usually working on a single option and then varying it, they
are involved in a process looking for marginal improvements rather than
testing systematic variations. That would not be a problem if they could
consciously satisfice, and ask themselves whether the option in its current
state is good enough.[94] But since lawyers perceive that there is a problem
about not knowing where to stop, it seems to follow that they must have no
clear idea of what counts as a good enough solution. One can only speculate as to why that should be the case, but the situation suggests that some
lawyers have no clear idea of what counts for their clients as acceptable

---

92 OPC (2011c) at 50.
93 Nancy Hupp, 'Short but Comprehensive', Practice Blawg 15 Feb 2010
(http://practiceblawg.com/2010/02/short-but-comprehensive/).
94 Cf. the procedures recommended in Paul Brest and Linda Hamilton
Kreiger, 'Lawyers as Problem Solvers' (1999) 72 Temple Law Review 811–32.

risk. A practising lawyer commented to the author, 'Good lawyers talk to their clients about what are acceptable risks', which is undoubtedly true and the issue is ultimately one of the accurate specifications of the client's requirements. But the persistence of the problem is itself interesting. One possibility is that lawyers might be experiencing difficulties in communicating risks to clients.

As an example of communications difficulties, a leading legislative lawyer explained to the author that one of the reasons for the inclusion in *Working With Parliamentary Counsel* of the passage cited above about the nature of the Office of Parliamentary Counsel's comments back to client departments was that the departments tended to take detailed comments as destructive criticism or as an attempt to shift all blame for lack of clarity to the department, not as an invitation to carry on a detailed correspondence that would clarify for drafters the department's requirements – and that was a difficulty that arose in communication not with lay clients but with other lawyers.

Assessment Costs

One important difference between law and engineering is the cost of assessing an option. Because of the combination of quantification and computing, engineers can assess and re-assess many options in a relatively short time. In contrast, although expert systems for lawyers exist and can help in such tasks as ensuring that definitions are held constant or that potential problems are comprehensively identified, the amount of human lawyer effort required to assess a draft is still considerable. In this regard the anti-specialisation bias of the Office of Parliamentary Counsel might have drawbacks, since assessment by non-specialists will usually take more time and effort than assessment by specialists. It is significant that the Office of Parliamentary Counsel emphasises that its clients, the departmental lawyers, are expected to be experts in the substantive law covered by the bill and to bring their expertise into play as drafts move between the Office of Parliamentary Counsel and the department.[95] Processes that help with option generation are not necessarily optimised for option assessment.

Moreover, we have seen that in engineering, the cost of option assessment feeds back to the option generation stage, so that engineering's combination of quantification and the use of computing resources has increased the number of options that can be assessed and the number of

---

[95]   OPC (2011c) at 17.

times those options can be adjusted and re-assessed. In legal contexts, where quantification is rarely achieved and computing, though extensively used, is necessarily limited in scope, the cost of option assessment and reassessment remains high. That cost alone might explain why lawyers generate so few options. One might hope that assessment costs would fall as computer-based expert systems for lawyers develop, and thus for option generation to become a more important activity, but the necessary conceptual work has not yet been done, or at least where it has been done it has not yet produced technology that lawyers use.[96]

Concurrence

The cost of option assessment might also explain the comparative lack in the legal context of concurrent engineering, the attempt to solve many aspects of a problem as possible early on in the process and avoiding 'throwing products over the wall'. Some of the demarcation disputes between lawyers and other professionals are notorious,[97] and debate continues to rage about whether lawyers should be allowed to practise in firms that include non-lawyers.[98] Nevertheless, the very fact that commercial lawyers are prepared to work on their clients' business problems shows a willingness to engage in a degree of concurrency. Even the OPC

---

[96] One promising area where conceptual work has been done is the analysis of complex statutes using techniques drawn from network analysis. See Scott Boorman and Paul Levitt, 'Blockmodeling Complex Statutes: Mapping Techniques Based on Combinatorial Optimization for Analyzing Economic Legislation and Its Stress Points Over Time' (1983) 13 Economics Letters 1–9 (which takes the cross-references between sections in statutes – including cross-references in commentaries, but one could also use the Explanatory Notes for new bills – and uses them to partition the statute, regardless of the statutory order of sections, into groups in which the sections relate to the rest of the statute in the same way). The importance of such techniques for legislative lawyers is yet to be fully explored, but one can see how they might considerably improve the dialogue between departmental lawyers and the Office of Parliamentary Counsel. They would help non-specialist Office of Parliamentary Counsel lawyers to understand the structure of the existing law and help both sides to identify issues and gaps in new bills that affect that structure.

[97] See generally for an account of 'jurisdictional' disputes between professions, Andrew Abbott, *The System of Professions: An essay on the division of expert labor* (Chicago: University of Chicago, 1988).

[98] See e.g. Nick Jarrett-Kerr, 'Alternative Business Structures – the Long Pregnancy' (2011) 11 Legal Information Management 82–85, and for a variety of perspectives, Robert Lawry and others, The Jonathan M. Ault Symposium, 'Professional Responsibility and Multi-Disciplinary Practice' (2001–2002) 52 Case Western Reserve Law Review 861–1004.

is aware of the need to deal with some concurrent issues, as long as they do not involve thinking about the real world effects of the legislation itself. It offers advice, for example, on the parliamentary handling of bills, not only on procedural matters but also on possible clashes between the wording of clauses and the way ministers want to present their policies to Parliament.[99]

Transactions lawyers are also used to working in teams with other experts. Caruth, for example, tells of an occasion in which a problem had arisen in the construction of an oil refinery. To add to the physical problems of completing the job, there was a legal complication that the principal contractor had agreed to work on a fixed-price basis but had taken on sub-contractors on a cost-plus basis, so apparently transferring to itself the whole of the risk of poor performance by the sub-contractors. Caruth was dispatched to negotiate a way out the problem with a joint team of lawyers and engineers.[100] Transactions lawyers frequently find themselves in teams that include, for example, accountants, surveyors and bankers. In the legislative context, even the Office of Parliamentary Counsel is willing to be seen as part of the team responsible for a bill, albeit a slightly distant and reticent member, and it treats departmental lawyers as part of the department's broad bill team together with policy advisers and process managers.[101]

Prototypes and Testing in Situ

The final stage of the engineering design process is making a prototype for testing. For lawyers this is rarely a plausible proposition. Although there might be extensive experience of similar contracts, companies and statutes, and some confidence about the way they will perform, each new artefact is sent untested into the world. Engineers nevertheless also encounter situations in which prototype testing is not a practical option – for example where the project is large scale and essentially a one-off. In those cases, engineers strive to build into the process of building the artefact opportunities for review and feedback. Lawyers could presumably act in a similar way, allowing for feedback and correction in the process of deploying a legal device. The evidence is mixed, however, on whether they in fact do so. Transactions lawyers sometimes give the impression that they are

---

[99] OPC (2011c) at 14.
[100] David Caruth, *A Life of Three Strands: A City Lawyer's Memoir* (London: Avon Books. 1998) at 47–48.
[101] OPC (2011c) at 16–19.

prone to somewhat slap-dash exercises in cutting and pasting, especially when they are under pressure of time, but researchers suspect that lawyers have tactical reasons for giving that impression, possibly that it suits their purposes that the market does not notice their innovatory deviations from standardisation, and that reality is quite different.[102] Another possibility is that timescales are important, with more care taken – more iterations between the parties, for example – for agreements designed for the longer term. In the legislative field, the division of labour between departmental lawyers and the Office of Parliamentary Counsel, and the iterative process between them, offers some protection, but in jurisdictions without such a division, for example in the United States, the process of reviewing while constructing might not be very elaborate.

In both the UK and the US, however, there is other set of processes that might play some role in adjusting a draft before it becomes law, namely the legislative process itself. In some countries, the legislative process might specifically include a revising stage, for example articles 38 and 39 of the French constitution, which entrench a consultative role for the Conseil d'État for governmental bills and secondary legislation.[103] Legislatures often claim that they are carrying out such a function themselves. For example the UK House of Lords is frequently said to act as a 'revising' chamber.[104]

Legislative lawyers, however, usually express little confidence in the ability of legislatures to act as quality control processes. In the UK, for example, standard operating procedures instruct ministers to refuse to accept any amendments offered by backbench or opposition Members of Parliament. Even if ministers accept the policy arguments behind a non-Office of Parliamentary Counsel drafted amendment, they are told that they should do nothing beyond promising to bring forward an officially drafted amendment later.[105] US legislative counsel have described the typical output of the legislative process of the Congress as 'blurry', all for good constitutional and political reasons, but nevertheless hardly high quality.[106] The problem of how to ensure that constant assessment is built into the legislative process itself is essentially as yet unsolved.

---

[102] Mark Weidemaier and Mitu Gulati, 'How Markets Work: The Lawyer's Version' (2011).

[103] For details of the legislative role of the Conseil d'État, see Bell (2000).

[104] See e.g. Donald Shell, *The House of Lords* (Manchester: Manchester U.P., 2007) at 35 and chapter 4.

[105] OPC (2011c) at 67–68.

[106] M. Douglass Bellis, 'Drafting in the US Congress' (2001) 22 Statute Law Review 38–44 at 40–41.

GENERAL PRINCIPLES OF SUCCESSFUL LEGAL DESIGN?

Is there a legal equivalent of the (albeit tentative) principles that emerge from engineering about how successful design can be organised? Little detailed work has yet been attempted about the question, but it is an area of work that might develop in the future. Possible sources for such principles include the various practitioners' guides to legal drafting[107] and the style guides issued by the UK Office of Parliamentary Counsel and US House of Representatives Office of Legislative Counsel.[108] If one examines these texts even superficially, one will see emerging, across the divide between the public and private sectors, a set of common themes. First, they invariably urge lawyers to make sure their main message gets across and is not obscured by subsidiary material. Second, they call for the elimination of ambiguity and obscurity (which, given the non-legal intended readership of legal documents, now often means eliminating old-fashioned 'legal' language). Third, they insist that often-used terms should be clearly defined and consistently used. And fourth, they urge the elimination of unnecessary material (the Office of Parliamentary Counsel, for example, refers to the 'tendency to turn septic of provisions in a Bill that are not legally necessary').[109]

These themes contain at least the starting point for developing some general principles of legal design. But they are largely concerned with avoiding bad solutions rather than finding good ones, and they seem narrowly focussed on the process of drafting rather than on the broader process of design. For example, the elimination of ambiguity and obscurity is a useful linguistic rule, but in terms of design, some lack of clarity might be important to get a deal going. Drafting clauses that, in effect, postpone dealing with disagreements to a later stage (which might include rights of first refusal or first offer) allow the parties to begin their joint work straightaway. For consideration of proper design we might look instead to a comparison of what lawyers do with some of the equivalent engineering principles. In particular, we might consider the engineer's principles of

---

[107]   E.g. Peter Butt and Richard Castle, *Modern Legal Drafting: A Guide to using Clearer Language* 2nd edition (Cambridge: Cambridge U. P., 2006), Thomas Haggard, George Kuney, *Legal Drafting: Process, Techniques, and Exercises* (Eagen, Minn.: Thomson-West, 2007), Eidson Espenschied (2010).
[108]   OPC (2011b), *House Legislative Counsel's Manual on Drafting Style* (1995) .http://www.house.gov/legcoun/pdf/draftstyle.pdf.
[109]   OPC (2011c) at 36.

precision in determining the client's requirements, redundancy, minimisation of the number of elements and modularity.

The importance of clarity about the goals and objectives of the project is, as we have seen, recognised by lawyers as much as by engineers. Lawyers do not share engineers' enthusiasm for quantification, but the gap might not be as large as it first seems. Not only do engineers sometimes face problems with non-numerical objectives,[110] lawyers, especially commercial lawyers, deal with clients whose goals are largely quantifiable. Clients could readily set quantifiable goals, for example, in tax matters or for financial instruments. Even where objectives for lawyers are not easily quantifiable, (for example the emotional satisfactions sought by the client of Nathanson's will lawyer) lawyers are, at least in an informal way, constantly modelling their clients' priorities or their trade-offs between their different objectives, and it might help some lawyers in the future to formalise those models. For example, it might be helpful for lawyers to be able to distinguish between a client who is prepared to trade one goal off against another from a client who requires a minimum level of success about one goal, but, subject to that constraint, wants to maximise the degree of success achieved in another goal.

Legal attitudes towards redundancy seem to parallel engineering attitudes, but again might benefit from a degree of formalisation. Some forms of legal drafting exhibit ludicrous levels of redundancy. For example, objects clauses in British company constitutions, the (formerly compulsory) clause that lays out what the company has legal power to do,[111] were traditionally drafted with very high levels of redundancy. To make sure that the power existed to do whatever the management of the company wanted to do, every conceivable business and type of transaction they might want to do was listed, whether or not items on the list overlapped. Even when the law was changed in 1989 to allow companies to state that their object was to act as a 'general commercial company', little changed, allegedly because banks were uncertain what the phrase meant.[112] Only with a further reform, making unrestricted objects a statutory default rule, has any change in drafting practice occurred.[113] One can also see

---

[110] Simon (1996) 145–46.
[111] See Companies Act 2006, section 31.
[112] See David Martin, *One Stop Company Secretary* 6th edition (London: ICSA, 2009) at 264.
[113] See e.g. the new, object-less, articles and memorandum of association of Prudential plc at http://www.prudential.co.uk/prudential-plc/storage/downloads/mems-and-arts-sep-2011.pdf. One can see a similar change also in the standard forms issued by mass market drafters such as Oyez. If banks still object to

contractual provisions for mediation or arbitration as a form of redundancy, as supplementary ways of meeting the parties' goals if unforeseen
obstacles arise (in the same way as engineers think about human beings
as means for adjusting systems that might otherwise drift away from their
goals or outside their safety zones).[114] But like engineers, lawyers are conscious of the costs of redundancy. Modern drafting style tends towards
eliminating long lists of overlapping items, which are seen as tending
towards confusion,[115] and favours dispute resolution procedures designed
to work in a defined sequence rather than in parallel.[116]

Minimisation of elements is also a plausible goal of successful legal
design. It appears most clearly in the Office of Parliamentary Counsel
principle that unnecessary provisions 'turn septic', but it also lies behind
the Office of Legislative Counsel's injunction to 'cast out idle words',[117]
and calls by writers on contractual drafting to excise unnecessary material,
albeit subject to a warning that words that might look like 'barnacles'
acquired through unthinking repetition might in fact have some important
but forgotten function.[118] The conventional explanation for economy in
drafting is that courts tend to believe that statutory or contractual words
must have some function, so that the danger of including unnecessary
words or provisions is that judges will attribute functions to them that
interfere with the intended meanings of other provisions. That is entirely
possible, but judicial interpretation is not the only possible source of confusion. It can arise just as easily from misunderstanding by those who read
the words for themselves.

Modularity also appears in legal design, in the sense of chunks of internally coherent text that can be slotted into larger documents and work well
within them. Examples include standard arbitration clauses that fit into

---

unrestricted objects, however, there must still be some doubt whether the new
style company constitutions will catch on, especially for start up companies. The
pressure of standardisation might, however, cause the banks to reverse their policy.

[114]   Pahl et al. (2007) at 42. One might also include the courts and the judiciary
as such a system, but the problem with the courts as a back-up redundant system is
that they are unreliable as means of ensuring that a legal device works.

[115]   Butt and Castle (2006) at 57.

[116]   Robert Dobbins, 'The Layered Dispute Resolution Clause: From Boilerplate
to Business Opportunity' (2005) 1 Hastings Business Law Journal 161–82. See
also Gary Poon, *The Corporate Counsel's Guide to Mediation* (Chicago: ABA
Publishing, 2010) 15–24.

[117]   *House Legislative Counsel's Manual on Drafting Style* (1995) at 5.

[118]   Eidson Espenschied (2010) at 23. For the description of prior contractual
language building up like 'barnacles', see Philip Wood, *Life after Lehman: Changes
in Market Practice* (London: Allen and Overy, 2009) at 9.

different kinds of agreements, including the increasingly popular 'layered' or 'multi-tiered' dispute resolution clauses that take the parties from mediated negotiation to full-scale arbitration.[119] Some market standard agreements now exist as 'suites' – collections of documents using consistent clauses that cover different possible deals in a market.[120] Re-using elements within statutes and between statutes (although the latter is not encouraged by the Office of Parliamentary Counsel) are also attempts at modularity (for example consistent definitions clauses). In the words of the House Office of Legal Counsel, drafting style should be 'one of the predictable, steady elements that attorneys use to reduce chaos to order, and not one of the fluctuating factors that contribute to the chaos'.[121] At a more macro-level, the Uniform Commercial Code is in effect a modular construction, allowing different states to opt for different variants but all within a common list of alternatives.

Whether there are limits to legal modularity at the macro-level lies at the heart of one of the central debates in comparative law: whether projects for supra-national codifications such as the projected European Civil Code are feasible.[122] In effect, such projects propose to insert into national legal systems a very large module that would replace existing national law across areas as broad as the whole of private law. Some argue that the project is bound to fail because there are unspoken system-wide characteristics of different legal systems that mean that rules, even using the same terms, are never truly interoperable with the rest of the receiving legal system. The result will either be failure or a form of colonialism.[123] Others argue that conceptual differences are smaller than opponents assert and that global economic convergence is more important than the remaining conceptual disparities.[124]

Settling that dispute is beyond the scope of the current work, but we can at least attempt to specify more precisely what these kinds of claim

---

[119] See e.g. Dobbins (2005).

[120] E.g. the Loan Market Association's model agreements. See http://www.lma.eu.com/pages.aspx?p=206.

[121] *House Legislative Counsel's Manual on Drafting Style* (1995) at 7.

[122] See e.g. Arthur Hartkamp, Martijn Hesselink, Edwoud Hondius, Chantal Mak and C. Edgar du Perron, *Towards A European Civil Code* 4th edition (Alphen aan den Rijn: Kluwer-Ars Aequi Libri, 2011).

[123] E.g. Pierre Legrand, 'Sens et Non-sens d'un Code Européen' (1996) 4 Revue internationale de droit comparé 779–812.

[124] E.g. Klaus Peter Berger, 'European Private Law, Lex Mercatoria and Globalization' in Arthur Hartkamp, Martijn Hesselink, Edwoud Hondius, Chantal Mak and C. Edgar du Perron, *Towards A European Civil Code* 4th edition (Alphen aan den Rijn: Kluwer-Ars Aequi Libri, 2011).

amount to. One can concede that the effects legal rules have on behaviour can differ not because of differences in the rules themselves but because of differences in the social, economic, political and cultural environment within which they operate. But that is not the same as arguing that rules taken from one legal system to another, or created by transnational bodies, are inherently incomprehensible in the receiving system. The former argument is an uncontentious claim that rules, like any engineering device, interact with their environment, so that designers who ignore variations in the environment might be surprised by the results. The latter is more akin to a claim that we cannot understand legal systems by understanding the rules within them and that there are emergent properties of the system as a whole that can only be understood at the level of the system, properties, moreover, that have 'downward' effects on the rules. Sceptics of such 'strong' emergent properties might suspect that the problem is merely that we have not understood the rules themselves in sufficient detail, but there might well be properties of human languages that have to be explained in terms of emergence.[125] Whether such problems are serious enough to prevent interoperability is, however, a different question. It is perfectly possible that, even taking into account 'downward' effects, the fit is within acceptable levels of engineering tolerance.

LITIGATORS AND JUDGES AS ENGINEERS

If we take the work of transactions lawyers and legislative lawyers as the central case of what lawyers do, the analogy with what engineers do is easy to see. We can perhaps start to go beyond simple analogy and look for ways to use engineering as a model for understanding what lawyers do and for providing ideas for practical improvement in both directions. Indeed, to the extent that engineering increasingly deals with sociotechnical systems, and law forms part of such systems, one can even start to contemplate integrating law into engineering.

But what about the types of lawyer whose work lies at the centre of the currently dominant paradigm, namely litigators and judges? Is there any way of incorporating them into the view that lawyers can be seen as engineers, or, to be more precise, that lawyers, like engineers, are concerned with design and that they are concerned with design in a manner that

---

[125] See e.g. Nick C. Ellis, 'Emergentism, Connectionism and Language Learning' (1998) 48(4) Language Learning 631–64. Cf. Simone Glanert, 'Speaking Language to Law: The Case of Europe' (2008) 28 Legal Studies 161–71.

makes comparing them with engineers at least as useful as comparing them with other types of designer? The answer is that there is a way of doing that, although we possibly take it at the cost of having to retreat from the edge of theory and back to the realm of analogy.

Turning first to litigators, the place we might start is to notice that for litigators, the main obstacle to achieving their clients' purposes is the activity of the other party, namely of some other lawyer's client. Overcoming that kind of obstacle does not sound much like an activity aimed at making people and objects work better together, and so does not sound much like engineering, although there are forms of litigation – in which the parties want a point clarified but otherwise intend to carry on working together – in which that is precisely what is happening. Oddly, however, there is a form of engineering that fits the more normal type of litigation, in which destruction of the other party is either an intended result of the process or one to which the client is indifferent, and it happens to be the original form of engineering in the modern world. It is military engineering.[126] The goal of military engineers is to contribute to the success of military operations, and, when those operations take the form of armed conflict, their goal is victory for their side over their adversaries.

It should be conceded, however, that the lessons for litigation from military engineering, and vice versa, are not as obvious of those of civil engineering for transactional and legislative lawyering. One of the classics of military engineering, P.S. Bond's *The Engineer in War*, posits three main areas of interest for the military engineer: transportation, fortification (including destroying the other side's fortifications) and sanitation.[127] Although one might be able to draw some analogies between military transportation and the need for litigators to construct flexible arguments that allow them to change tack at short notice, and between fortification and the way litigators seek to build impregnable arguments by thinking about how the other side might attack them, it is difficult to see a litigation parallel for sanitation, although one might think about whether litigators have any responsibility to clear up the mess in human relations that litigation often leaves behind.

There is, however, one aspect of military engineering that lawyers, especially those brought up in common law systems, might fruitfully consider. Bond pointed out that unlike civil engineers, who seek to build roads and bridges to work for a long time, on firm foundations and with long-lasting materials, military engineers build for the moment using whatever they

---

[126] I am grateful to Scott Boorman for this suggestion.
[127] P.S. Bond, *The Engineer in War* (New York: Magraw-Hill, 1916) at 14.

have to hand.[128] Military roads and bridges on or near the battlefield are designed for speed of construction and immediate effectiveness, not for permanence. The arguments of litigators are similarly designed for immediate effect in winning the current battle. They are not designed for long-term stability or for solving problems beyond the immediate ones facing the litigator's client. But in a common law system, where much of the law is built up from judicial decisions arising out of litigation, the result is that we can be left with legal structures built out of the legal equivalent of the detritus of war. It is not as far-fetched as it might first appear to draw an analogy between, for example, the entirely judge-made English law of psychiatric injury in negligence, once described by a leading scholar as confused, unedifying and, in some respects 'grotesque',[129] and the transport infrastructure of a recent battlefield. Both are full of roads that lead nowhere, bridges that cross obstacles that once seemed important but no longer matter and vehicles that were once useful in getting somewhere but are now burnt out and abandoned.

Moving onto judges, it is possible to conceive of their work precisely as building long-lasting and useful legal structures out of the temporary and improvised material of litigation. They would be the judges in the tradition of, for example, Karl Llewellyn's Grand Style or Ronald Dworkin's Hercules.[130] But most judges are reluctant designers. They tend to decide cases on the narrowest plausible grounds, disturbing the existing structures as little as possible. One of the reasons for their reluctance is they face a fundamental problem that they have no client whose objectives and goals they can work towards. They might attempt to construct a client – 'the public interest' or 'the people' – out of the constitution they work within or the values inherent in the law,[131] but that exercise is full of peril, not least because it threatens to bring them into the heart of politics. Another, more realistic, way to think of judges is as bricoleurs, as do-it-yourself bodgers who use whatever is to hand to keep the structure of the law from falling apart.[132] If that seems too lowly, perhaps we could describe judges

---

[128]   Bond (1916) at 12–13.

[129]   Jane Stapleton, 'In Restraint of Tort' in Peter Birks (ed.), *The Frontiers of Liability* vol. 2 (Oxford: Oxford U.P., 1994) at 87.

[130]   For the Grand Style, see e.g. Llewellyn (1960b). For Hercules, see Ronald Dworkin, *Law's Empire* (London: Fontana, 1986).

[131]   Simon (1996) at 153 describes a similar process of constructing society as one's client.

[132]   See Nigel Simmonds, 'Bluntness and Bricolage' in Hyman Gross and Ross Harrison (eds), *Jurisprudence: Cambridge Essays* (Oxford: Oxford U.P., 1992) and, in a narrower context, Gerald Garvey, *Constitutional Bricolage* (Princeton: Princeton U.P., 1971).

as consulting engineers who are asked to decide what to do about problems that have arisen in structures and devices designed and built by others. One might even be able to identify parallels between judicial techniques and engineering methods. For example, judges often include an element of redundancy in their judgments, especially in the lower courts where it is common for judgments to be structured in the alternative ('if I am wrong about point X, there is also point Y, which produces the same result'). The narrowness of judicial reasoning might be seen as a consequence of the judges' lack of capacity for option testing and thus an understandable reluctance to make changes the effects of which are uncertain. But even if we can describe judges as consulting engineers, we should recognise that they often seem to be working without access to the original drawings and to be trying to guess the function of the device they are called upon to repair entirely from the complaints of those who claim that it has stopped working. It is a form of reverse engineering without the benefit of understanding much about what the product does.

One might justify the processes of the common law as an exercise in the co-evolution of problems and solutions, or what Simon called 'designing without final goals', in which each solution changes our understanding of the problem, and so also changes what the next solution needs to achieve.[133] When the process works, the very act of designing solutions leads to a better understanding of the problems. Where it does not work, at least it might have revealed that the problems we face exhibit the third kind of impossibility, that there is no satisfactory way of stating the problem so that it can be solved. It is difficult, however, to see how even this kind of process can work without judges having some initial view of what the problems are and without engaging in a conscious effort at designing solutions. Where judges refuse to see themselves as engaged in any form of engineering, or any form of conscious design, they are unlikely to gain enlightenment.

NEXT STEPS

The purpose of this chapter was to show that there is a unifying theme for what lawyers do, namely the theme that lawyers, like engineers, make useful devices. It has gone on to show that we can use the analogy between law and engineering, especially between law and engineering design, to illuminate further how lawyers achieve their effects, and even to use the analogy

---

[133] Simon (1996) at 162–64.

to suggest possible improvements in legal practice. The rest of this book is devoted largely to teasing out some initial thoughts about the implications of treating lawyering as principally a form of engineering, first for practising lawyers in the field of legal ethics and then for academic lawyers, in terms of what they research and teach.

4. Implications (1) – Professional ethics

We now turn to the question of what difference widespread acceptance of the law-as-engineering perspective would make. We look at the implications in three areas: lawyers' professional ethics, legal education, and legal research. In this chapter we consider the first item on that list

We start with a problem of legal ethics that currently has no satisfactory answer, namely the responsibility of lawyers for the effects of devices they design on third parties. We then suggest that engineers have been thinking about ethical questions with many parallels with that issue, and that the way engineers have reasoned about their ethical issues provides a way forward for lawyers. We conclude with asking how legal ethics might work if it started with the concerns of lawyers whose main work is comparable to that of engineers.

THE FALL OF LEHMAN BROTHERS AND REPO 105S

What responsibility do lawyers bear for harmful effects on third parties of the transactions they facilitate? This is not a trivial problem. The clearest examples arise from an event of global significance, namely the collapse of the world's financial markets in 2007–9, a disaster in which lawyers played an important, but as yet under-reported part.

Let us start with the fall of the investment bank Lehman Brothers in September 2008, one of the crucial events in the financial crisis. The collapse of Lehman, including the failure of attempts to rescue it, is often taken by economists to be the central event of the Great Crash, and the point at which the effects of a crisis in the financial markets started to leech into the rest of the economy.[1] Lehman's collapse came at the end of long

---

[1] E.g. Charles Bean, 'The Great Moderation, the Great Panic and the Great Contraction' (2010) 8 Journal of the European Economic Association 289–325, Jagjit Chadha, Sean Holly (eds), *Interest Rates, Prices and Liquidity: Lessons from the Financial Crisis* (Cambridge: Cambridge U.P., 2012) at e.g. 108, 172–74, 197–201, 218–22, 240, 253–58. For a somewhat breathless account of the events,

complex series of events, but essentially the problem originated in the sub-prime mortgage market. The sub-prime market consisted of mortgages that had been granted by commercial banks to clients who were poor credit risks, often on terms that attracted such clients into the market but which were unsustainable in the longer term. Sub-prime lenders were, however, able to carry on lending because, first, a rising property market – itself later fuelled by sub-prime loans – seemed to offer the lender built-in protection, and second, because the risks could be spread and managed by securitising the loans and packaging them with other mortgage loans. The proceeds of sale of packages of securitised mortgages could then be used to finance further loans. Lehman became heavily involved in these markets. In 2006, it embarked on an aggressive growth strategy that involved taking on more and more risk.[2] Lehman failed, however, to spot the downward economic trends that undermined the borrowers' payments on their mortgages, on which the entire edifice of derivatives was built. Instead, Lehman bet even more heavily in the hope of making money by contrarian means. The attempt ended in disaster. Efforts at rescue ran into the sand (including an abortive rescue by the British bank Barclays, one of the problems of which was a legal obstacle concerning a need to obtain shareholder consent at short notice).[3] Lehman collapsed. There then ensued what some authors have called the Great Panic of 2008–9, the consequences of which will remain with us for a very long time.

One of Lehman's practices revealed by the investigations into the bank's failure was that Lehman had been hiding some of its assets and liabilities from regulators and from the market.[4] Lehman was downplaying the

---

see Andrew Sorkin, *Too Big to Fail* (London: Penguin, 2010). For more measured account see Statement by the Financial Services Authority 20 January 2010, http://www.fsa.gov.uk/pubs/other/lehman.pdf.

[2] Report of the Examiner in Bankruptcy in Lehman's Case (the Valukas Report) vol 1, 3–5 (http://jenner.com/lehman/lehman/VOLUME%201.pdf).

[3] The relevant requirement was that the UK Listing Rules required prior shareholder approval for substantial guarantees of the type demanded by US regulators. No meeting could be organised in time and the UK authorities were not enthusiastic about waiving it. Lawyers looking back on the situation might now ask whether Barclays might have gone ahead anyway, since the Listing Rules do not limit the powers of companies, but only create obligations about how those powers ought to be used. Breach of the rules might invite sanctions from regulators, such as the UK Listing Authority, and might have caused practical problems later, but the exercise of the powers would have been valid. The question never arose as a live issue, however, because Barclays seems not to have considered commercially viable any deal including such guarantees. See Statement by the Financial Services Authority 20 January 2010, http://www.fsa.gov.uk/pubs/other/lehman.pdf.

[4] The account here is based on the Valukas Report vol 3, 'Repo 105'.

extent to which it held risky assets and liabilities, so making the bank appear safer than it really was. The principal method Lehman employed to downplay the degree to which its position was risky was to take some of its assets and liabilities off its balance sheet for a few days at a time, especially at the point, usually quarterly, when the bank was required to report its assets, liabilities and capital to the US regulator. The technique used to achieve this effect was known as Repo 105 (or the similar Repo 108), a transaction that on its face looked fairly standard, but which in reality exploited differences in the various legal and accounting regimes under which Lehman operated.

A 'repo' is a standard method of raising short-term finance using securities. The organisation wishing to raise money sells some of its securities to a counterparty for cash, agreeing simultaneously to buy back equivalent securities (which may or may not be the precise securities sold) at a specific price at a later date.[5] The seller gains cheaper financing than by an unsecured loan, and but retains the possibility of benefiting from any increase in the value of the securities. The buyer gains security for the cash advanced, is able to use the securities sold to cover any obligations it might have in the meantime to deliver such securities to any third parties with whom it might have a 'short' position (i.e. promising to sell something at a price lower than one has to pay to buy it) and usually earns a small return from the repurchase price being set slightly higher than the sale price.[6]

Repo transactions were very useful for Lehman, as for other institutions, in generating short-term finance and in themselves were perfectly acceptable to the regulator, but there was a snag. The relevant US accounting rule, the US Generally Accepted Accounting Principles' Statement of Financial Accounting Standards number 140 (GAAP SFAS 140), requires some repos to be treated as if they were loans rather than sales. In particular, GAAP SFAS 140 says that a repo should be accounted for as a loan if the transferor retains effective control over the asset. The standard repurchase provision was seen as retaining control. As a result, the effect of a repo transaction was that, in accounting terms, Lehman's assets grew by the amount of the sale price and its liabilities grew by the amount of

---

[5] My thanks to Nicholas Aleksander for helping me unpick the intricacies of these transactions. See also Kingsley T.W. Ong and Eugene Y.C. Yeung 'Repos & Securities Lending: the Accounting Arbitrage and their Role in the Global Financial Crisis' (2011) 6(1) Capital Markets Law Journal 92–103. Responsibility for any remaining inaccuracies or over-simplifications, however, remains with the author.

[6] See e.g. Ong and Yueng (2011) at 92–93. The return to the buyer is usually subject to a margin call mechanism that adjusts for changes in market conditions.

the repurchase price. Lehman looked for a way that they could continue to use repo transactions, but without the inconvenient increase in their total assets and liabilities. Lehman came up with the idea that they could officially lose control of the assets that had been relinquished if the transaction did not generate enough cash for them to buy the assets back in the market. That is, the repurchase agreement would not count as maintaining control if the repurchaser had to go beyond the funds generated by the deal itself to regain the assets. If instead of a loan, the deal counted only as a futures contract, the increase in Lehman's assets and liabilities would be limited to the difference between the sale price and the repurchase price.

The crucial figure was how big the difference had to be between the market value of the assets and the sale price for control to count as relinquished. In the normal deal, assets would be sold at below their market value with an agreement to repurchase at their market value, with the difference between the two set at 2 per cent. For the accounting authorities, that was near enough to count as control. Lehman was advised that the difference had to be 5 per cent for bonds and 8 per cent for equities for control to count as relinquished. Those differences were the origin of the names 'Repo 105' and 'Repo 108'.[7]

There was, however, a further problem. Another requirement of the US accounting rules was that the transaction had to result in the isolation of the assets from the transferor in the event of insolvency ('bankruptcy', in US terms).[8] That was interpreted as meaning that the transaction had to count in law as a sale of the assets and not, for example, as secured lending. Lehman took this 'true sale' problem to a series of US law firms, but none of them was prepared to stake their professional reputation on the assertion Lehman was hoping for.[9] Eventually, Lehman turned to the London Magic Circle firm of solicitors Linklaters, advisers to Lehman's London operation.[10]

---

[7] One difficulty of this field is that although repo deals are formally sales combined with promises to repurchase, in the language of the market – more realistic than that of the lawyers – they are often treated as collateralised loans, to the extent that the seller is sometimes described as 'selling collateral'. '105' indicates that, in these terms, the 'collateral' sold is worth 105 per cent of the 'loan'.

[8] SFAS 140.9(a).

[9] See Valukas Report vol. 3 at 783–84.

[10] See Valukas Report vol. 3 at 784. See also Jeremy Hodges, 'Linklaters opinion letter at centre of Lehman funding controversy' legalweek.com 12 Mar 2010, Michael De La Merced and Julia Werdigier, 'The Origins of Lehman's "Repo 105"' New York Times, 12 March 2010 (http://dealbook.nytimes.com/2010/03/12/the-british-origins-of-lehmans-accounting-gimmick/), Gavriel Hollander, 'Lehman exploited Linklaters opinion to tidy up balance sheet' The Lawyer 12 March

The situation in England was fundamentally different from that in the US. The relevant accounting rules (the International Financial Reporting Rule 39) require that for a repo to go off balance sheet in the way Lehman wanted, it was not enough for there to have been a legal sale. The rule was that, in addition to control having been relinquished, substantially all the risks and rewards of ownership must be passed over to the counterparty. In England, therefore, whether a repo involves a true sale of the assets is insufficient to settle the relevant accounting issue. Nevertheless, Linklaters was prepared to put in writing an opinion that, as a matter exclusively of English law, assuming that no other legal system was relevant to the transaction, and assuming that the assets transferred were liquid assets (in the sense that there was a ready market where they could be bought and sold), the transfer of assets to the buyer counted as a sale and not as anything else.[11]

On the basis of Linklaters' letter, Lehman proceeded to carry out vast numbers of Repo 105 transactions, using its London subsidiary as an intermediary to ensure that the transactions were subject to English law and thus, in the relevant system, counted as true sales. At the same time, however, relying on the fact that its London subsidiary, in common with all of its subsidiaries, was treated for accounting purposes as subject to US accounting rules rather than British rules, Lehman used the English true sale opinion to satisfy the US accounting standard. By combining the English true sale point with relinquishing control according to GAAP standards by increasing the difference between the selling price and the market value of the assets, Lehman was able to justify removing the full value of the assets involved in the repo transactions from its balance sheet, and also from the returns it made to the US authorities. It had, in effect, arbitraged the differences between the English and US legal systems and the British and US accounting rules.

The precise circumstances in which Linklaters first gave, and later repeated, their opinion are not clear, and we do not know whether Linklaters had any prior involvement in the development of the Repo 105 programme.[12] It should also be made clear that we cannot say that the

---

2010, Megan Murphy and Michael Peel, 'Linklaters faces fall-out from Repo 105' Financial Times 13 March 2010, Heather Stewart, 'Lehman's advisers were guard dogs that didn't bark' The Observer 14 March 2010.

[11]   See Valukas Report vol. 3 at 784–86. Linklaters' opinion letter is reproduced in full in Appendix 17 to the Valukas Report at 20–31.

[12]   See Valukas Report vol. 3 at 765 note 2950, where the Examiner in Bankruptcy remarks that Linklaters' opinion letter is silent about the issue of whether the firm had any role in the earlier development of the Repo 105 programme.

opinion was in any way wrong as a statement of English law,[13] and since it made no reference at all to the accounting position under the US GAAP SFAS 140, the interpretation of the US accounting rules were not part of its remit.[14] In any case, it is not even clear that Lehman had misinterpreted those US accounting rules. It had merely taken advantage of differences between US and non-US rules. The Examiner in Bankruptcy in Lehman's case, however, was clear that there was never any commercial justification for the Repo 105 transactions (or, more accurately, there was no commercial justification for the '105' part of the deals) and that from the start they could only have been a device to manipulate Lehman's balance sheet.[15] To qualify for accounting treatment as a sale, Lehman effectively had to promise to pay more than the going market rate for repo deals. The Examiner found that officers of Lehman had breached their fiduciary duties 'by exposing Lehman to potential liability for filing materially misleading periodic Reports'. A spokesperson for Linklaters, however, denied any responsibility for those breaches. She told the *New York Times*:[16]

> The U.S. examiner's Report into the failure of Lehman Brothers includes references to English Law opinions which Linklaters gave in relation to a number of Lehman transactions. The examiner – who did not contact the firm during his investigations – does not criticise those opinions or say or suggest that they were wrong or improper. We have reviewed the opinions and are not aware of any facts or circumstances which would justify any criticism.

---

[13]   See e.g. Ong and Yeung (2011) at 94–97. The technical accuracy of Linklaters' opinion was generally assumed at the time even among those who had concerns about wider issues. See e.g. Elizabeth Fournier, 'The Reality of Repo 105' (2010) 29(3) International Financial Law Review 60. There is a possible hole in Linklaters' advice concerning the point that under the terms of Lehman's repo deals, including Repo 105 deals, any dividends or interest payable to the owners of the financial assets remained payable to Lehman during the period they were placed with the buyer. That does not look much like a 'sale' of the assets, since receiving dividends and interest is a normal incident of owning shares or bonds. Linklaters, however, said that this was not a problem because the buyer was under no obligation under the deal to restore the precise assets transferred to it by Lehman, only equivalent assets. Since the obligation to pay over dividends could apply to assets that Lehman had never owned, it could not be used to establish that Lehman still owned the assets they had purported to sell. In *Lehman Brothers International (Europe) (in administration) v Lehman Brothers Finance* [2010] EWHC 2914 (Ch), the court accepted the parties' assumption that the repos did effectively transfer ownership. See Ong and Yeung (2011) at 96–97.

[14]   See Valukas Report vol. 3 at 786.

[15]   Valukas Report vol. 3 at 735, 746–47, 761ff.

[16]   De La Merced and Werdigier (2010).

GOLDMAN SACHS AND THE BIG SHORT

We can also turn to another of the sources of financial catastrophe in 2007–9, the conduct of the investment bank Goldman Sachs. In particular we might examine the ABACUS 2007-AC1 affair.[17] Goldman Sachs was the first big player in the financial world to realise that there was something deeply wrong with the sub-prime mortgage market. Goldman had been heavily involved in designing and selling complex financial products derived from the mortgage markets, not only packaged securitised mortgages but also re-securitisations which packaged together packages of mortgages with other securitised investments. These became known as CDOs – collateralised debt obligations. CDOs could also be created out of other CDOs, in which case they were 'CDO²s'. Goldman's activities, however, had not been confined to brokering deals between others for a fee. It also had participated as an investor on its own account, as a result of which it found itself faced with considerable losses if the value of its CDO products fell. As the US housing market faltered and various types of sub-prime borrower began to default, some Goldman employees began to argue that the firm should protect itself from the coming drop in values. There were various devices it could use. It could, for example, use credit default swaps (CDSs), in effect bets that a particular business would fail, to bet that the sub-prime deals would fail. More effectively, it could combine CDSs with taking 'short' positions on the mortgage-related investments themselves – in other words instead of holding investments and hoping their value would rise before selling them (the 'long' position), they would sell investments in the hope their value would fall before they had to buy them. Initially, Goldman's intention seems to have been merely to reach 'home' – a neutral overall position – but subsequently it shifted to hoping for the market to fall, to a position described internally as 'The Big Short'.[18]

One of the difficulties of massively shifting one's position from long to short is finding enough investment opportunities to short. Goldman

---

[17]   See *SEC v Goldman Sachs and Tourre*, Complaint 10 April 2010. http://www.sec.gov/litigation/complaints/2010/comp-pr2010-59.pdf, Consent 14 July 2010 http://www.sec.gov/litigation/litreleases/2010/consent-pr2010-123.pdf, (agreeing to Proposed Judgment http://www.sec.gov/litigation/litreleases/2010/judgment-pr2010-123.pdf).

[18]   Carl Levin (chair), *Wall Street and the Financial Crisis: Anatomy of a Financial Collapse* (United States Senate, Permanent Subcommittee on Investigations of the Committee on Homeland Security and Governmental Affairs, 13 April 2011) at 386–87.

decided to improve their chances by continuing to create more and more
CDOs. A further problem was that no matter how many times mortgages
are re-securitised, ultimately the CDOs depend on flows of income from
a finite number of real borrowers who steadily repay their loans. The
way around that problem was the 'synthetic' CDO, in which investors
in effect placed bets that the market value of a real CDO would rise or
fall. The synthetic CDO allowed investment in CDOs beyond the value
of the underlying assets. Goldman proceeded to sell products – including
synthetic CDOs and partially synthetic CDO^2s – to unsuspecting institutions without disclosing its own short position on those products. Its sales
techniques included using ambiguous language (for example describing
the underlying assets as 'sourced on the Street' to suggest, without actually saying, that they were newly acquired, not just part of Goldman's own
inventory that it wanted to offload) and by pointing to small long positions that Goldman was taking on the investment (for example taking the
'equity' tranche of a CDO – the tranche last to be paid) without mentioning that the value of that long position was tiny compared with its short
position.[19]

The ABACUS 2007-AC1 CDO was one of the CDOs Goldman spon-
sored at the time. In some ways, it was a special case, since Goldman's
role was not as comprehensive as in other deals. In effect, Goldman set up
the deal to deliver a $1bn profit to a favoured client, a hedge fund whose
managers had also formed a very negative view of the mortgage market.[20]
More is known about this deal than the others, however, because it was
the subject of legal action by the Securities and Exchange Commission.
The essence of the deal was that Goldman would allow the hedge fund to
choose the securities that a synthetic CDO would use as reference points.
Because of the risk that the hedge fund's involvement in choosing the
securities would discourage investors, Goldman arranged for another firm
to take on formal responsibility for the selection, a firm that subsequently
claimed that it believed that the hedge fund would be taking an 'equity'
stake and thus had a long position. Investors were found who took long
positions. The value of the reference securities began to fall almost immediately, wiping out the long investors' positions and producing the envisaged $1bn profit for the hedge fund. Goldman eventually paid $550m in
compensation and civil penalties as a result of the SEC action.

The role of lawyers in the ABACUS 2007-AC1 CDO is less clear than
in the Lehman Repo 105s, but the evidence taken on the crisis by the US

---

[19] See generally Levin (2011) at 390ff.
[20] Levin (2011) at 396.

Senate Permanent Sub-Committee on Investigations of the Homeland Security and Government Affairs Committee shows that both Goldman's in-house lawyers and external counsel (McKee Nelson) had sight of the deals over a long period and took responsibility for questions of disclosure and conflicts of interest. Moreover it seems that one of the senior executives in Goldman's mortgage team was a lawyer, an ex-associate at the same outside law firm. Although lawyers do not necessarily take part in the selling of securities to particular investors, they are intimately involved in creating the securities and preparing for sales, including the drafting of formal offer documents. The importance of lawyers can be seen in the fact that the choice of lawyer is a significant matter for the parties to the deal. In the ABACUS deal, for example, we have an exchange of emails between Goldman and the firm who took formal responsibility for selection of the securities in which Goldman insisted on installing McKee Nelson as 'deal counsel' rather than the law firm proposed by the selection agents.[21] The Goldman executive explained:

> We are using McKee Nelson as deal counsel since they have a deep knowledge of the ABACUS transaction documents. I am afraid that if we use counsel not familiar with our deal structure, legal expenses might be significantly higher than otherwise, and the transaction execution might take more time.

What the lawyers knew of Goldman's intentions and when they knew it does not appear in any of the written evidence given to the Senate Sub-Committee or in the published SEC documents. But there is a clue about what might have happened, or at least what in-house counsel and the external lawyers might have said happened, in the terms of the judgment against Goldman (to which Goldman consented). Goldman agreed to ensure that in future all their marketing material would be reviewed by their in-house lawyers and to establish a centralised system of recording which lawyer reviewed which document and when, and, if Goldman used external lawyers for a deal, that those lawyers would also review all the marketing material. The lawyers are also to see the minutes of the firm's committee that approved the deal. An obvious interpretation of these requirements is that, despite the repetition of the assurance that disclosure issues were under the control of the in-house and external lawyers, there was some confusion about the extent to which Goldman's lawyers had reviewed the ABACUS marketing material and some question about the extent to which the lawyers appreciated Goldman's intentions.

---

[21]   Levin (2011) Exhibit #111 at 407.

LAWYERS AND THE CRASH

Deals such as the Repo 105s and the Goldman Big Short were not in themselves the only or even the principal causes of the financial crash of 2008,
but they and transactions like them formed part of a larger process that
resulted in economic losses and personal insecurity for millions of people.
In most, if not all, of the transactions that fuelled the initial bubble conditions of the early 2000s and the great expansion in the number, complexity and value of financial instruments that accompanied and encouraged
those conditions, lawyers must have been at some point involved.[22] The
Permanent Sub-Committee on Investigations identified four related causes
of the crash:

> Lenders introduced new levels of risk into the U.S. financial system by selling
> and securitizing complex home loans with high risk features and poor under-
> writing. The credit rating agencies labeled the resulting securities as safe invest-
> ments, facilitating their purchase by institutional investors around the world.
> Federal banking regulators failed to ensure safe and sound lending practices
> and risk management, and stood on the sidelines as large financial institutions
> active in US financial markets purchased billions of dollars in mortgage related
> securities containing high risk, poor quality mortgages. Investment banks
> magnified the risk to the system by engineering and promoting risky mortgage
> related structured finance products, and enabling investors to use naked credit
> default swaps and synthetic instruments to bet on the failure rather than the
> success of U.S. financial instruments. Some investment banks also ignored the
> conflicts of interest created by their products, placed their financial interests
> before those of their clients, and even bet against the very securities they were
> recommending and marketing to their clients.[23]

Repo 105s and ABACUS were examples of the fourth category – the risk
multiplication effects of irresponsible behaviour by the investment banks,
behaviour whose catastrophic effects were in part triggered by Goldman's
own strategy of shorting the whole market. The role of lawyers in that
category is clear. But one could point to the role of legal advice in every
part of the story. The transactions required to create all the relevant investment instruments were complex enough to need repeated legal activity.
For example, structured finance, at an absolute minimum, requires, well
before the sale of securities to investors, the creation of a new company,

---

[22]   John Flood and Eleni Skordaki, 'Structuring Transactions: The Case
of Real Estate Finance' in Volkmar Gessner (ed.), *Contractual Certainty in
International Trade: Empirical Studies and Theoretical Debates on Institutional
Support for Global Economic Exchanges* (Oxford: Hart Publishing, 2009) chapter 6.
[23]   Levin (2011) at 12.

the special purpose vehicle, and the transfer to it of assets, a process that requires detailed knowledge and use of the rules concerning the assignment of obligations. All of these effects have to be achieved in specific jurisdictions using the law of that jurisdiction and understanding its relationship to other jurisdictions.

Offering securities to the market, as we have seen, requires a constant flow of legal advice and guidance. In-house lawyers were especially important, often sitting on important internal committees in both the lending banks and the investment banks and taking a lead on drafting and reviewing transactions documents. Moreover, the regulators, at least in the US, were stuffed full of lawyers who needed to understand the structure and risks of the transactions undertaken by the businesses they were regulating, and who tended to communicate to those businesses through their lawyers. Even the least lawyered part of the story, the behaviour of the ratings agencies, must at least have involved advice about the legal principles underlying the characteristics of the securities being rated, even if it involved little legal engineering of its own.

As the Repo 105 story shows, the issues are far from confined to the USA. London law firms are as much at the heart of the world financial system as New York firms. Indeed, the whole concept of law firms having a home jurisdiction is beginning to collapse as lawyering becomes as inherently multinational as the markets it facilitates. Jurisdiction-crossing is also important because of its implications for regulation, as the connection between ABACUS and the Cayman Islands illustrates. The Turner Review on the global banking crisis, commissioned by the UK government and published by the UK Financial Services Authority, pointed to the lack of global regulation of banking as one of the longer term causes of the crisis.[24] Banks' lawyers could engage in what Turner calls 'regulatory arbitrage' – what lawyers would call 'forum shopping' – to shift activity into the most favourable jurisdiction for what they wanted to do. In contrast, when banks failed, the responsibility for rescuing them (or, as in the case of Lehman, not rescuing them) fell on national authorities. As the Governor of the Bank of England remarked, banks live globally but die nationally. The crucial point is that lawyers are essential in the identification and exploitation of regulatory arbitrage opportunities. Repo 105s provide a clear example of regulatory arbitrage, and there is also an element of forum shopping in the setting up of the ABACUS special purpose vehicle as a company registered in the Cayman Islands. Turner's big picture of the

---

[24]   Adair Turner, *The Turner Review: A Regulatory Response to the Global Banking Crisis* (London: Financial Services Authority, 2009) 36.

banks' strategy of freeing themselves from national regulation is the result of a great number of small decisions at the heart of each of which lay legal engineering.

Not all the causes of the crash directly implicate lawyers. On Turner's account, for example, a major factor was that bankers became over-impressed by the sophisticated mathematics employed by analysts to estimate the future riskiness of assets,[25] and it is difficult to see how lawyers could have prevented that development. Moreover, Turner's overall explanation of the crash includes a factor over which no one had much control, namely the massive funds looking for investment opportunities that came into existence as the result of high oil prices and the economic rise of China. But those factors explain only why bankers wanted to create innovative financial products (for example the multiple level securitisations) and structural devices (for example the offshore special purpose vehicles and near-bank 'conduits') that multiplied the risk. The people who took that demand and turned it into working devices were lawyers.

TRANSACTIONAL LAWYERS' ETHICS

What is the ethical position of the lawyers involved in transactions such as the Repo 105s and the Big Short synthetic CDOs? Is there a point at which they should tell their client that they are not prepared to work on deals that might adversely affect the other side of the transaction or third parties? Do lawyers have an obligation to preserve the stability of markets, including financial markets, an obligation that goes beyond their duties to their clients?

Lawyers' professional ethics do not at present seem well-suited to answering such questions. In England, the Solicitors Regulation Authority's Code of Conduct lays down ten high level principles that lawyers should follow:

1. uphold the rule of law and the proper administration of justice;
2. act with integrity;
3. not allow your independence to be compromised;
4. act in the best interests of each client;
5. provide a proper standard of service to your clients;
6. behave in a way that maintains the trust the public places in you and in the provision of legal services;
7. comply with your legal and regulatory obligations and deal with

---

[25]   Turner (2009) at 44.

your regulators and ombudsmen in an open, timely and co-operative manner;

8. run your business or carry out your role in the business effectively and in accordance with proper governance and sound financial and risk management principles;

9. run your business or carry out your role in the business in a way that encourages equality of opportunity and respect for diversity;

10. protect client money and assets.

The lawyer's own client is mentioned three times, regulators once and the legal profession ('the provision of legal services') once. Parties to a transaction other than the lawyer's own client are not mentioned at all, and third parties appear if at all only by implication, for example in the duties to uphold the rule of law, to act with integrity and to maintain public trust in the profession. But even those principles are in some way restricted. The duty to uphold the rule of law seems to be defined narrowly, that lawyers should not break the law or assist in breaking the law. It goes no further than the boundary of the law itself. The duty to act with integrity is directed inwards, at the lawyer's sense of self-worth, rather than outward to other people the lawyer's action might affect. And the duty to maintain public trust is arguably more about the profession than the public. It is prudential rather than ethical.

Moving from high level principles to more concrete provisions, few of the Code's required 'outcomes' or 'indicative behaviours' apply outside the closed world of lawyer, client and court. Even those that do apply, although they recognise that lawyers might create risks for others when they advise on deals, seem on closer inspection to be restricted to fairly narrow circumstances. The required 'outcomes' that refer to the other party in a deal or to third parties are: (1) that solicitors must 'not take unfair advantage of third parties in either your professional or personal capacity'; (2) that they must 'perform all undertakings . . . within an agreed timescale or within a reasonable amount of time'; (3) that 'where [they] act for a seller of land,' they must 'inform all buyers immediately of the seller's intention to deal'; and (4) that they must 'properly administer oaths, affirmations or declarations'. Only the first rule is of general application. The others apply to specific situations, the third and fourth to very specific situations. And if one looks further, into the 'indicative behaviours', which the Code lays down to explain the 'outcomes', even the first rule starts to look quite narrow in scope. Indicative behaviours for the first outcome include matters such as communicating with the other side in litigation only through their own lawyers and not 'demanding anything for yourself or on behalf of your client, that is not legally recoverable' – in other words anti-intimidation rules designed to protect the reputation of the profession against accusations that litigators are ruthless. One other 'indicative behaviour' looks more promising, namely not 'taking unfair advantage of an opposing party's lack of legal knowledge where they have not instructed a lawyer', but even there the rule is drafted on the assumption that the lawyer is taking part not in transactional law but in litigation ('opposing party') and only applies if the other side is not legally represented. Presumably, if the other side does retain a lawyer, no problem arises. Only in the Code's provisions about conflicts of interest can we see a concern with transactional law being brought to the fore.[26] The Code requires lawyers, for example, to identify situations in which they might be at risk of acting for more than one party to the same transaction, and if they do find themselves in such a situation, to withdraw their services from at least one of the parties. Another concern is that acting for one client might reveal information of use to another client, thus creating a conflict between the duty not to breach the first client's confidentiality and the duty to act in the interests of the second client. But even in these situations, the primary purpose of the rule is not so much to protect third parties as to protect existing clients, though the two might to some extent become intertwined.

In the United States, the nearest equivalent of the SRA's Code of Conduct, the ABA's Model Rules of Professional Conduct, although historically also dominated by the perspective of the litigator,[27] at least now recognises lawyers' different roles as advocate, adviser and negotiator and differentiates between them:

> As a representative of clients, a lawyer performs various functions. As advisor, a lawyer provides a client with an informed understanding of the client's legal rights and obligations and explains their practical implications. As advocate, a lawyer zealously asserts the client's position under the rules of the adversary system. As negotiator, a lawyer seeks a result advantageous to the client but consistent with requirements of honest dealings with others.[28]

The Model Rules follow up on the 'advisor' role with more specific rules that have the effect of protecting third parties. They include a rule that lawyers 'shall not counsel a client to engage, or assist a client, in conduct that the lawyer knows is criminal or fraudulent',[29] rules that allow

---

[26] Solicitors Regulation Authority Code of Conduct, chapter 3.
[27] Sung Hui Kim, 'Lawyer Exceptionalism in the Gatekeeping Wars' (2010) 63 SMU Law Review 73–136, 99 (note 174) for a useful survey of the literature on this point.
[28] ABA Model Rules Preamble [2].
[29] ABA Model Rules Rule 1.2(d).

disclosure of clients' confidential information to prevent injury, including financial injury, caused by a client's crime or fraud,[30] rules allowing lawyers to include advice about broader ethical concerns in their legal advice, and, where the client is not an experienced user of legal services, to go beyond purely technical advice even where the client asks only for technical advice.[31] There is also a rule that lawyers should not misrepresent facts or their opinion of the law to third parties.[32]

But although the Model Rules recognise the risks lawyers' activities might have beyond the narrow limits of the interests of the client and the administration of justice, apart from the reference to 'honest dealing' in the negotiator role, the emphasis is on avoiding participation in criminal activity and fraud, which is to say unlawful actions rather than any broader category of activities that carry risk for third parties.[33] As for the 'honest dealing' requirement, it creates obligations to third parties, even third parties with whom a client might deal after the lawyer no longer works for the client, but the meaning of the word 'honest' is, perhaps bizarrely, unclear, having different meanings in different contexts, and having its weakest meaning with regard to third parties, in which it is fully constrained by the competing duty of client confidentiality.[34] In particular, it seems that US lawyers accept as 'honest' a range of behaviour, including taking advantage of the other side's errors and even inducing such errors, that non-lawyers would find very surprising.[35]

In the absence of a comprehensive set of rules, or even higher level principles, designed to deal with transactional situations, US lawyers have been tempted to fill in the gaps using the Model Rules' standard for the conduct of advocacy, a standard with which they are very familiar, namely 'zealously assert[ing] the client's position'. But zeal in the client's interest is not always compatible with the public interest. Similarly, the Model Rules allow trial lawyers to resolve any doubts they might have about the honesty of their client's claims in favour of the client and to continue to press the

---

[30] ABA Model Rules Rule 1.6(b). See Geoffrey Hazard, 'The Client Fraud Problem as a Justinian Quartet: An Extended Analysis' (1996–97) 25 Hofstra Law Review 1041–61.
[31] ABA Model Rules Rule 2.1.
[32] ABA Model Rules Rule 4.1. See further Geoffrey Hazard, 'Lawyer Liability in Third Party Situations: The Meaning of the Kaye Scholer Case' (1992–93) 26 Akron Law Review 395–406.
[33] Moreover the Rules omit any elaboration on 'honest dealing' or, indeed, place such obligations on the 'negotiator' as opposed to the 'advisor'.
[34] See John Humbach, 'Shifting Paradigms of Lawyer Honesty' (2009) 76 Tennessee Law Review 993–1037, 996–97
[35] Humbach (2009) at 999–1000.

client's case,[36] but whether the same view is compatible with the public interest when the client makes implausible claims to the lawyer about its marketing strategy for a synthetic CDO or the possible uses of Repo 105s is an entirely different question.

In the wake of a previous round of corporate misconduct, the Enron scandal, in which legal engineering was also at the core of what went wrong (alongside inadequate auditing), suggestions for reform of legal ethics came forward that recognised the special position of the transactions lawyer. But instead of concentrating on the issue of the risks for third parties created by lawyers' artefacts, reformers attempted to make fine distinctions between the lawyers' duty to the management of a corporation and the lawyers' duty to the corporation 'itself' or to the shareholders.[37] That is a difficult solution to apply, since it requires lawyers in effect to construct the interests of a client for themselves in opposition to the authorised organs and agents of the corporation and it misses the point that the dangers created by Enron and by Lehman and Goldman were not just to their shareholders but to the entire financial system.

The characteristics of the ethical problems posed by lawyers' involvement in the Crash are better stated in their own terms, rather than as an incident of issues surrounding the meaning of 'representation'. The first set of issues arise most immediately from the ABACUS CDO, namely what kind of responsibility do lawyers have for any harm transactions might cause to the other parties to the deal? Can lawyers maintain the position that, as a default position, lawyers have no responsibility for what documents are used for? Is it really enough for lawyers to be able to show that a deal was not inherently criminal and that they had no knowledge of their client's motives and purposes? Is there any relevance at all that the other parties engaged their own lawyers? Is it relevant that lawyers worked as part of multi-disciplinary teams – including accountants, financial analysts and the bankers themselves?

A second set of issues arises out of the Repo 105 deals. What responsibility do lawyers have for harm transactions cause not to the other parties to the deal (in the Repo 105 deals, the counterparties were paid in full as they expected), but to third parties such as Lehman's investors. One might also point to entirely different sorts of third party loss cases, for example where lawyers draft contracts whose implementation will create environmental

---

[36] Model Rules Comment 8 to Rule 3.3.
[37] See e.g. Rutheford Campbell and Eugene Gaetke, 'The Ethical Obligation of Transactional Lawyers to act as Gatekeepers' (2003–2004) 56 Rutgers Law Review 9–71.

costs. There is an overlap with the first set of issues on questions such as whether lawyers can deny responsibility for what their clients do with what is made for them, but in circumstances in which identifying victims might be more difficult, so that warning the victims might not be an option.

A third set of issues arises out of both incidents. What responsibility do lawyers have for the wider effects of what they do, such as responsibility for the Crash itself, not only for harm suffered by market participants but also for the real economy effects – the millions of lost jobs? Does it matter that others, for example bankers over-impressed by clever mathematics, played a role in creating the risks? Does it matter that others, especially accountants, were better trained to recognise the risks? Does it matter that others, regulators and central bankers, purport to control the financial system as a whole?

Before we attempt to answer those questions, for which legal ethics currently provides no satisfactory answer, we should turn for inspiration to the way engineers think about the ethical problems that face their profession.

ENGINEERING ETHICS

Engineers, like transactions lawyers, make things for clients that might turn out to harm their client's customers or third parties. Engineering ethics, a relatively new but rapidly expanding field, asks what responsibility engineers should take for such harm.

The Debate about the Ethical Principle of Technological Neutrality

The starting point for discussion in engineering about engineers' responsibilities for what their clients do with the artefacts engineers make for them is the contested notion of ethical technological neutrality.[38] Proponents of ethical technological neutrality claim that objects themselves are morally

---

[38] See e.g. Maarten Franssen, Gert-Jan Lokhorst and Ibo van de Poel, 'Philosophy of Technology' in Edward Zalta (ed.), *The Stanford Encyclopedia of Philosophy* (Spring 2010 Edition) section 3.3.1 http://plato.stanford.edu/archives/spr2010/entries/technology/. There is another form of technological neutrality, namely regulatory technological neutrality, which claims that public policy should not discriminate in favour or against particular types of technology. See e.g. Bert-Jaap Koops, 'Should ICT Regulation be Technology-Neutral?' in Bert-Jaap Koops, Miriam Lips, Corien Prins and Maurice Schellekens, *Starting Points for ICT Regulation: Deconstructing Prevalent Policy One-liners* (The Hague: TMC Asser Press, 2006) 77.

neutral and that those who design them have no responsibility for what other people do with them.[39] Designers of guns are not responsible for people being shot. Designers of planes are not responsible for noise and pollution around airports.[40] Several engineers have argued strongly for the neutrality principle, and even Herbert Simon seems to have been an advocate of it, telling an interviewer:

> There are no morals about technology at all. Technology expands our ways of thinking about things, expands our ways of doing things. If we're bad people we use technology for bad purposes and if we're good people we use it for good purposes.[41]

But the tide has now turned.[42] Two principal arguments against ethical technological neutrality stand out.

First, the very fact that the engineering engages in a process of design puts the objects it produces in a different category from other objects. Design starts with the goals and objectives of the client. That means that engineering produces objects that have purposes, not just objects that have a brute existence. Those purposes form, either explicitly or implicitly, a plan for the use of the object, a plan the engineer has to adopt to be able to design the object. Although one might plausibly argue that engineers are not responsible for use of the object that falls outside the usage plan assumed in its design, so that, for example, one should not hold aircraft designers responsible for the 9/11 attacks, one cannot exclude their responsibility for acts that fall within it. Furthermore, where there are effects that follow inevitably from any form of usage of the object – for example,

---

[39] E.g. Joseph Pitt, *Thinking About Technology: Foundations of the Philosophy of Technology* (New York: Seven Bridges Press, 1999).

[40] See Pieter Vermaas, Pieter Kroes, Ibo van de Poel, Maarten Franssen and Wybo Houkes, *A Philosophy of Technology: From Technical Artefacts to Sociotechnical Systems* (Morgan and Claypool, 2011) at 16–18.

[41] See Byron Spice, 'CMU's Simon reflects on how computers will continue to shape the world' Pittsburgh Post-Gazette, 16 October 2000. The full exchange is that in answer to Spice's question, 'This week's symposium addresses whether computers will help or hinder efforts to create a "good world". Does that assume a technology can be inherently good or bad?' Simon replied, 'No, not inherently – inevitably. (Laughs). There are no morals about technology at all. Technology expands our ways of thinking about things, expands our ways of doing things. If we're bad people we use technology for bad purposes and if we're good people we use it for good purposes. That's why I'm less interested in questions of forecasting and more interested in what kinds of decisions we can make so that we do get a positive balance of the good uses of technology.'

[42] See e.g. Franssen, Lokhorst and van de Poel (2010).

currently, pollution arises whenever aircraft fly – it makes little sense to claim that such effects are outside the usage plan.

Perhaps the clearest exposition of why the concept of design undermines the neutrality principle can be seen in Tom Lehrer's satirical song about the German-US rocket scientist Wernher von Braun, who developed the V2 rocket for Nazi Germany but then, at the end of the Second World War, switched to working for the USA and went on to design ballistic missiles for the US military as well as rockets for the US space programme. Lehrer's song contains the immortal line: '"Once the rockets are up, who cares where they come down? That's not my department," says Wernher von Braun.' But, of course, rockets exist to be used. Where they come down is entirely the engineer's department, because no plan for using a rocket can exclude where it lands. No doubt the precise decision of where they are intended to land is someone else's but the capability for making that choice too has to be part of the plan for using the rocket.

More generally, Simon's point that designing new useful objects expands the range of actions at the disposal of clients needs to be supplemented by the point that any such expansion is an intentional act. It is not an accidental side-effect of the design process but rather its principal purpose. It might be that with some objects, for example computers, the range of possible uses is vast, but that does not by itself exonerate designers for all of those uses. One reason is that some of the large number of uses might have been intended, and so form part of the usage plan. Another reason is that it might have been possible to design the product so that users are not able to achieve some ends or to create certain types of risk (for example inserting in filters into networking software or fitting vehicles with speed limitation devices).

The idea that designers might anticipate and design out harmful uses of an object takes us to the second principal argument against ethical technological neutrality. As we saw when we examined the process of engineering design, engineers take into account constraints and objectives about which their clients might not be aware or with which they might not concern themselves. For such constraints and objectives, the engineer remains responsible, regardless of the client's purposes. Some of those concerns might be explained as self-interested worries about the reputation of the individual engineer, for example concerns with quality of performance. Similar concerns might arise from worries about the reputation of the profession as a whole, which, although not entirely self-interested from the point of view of the individual engineer, are not entirely focused on the welfare of others either. But some such concerns raise issues more clearly characterised as ethical, where the reputation of the individual or the profession might be relevant but the principal concern is with the interests of other people. The most widely accepted example of such a concern is public safety. Engineers now recognise, as a profession and individually, that they have an obligation of safety to the public at large, an obligation that ranks above satisfying the client's requirements.[43] It might be that clients have used the object in so unlikely a fashion that, despite the harm, engineers can still claim reasonably to have fulfilled their professional obligations about safety. But even then, one might ask whether the object could have been designed to react safely even to unexpected events (which is what 'fail safe' devices are supposed to do).

The effect of the second argument against ethical technological neutrality is that it raises to the level of an ethical requirement for all engineers the need to carry out safety engineering on any project they take on. Professional standards for safety engineering thus constitute important ethical standards for the profession as a whole.

Traditional safety engineering emphasised the reliability of designed objects, which is to say the probability that they will do what they were designed to do, and so seemed to merge safety into questions about the client's requirements.[44] Engineers' responsibility for accidents seemed limited to their responsibility for preventing component failure. Increasingly, however, safety engineers are recognising that reliability and safety are not the same thing – for example a chemical plant might reliably produce chemicals but also occasionally release toxic materials into the environment.[45] Reliability and safety might even conflict, as when increasing the reliability of a component increases the damage when it fails.[46] Safety, the avoidance of unintended unacceptable loss, requires its own separate approach, which treats safety as a property of the whole system and treats all aspects of the system, including its environment, the people within it and their environment, as relevant to the design problems it poses.[47] Ultimately, safety results from the successful imposition of safety

---

[43]   See e.g. H. Luegenbiehl, 'Ethical Principles for Engineers in a Global Environment' in Ibo van de Poel, David Goldberg and Michael Davis, (eds) *Philosophy and Engineering: An Emerging Agenda* (London: Springer, 2010) 147 at 154–55. See also Charles E. Harris, Michael S. Pritchard and Michael Jerome Rabins, *Engineering Ethics: Concepts and Cases* (Belmont, CA: Wadsworth Cengage, 2009) 172–73.
[44]   See Jens Rasmussen, 'Risk Management in a Dynamic Society' (1997) 27 *Safety Science* 183–213, Nancy Leveson, *Engineering a Safer World: Systems Thinking Applied to Safety* (Cambridge, MA: MIT Press, 2011) chapter 2 (Leveson 2011a).
[45]   Leveson (2011a) at 11.
[46]   Leveson (2011a) at 11.
[47]   Leveson (2011a) at e.g. 15.

constraints on a system, and, although failure to impose such constraints will invariably involve acts by people other than the designing engineer, the engineer's ability successfully to understand the system is always relevant to its safety and remains the engineer's responsibility.

Safety engineering emphasises a number of practices. Foremost is the need for systematic identification of hazards, and what controls each hazard. Another is the importance of dynamic effects, such as the tendency of competition and cost pressures to give rise to higher risk behaviour. Safety engineers also train themselves to bear in mind a number of common mistakes, such as the dangers of ignoring the unquantifiable, of thinking about the causation of accidents as simple linear chains, and of confusing causation with blame (especially ignoring the importance of the environment within which people make 'errors'). They also think about the technology of safety engineering itself, such as the importance of easy monitoring of the condition of the system and the benefits of reducing complexity.[48]

Safety engineering requires engineers to understand sociotechnical systems, not just technical ones. That does not mean that their interventions in design are always or even frequently social. Indeed they might have to treat much of the social behaviour that affects safety as essentially beyond their control, as part of the environment within which the system operates rather than within the system. But their interventions will be aimed at counteracting risks however they are caused. Just because the social environment might be uncontrollable does not mean that hazards created in it are uncontrollable.[49]

Engineers and Sustainability

Engineers' concern with safety has a long history. Of more recent origin, but increasingly important in the education of engineers, is sustainability. The realisation that engineering not only uses the great forces of nature for human benefit but can also have immense adverse impact on the natural world is bringing about a re-evaluation of the relationship between engineering and the environment. Increasingly, engineers are taught that they

---

[48] See Leveson (2011a) chapters 2 and 3. See also Nancy Leveson, 'The Role of Complexity in Safety Management and How to Manage It' http://tx.technion. ac.il/~gordoncn/05072011/3.Nancy_presentation.ppt.

[49] We should also note at this point a form of engineering related to safety engineering but with a different aim, namely resilience engineering, the engineering of the ability of a system to bring itself back to functionality after a breakdown. Resilience engineering is discussed in Chapter 5.

should take responsibility for environmental impacts and should attempt to design their products so that they promote sustainability. In particular, engineering professional bodies have become interested in encouraging engineers to think about the long-term effects of their professional activity, to consider the whole life-cycle of their products from the point of view of sustainable resource use (including final disposal), to choose sustainable options at all stages of the design process and to resist the temptation to cut costs by reducing sustainability.[50]

Sustainability, like safety, is a constraint on design for which engineers themselves take responsibility. Some clients might themselves strongly favour sustainability, and might even want to make sustainability not only a side-effect of their business but its main selling point – for example the renewable energy sector. But engineers' responsibility for sustainability goes beyond the desires of clients. It is a professional obligation of engineers themselves.

Engineers' Public Welfare Obligation

Michael Davis argues that the practice of engineering involves, both empirically and normatively, a commitment not just to the avoidance or minimisation of harm – whether accidents or environmental damage – but also to making life better.[51] There is evidence of such a commitment in the statements of ethical principle issued by engineering professional bodies. Statements endorsing public welfare or benefit as the paramount goal and ethical principle of engineering are now commonplace. The Royal Academy of Engineering's Statement of Ethical Principle, for example, begins, 'Professional Engineers work to enhance the welfare, health and

---

[50]   See e.g. Richard Dodds and Roger Daniels (eds), *Engineering for Sustainable Development: Guiding Principles* (London: Royal Academy of Engineering, 2005), Richard A. Fenner, Charles M. Ainger, Heather J. Cruickshank and Peter M. Guthrie, 'Embedding Sustainable Development at Cambridge University Engineering Department' (2005) 6(3) International Journal of Sustainability in Higher Education 229–41. On the final issue, the longevity of products, has long been a matter of contention between engineers and managers. Engineers have long liked to design products that last well beyond the period buyers are likely to want to use them, whereas managers are not concerned if products fail as long as buyers continue to buy them or the firm's other products. The practice of built-in obsolescence, where products are effectively designed to fail prematurely as a way of increasing future sales has been controversial with engineers since it was first revealed by Vance Packard in the 1960s.
[51]   Michael Davis, *Thinking Like an Engineer: Studies in the Ethics of a Profession* (Oxford: Oxford U.P., 1998) at 16.

safety of all'. Fundamental Canon Number One of the American Society of Civil Engineering reads: 'Engineers shall hold paramount the safety, health and welfare of the public.' How precisely engineers might decide whether a specific project provides a public benefit is, of course, a matter of debate, and economists, perhaps not the best guides to ethics, will continue to squabble about whether their notion of a social welfare function makes sense, at least to economists. The importance of accepting the principle, however, is that engineers have taken responsibility for the question. They accept that the responsibility of others is no excuse. In particular, what the client wanted is no answer to the charge that the system ought to have been designed differently.

The Problem of Many Hands

Since engineers work in teams that work with and for other teams, and work within and on systems of immense complexity, it is not surprising that ethicists of engineering have begun to think about situations in which complexity combines with the fact that the final result is the work of many different people to produce a situation in which responsibility for the result is unclear. This is the problem of 'many hands', consideration of which began in the arena of public policy. [52] The field of software engineering is particularly prone to such problems, but they also occur in, for example, environmental engineering or in any field in which 'sociotechnical' features of the system (i.e. people) are important.

A lively controversy has broken out in the pages of the journal *Science and Engineering Ethics* about the ethical responsibility of engineers in 'many hands' situations. [53] One of the themes of the debate is whether professional ethical standards should adopt a broader idea of responsibility

---

[52] See e.g. D. Thompson, 'Moral Responsibility of Public Officials: The Problem of Many Hands' (1980) 74 American Political Science Review 905–15.

[53] See Donald Gotterbarn, 'Informatics and Professional Responsibility' (2001) 7 Science and Engineering Ethics 221–30, James Stieb, 'A Critique of Positive Responsibility in Computing' (2008) 14 Science and Engineering Ethics 219–33, Donald Gotterbarn, '"Once more unto the Breach": Professional Responsibility and Computer Ethics' (2008) 14 Science and Engineering Ethics 235–39, Chuck Huff, 'It is Not All Straw, But it Can Catch Fire: In Defense of Impossible Ideals in Computing' (2008) 14 Science and Engineering Ethics 241–44, James Stieb, 'Response to Commentators of "A Critique of Positive Responsibility"' (2009) 15 Science and Engineering Ethics 11–18. The field to which the discussion principally related, software engineering, suffers from the specific complicating factor that software is easily replicated and errors can quickly flood out from their origins – a characteristic perhaps shared by legal documentation in the wrong circumstances.

than that which applies to non-professionals. In particular, although the 'many hands' problem might lead us normally to say that individual responsibility was excluded because, from the point of view of the individual concerned, the harm was difficult to predict and even more difficult to prevent, should a professional person nevertheless accept responsibility for what happened, including responsibility for what their clients did or what many other people did in consequence of what the client did?

There are various arguments that professionals should accept responsibility on a broader basis than other individuals. One strategy is to try to establish that in the case of professionals there is more likely to be some kind of causal link to the harm than in the case of non-professionals. For example, other actors might refrain from acting to prevent the harm out of deference to the professional's reputation. But establishing causation by such effects in real cases is far from easy.

Another strategy is to point out that the position of professionals is different from that of non-professional because the professionals' functions specifically include dealing with uncertainty produced by the actions of other people. One of the marks of a professional, according to this view, is that the professional absorbs the uncertainty inevitably faced by lay clients who know little or nothing about the professional's field of expertise.[54] Some might see that professional absorption of uncertainty as an unfortunate fact of life, but another view is that the absorption of uncertainty has beneficial effects. The absorption of uncertainty by managers, for example, helps organisations to function, because without it, too many people become so anxious about what might or might not happen that they fail to carry out their own tasks. The absorption of uncertainty, on this view, is an aspect of the division of labour, and so of specialisation and greater productivity. The argument continues that just as managerial absorption of uncertainty enhances the productivity of organisations, so the absorption of uncertainty by professions allows societies to function. Professionals should therefore be prepared to accept responsibility as a way of confirming that they are absorbing the relevant uncertainties. If they refuse, the uncertainty would spread back into

---

[54] For the concept of uncertainty absorption, see originally James March and Herbert Simon, *Organizations* (New York: Wiley, 1958) and for the more general idea of the management of uncertainty, see Renée Fox, 'Training for Uncertainty' in Robert Merton et al., *The Student Physician: Introductory Studies in the Sociology of Medical Education* (Cambridge, MA: Harvard U.P., 1957). As for its application to lawyers, one lawyer commenting on the draft of this book commented 'Many clients will say to themselves "this looks OK, but we had better get [a major firm] to OK it"'.

society at large and inhibit much activity. The problem with this strategy, however, is that, ultimately, it also depends on an empirical speculation, this time about productivity. Is it really the case that a society in which a wide range of uncertainties were openly admitted and submitted to the public at large would be less productive? Do we have any examples of such societies?

A third, and possibly better, strategy for establishing the broader responsibility of professionals is to concentrate specifically on design professionals and to start with the position of a designer in a complex system. The very fact that designers take on the task of altering the performance of the system puts them in a different position from those who are merely part of that system. Part of the task of design is thinking about, and taking responsibility for, matters such as safety and sustainability, and possibly for overall public welfare. Those tasks themselves inherently involve thinking about the consequences of complex processes, including the actions of other people. The position of designers is different from that of non-designers precisely because the obligations of the safety engineer attach to designers but not to non-designers.

One crucial point is that if one thinks about designers themselves in system terms, one will see that designers occupy a position within the system from which more can be influenced than from other positions, including the actions of other people. Even when those actions could not have been influenced, and there was nothing that could have been done to prevent the harm done to third parties, the designer is still central because of the object's very existence. The judgment of whether to create the object, given its risks and its benefits, is that of the designer. The client might decide whether to use the object, but without the designer there would be no decision for the client to make.

The Challenger Disaster

An example often used to encourage engineers to think about their wider responsibilities is the tale of the tragedy of the O-rings. In January 1986, engineers at Morton Thiokil, the company that built the space shuttle, unanimously recommended that a forthcoming launch of the space shuttle 'Challenger' should be postponed. The problem the engineers had identified was that, because the temperature at the launch site was near freezing, the O-rings that sealed together the segments of the launch boosters (and the use of which had allowed efficient off-site assembly of the shuttle) might become brittle and suffer erosion. If the O-rings failed in flight, the boosters would, quite simply, explode. The engineers were not certain of the effects of freezing temperatures on the O-rings, since they had not carried out tests at below 40 degrees Fahrenheit (4.5 degrees Celsius), but they could extrapolate from what they knew.

NASA, Morton's clients, reacted badly to the recommendation. For political and public relations reasons, they needed the launch to go ahead. NASA vehemently called into question the engineers' evidence-base for their conclusion, which was, after all, not grounded in direct testing but on extrapolation. Morton Thiokil's management wobbled. The client's desires were clear and no one could say that the engineers had failed to inform NASA of the risks. Moreover, the space shuttle contract had earned Morton Thiokil $150m and many jobs depended on it. The protocols for launching the shuttle, however, gave Morton Thiokil's senior engineer a veto over any launch. That engineer was originally inclined to halt the launch. But NASA put pressure on Thiokil Morton's senior management, who in turn pressured the senior engineer. Eventually, after management told the senior engineer to 'take off [his] engineering hat and put on [his] management hat'[55] he caved in and withdrew his veto. The launch went ahead. Just over a minute into the flight, an O-ring failed, the booster exploded and seven crew members died.

The Challenger disaster sparked a whole series of investigations, reports and debates.[56] But for our purposes it illustrates both of the reasons why both technological neutrality and many hands excuses are now usually thought to be unconvincing. First, if one thinks about the implied usage plan for the shuttle, it becomes immediately apparent that it included the very decision by the senior engineer to give permission for the shuttle to fly. A shuttle launch resulted from the operation not just of a physical system but a sociotechnical system, which included the exercise of judgment by the senior engineer. As soon as the senior engineer moved away from the implied plan, he was making himself responsible for the launch. Yes, NASA was responsible too, as was senior management at Morton Thiokil. But given the implied usage plan for the object, the engineer was responsible.

Second, the engineer's concern for safety – in this case for the safety of

---

55   Davis (1998) at 44.
56   See the documents listed at NASA History Office 'Challenger STS 51-L Accident' http://history.nasa.gov/sts51l.html particularly William Rogers (chair), *Report of the Presidential Commission on the Space Shuttle Challenger Accident* (Washington, DC: NASA, 1986) and especially Richard Feynman, 'Personal Observations on Reliability of the Shuttle' *Rogers Commission Report, Volume 2 Appendix F* (Washington, DC: NASA ,1986). See generally Rosa Lynn Pinkus, *Engineering Ethics: Balancing Cost, Schedule, and Risk* (Cambridge: Cambridge U.P., 1997).

the shuttle's crew – should have been paramount. That responsibility was not switched off by the fact that NASA was also responsible for the safety of the crew. There are some aspects of a project for which engineers remain responsible regardless of the desires of the client, and the Challenger disaster concerned one of them. Looked at from the viewpoint of safety engineering, the harm occurred not just because of a single linear set of causes (or a line of gaps in preventative measures – the 'Swiss Cheese' model) but because of failures to understand the system as a whole and to provide for controls for all the relevant hazards. For example, we might concentrate not on the failure of the physical component, the O-ring, but on the conditions that made that failure possible. In particular, the client's political environment created a tendency towards higher risk behaviour. The controller for that hazard was merely the senior engineer's sense of professionalism, which turned out not to be enough. Nothing in the system reinforced it or provided for cases in which it failed.[57]

Moreover, although the accident occurred because of multiple failures involving many hands, the position of the designers is different from that of others because they were in a position to think about how the behaviour of others might affect the safety of the product. Failing to think about the whole system, including the pressures on the client, is a failure of design by the engineers, not just a failure of the client.[58]

LAWYERS AS ETHICAL ENGINEERS

Let us return to the questions of what ethical responsibility lawyers carry for the Lehman's Repo 105 deals, Goldman's Big Short and the Great Crash in general. Let us assume that in both cases, the lawyers were not

---

[57] Another element in the problem is that human beings seem to be programmed to deceive themselves (possibly as a way of better deceiving others), so that the NASA officials putting on the pressure and the Morton Thiokil engineers giving way to it might easily fool themselves into thinking that what they were doing was justified and safe. System design needs to anticipate such powerful tendencies and not just (self-deceptively) wish them away. See Robert Trivers, *Deceit and Self-Deception: Fooling Yourself the Better to Fool Others* (London: Penguin, 2011) chapter 9.

[58] There is one particular design point that perhaps requires more thought – what are the conditions under which clients will accept the advice of engineers? The Challenger contract effectively gave the engineers a veto, the exercise of which they were talked out of, but in other situations, there is no veto and the engineer has to be persuasive. Long-term relationships of trust might be important, as might wider respect in society at large for engineers.

made aware of their client's precise purposes – that in the Repo 105 transactions, Lehman did not tell Linklaters why they wanted to carry out this
form of transaction and in the ABACUS transaction Goldman's lawyers
were not made aware of the Big Short. Under current professional ethical
rules, all the lawyers would have a good case that they did nothing wrong.
In both cases, the lawyers carried out work for their clients with which
the clients were more than happy. In both cases, at least as we assume, the
lawyers did not themselves break the law or mislead or intimidate anyone.
In the Lehman case, the other parties to the deal were also happy with the
deal. In the Goldman case, in which other parties to the deal were let down,
those other parties were experienced investors and were presumably legally
represented, and so, whatever Goldman did to mislead them, Goldman's
lawyers are in the clear because the adverse consequences did not come
about because they took advantage of any lack of legal assistance provided
to the other parties.

But there is something unsatisfying in this complete exoneration of the
lawyers. In particular, if one looks closely at Linklaters' defence of what
it did for Lehman ('We have reviewed the opinions and are not aware of
any facts or circumstances which would justify any criticism') one receives
a distinct scent of two arguments that engineers increasingly reject, the
argument from technological neutrality and the equation of safety with
reliability. Linklaters says it has reviewed 'the opinions' it created. It has
not, one might surmise, reviewed Lehman's use of those opinions and
given any thought to its possible responsibility for that use. The implication seems to be that as long as the opinion was not flawed, that it reliably
produces the effects the client asked for, no ethical problems can arise.
But that point confuses reliability and safety and fails to deal with the
first argument against technological neutrality, namely the argument from
design. What was the usage plan, implied or explicit, for Linklaters' Repo
105 opinion? Linklaters' opinion itself contains part of the answer. It says
'You [Lehman] have asked us to review the Global Master Repurchase
Agreement ["GRMA"] that you intend to use for Repos or reverse Repos
and buy/sell backs of securities and financial instruments ["Securities"]
with various counterparties.'[59] The difficulty for Linklaters is the comment
of the Examiner in Bankruptcy in Lehman's case that the 105 form of
Repo had no obvious commercial purpose. Lehman might well not have
made Linklaters aware of the Repo 105's intended use, namely to manipulate the numbers reported to the US authorities, but lawyers thinking at all
carefully about what a usage plan for the opinion could possibly contain,

---

[59]   Valukas Report Appendix 17, Linklaters Opinion para. 1.1.

realising that it had no obvious commercial purpose, would be hard pressed not to conclude that the plan included changing the numbers reported to the US authorities. As a partner in a London law firm commented shortly after the publication of the Valukas Report, 'It's making us think internally about exactly what our opinion is being used for. . . . Previously we have assumed that you don't need to know anything about the economics of a situation to say that a transaction is what it is.'[60]

In fact, there is a hint that Linklaters had worked out to what use the Repo 105 might be put. The opinion warns, 'In coming to the conclusions set out in this opinion, we have assumed that the GMRA accurately reflects the agreement of the parties. If it is merely a "sham" . . . extrinsic evidence may be adduced to enable the courts to discover what was actually agreed',[61] a possibility against which Linklaters had covered itself by stating earlier that it had examined the GMRA 'but no other documents'.[62] One analyst has consequently described Linklaters as engaging in 'loophole engineering', artfully guiding its client around the law while also avoiding any suggestion of its own responsibility for the client's action.[63] But even if Linklaters' statements about shams and about the limitations on which documents its lawyers had read arise from caution rather than suspicion, a possibility that cannot be excluded given the rise of law firms' use of risk management techniques with respect to their own clients,[64] the question remains how experienced commercial lawyers could fail to spot a deal that had no obvious commercial purpose and then fail to think about what purposes it might have. Linklaters' defence has the quality of a Wernher von Braun argument, that where the Repo 105s fall is not its department.

---

[60]   Fournier (2010). There are echoes in these debates of the issues surrounding tax avoidance, particularly the creation of lawful structures lacking any commercial purpose apart from reducing liability for tax. Tax lawyers currently seem to have little problem in creating such structures, although whether they might take the same ethical view if a general anti-avoidance rule applied is an interesting question. Given the intimate connections between transaction design and tax, the suspicion arises that there has been some leakage from the culture of tax law into the culture of transactional law.

[61]   Valukas Report Appendix 17, Linklaters Opinion para. 2.6.

[62]   Valukas Report Appendix 17, Linklaters Opinion para. 1.2.

[63]   Richard Painter, 'Transaction Cost Engineers, Loophole Engineers or Gatekeepers: The Role of Business Lawyers after the Financial Meltdown' in Brett McDonnell, *Research Handbook of the Economics of Corporate Law* (Cheltenham: Edward Elgar, 2012) chapter 14.

[64]   See Stephan Landsman, 'The Risk of Risk Management' (2010) 78 Fordham Law Review 2315–27.

In the wider profession, the reaction to the Repo 105 affair has included elements the many hands excuse. In an informal survey carried out by the International Financial Law Review shortly after the publication of the Valukas Report, a considerable proportion of lawyers, on both sides of the Atlantic, were of the opinion that since accountants were in a better position and better qualified than lawyers to ask pertinent questions of clients about the purposes of the advice they received, the accountants, but not the lawyers, should accept responsibility for what the clients did with it.[65] The question arises whether anyone who claims to be a professional should take such a narrow view of their responsibilities. No doubt lawyers are influenced by the standards of the law of tort, in which, for the purposes of establishing legal liability in a complex case, one might take into account the arguments that another person's intentional intervention can break the 'chain of causation' and that liability can be limited by the extent to which other people assume responsibility for the situation, but the issue here is ethical rather than legal. The responsibility of other advisers, or indeed that of the client itself, is not particularly relevant. Ethical responsibility, especially in the sense of accepting responsibility for reducing the risk that a disaster will happen again, can be concurrent.

The Safety of Synthetic CDOs

The Goldman case is different. Lawyers had created large numbers of CDOs for Goldman in which the bank was not betting against its own clients. There is no difference in form or construction between a CDO designed to succeed and a CDO designed to fail. What made the difference in the ABACUS example was not how the CDO worked but who was choosing the underlying securities. If one hands over the selection function to someone with a short position – or someone paid by someone with a short position – one might expect the whole transaction to end in a collapse in value. Unlike the Repo 105, therefore, there is nothing inherent in the design itself that implies a usage plan that includes harming third parties.

But, although the implied usage plan for CDOs does not inherently include misleading clients of the issuing bank, the risk that CDOs might be used in that way is inherent. Such use might be improper, but the design did not eliminate the risk of improper use. That means that the Goldman case raises issues similar to those raised under the second argument against

---

[65]   Anon., 'Who Should be Responsible?' (2010) 29(4) International Financial Law Review 15.

technological neutrality, that there are matters, for example matters of safety, of which designers are seized even if their clients are not, and of which they remain seised regardless of their clients' instructions.

How should we assess the conduct of Goldman's lawyers if we accept that, as professionals, and like engineers, they have responsibility for the safety of their products for people other than their clients? There might have been clues that in the particular case the client's usage plan included misleading customers. For example, the lawyers' work might well have revealed the identities and the inter-relationships between those taking short positions and those selecting the securities. In that kind of case, the issue of 'gatekeeping' arises, namely the obligation of lawyers to prevent misuse of their products. But, even assuming no such clues were forthcoming, there is a question of design – had enough been done to reduce the risk of improper use? Would it have been possible, for example, to design a CDO so that those with short positions cannot influence the selection of securities? Or might it be possible to hit the specific technique of using the equity slice to give the impression that the bank had a long position by designing the transaction so that the equity holder has to declare short positions? Without more facts about what Goldman's lawyers knew, and more expertise about what the options were in CDO design, one cannot come to final judgment on such questions but at least they are questions that should be answered, not only with regard to the past, but also, putting to one side the often unproductive issue of blame, for the future.

Lawyers' Responsibility for the Crash

The final question is the extent to which lawyers should accept responsibility for the Great Crash itself. Essentially the question is whether lawyers have any responsibility for the safety of their designs at the level of the market. A number of additional considerations come into play. First, there is the question of the relationship between the nature of the risk and lawyers' field of expertise. When engineers take responsibility, and keep responsibility, for the safety and the sustainability of the objects they create, they presuppose that they at least possess the expertise necessary to assess the relevant risks, even though the action they take to control those risks might be aimed at other parts of the system. In contrast, we might wonder whether lawyers possessed sufficient expertise in how financial markets work to put them in a position to assess the dangers they were creating. That is clearly the case where lawyers were producing risk-multiplying devices such as synthetic CDOs. It might even be the case for regulator-confusing devices such as Repo 105s. At its most basic, the

proportion of mathematically-trained lawyers is low and even the proportion of economically literate lawyers is not high, especially in Britain where
it is common for lawyers to hold degrees in nothing except law and for law
schools to eschew economics.[66]

The attitude of engineers to understanding complex systems is,
however, instructive. Engineers started out with physical objects, but
have realised that limiting their understanding to physical science is not
enough. Safety engineering has had to develop an understanding of
human behaviour, to incorporate the insights of physiology, psychology,
economics, organisational behaviour, anthropology and even politics.
To take on the issue of sustainability, and to take responsibility for it,
engineers needed to expand their understanding of both the natural and
social worlds. It might well be the case that lawyers lacked the expertise
necessary to understand the impact of their activities on the financial
markets, but that should have been a spur to change, not an excuse for
inaction. Establishing relationships of strict causation between what specific lawyers did and specific aspects of the subsequent disasters might
be difficult, since one cannot rule out the possibility that bankers and
accountants might have tried to set up risk-multiplying transactions by
themselves, without the benefit of legal input, but that does not relieve
lawyers of all obligation to think about the consequences of what they
were asked to do and in particular of an obligation to engage in the legal
equivalent of safety engineering.

A different defence of lawyers is that if economists failed to predict the
financial crisis, why should lawyers be expected to do so? The same economists who dismiss the quantitative abilities of lawyers, and who complain
that regulatory bodies contain too many lawyers and not enough economists, themselves remained silent while the markets multiplied risk. What
could lawyers do in those circumstances? There is a line of defence that
goes 'lawyers are not economists or accountants and so are not responsible
at all for making judgments that economists or accountants would be much
better at making.'[67] There is some force to these points. But engineers who
have relied on faulty scientific work, with catastrophic results, would not
so easily let themselves off. Problems with the underlying scientific theory
should have become apparent during the testing of the product, a process
for which engineers, rather than scientists, are responsible. One might

---

[66]   Cf. the comment of a US lawyer to the International Financial Law Review
survey of 2010, that 'Most lawyers go to law school because they are not good with
numbers!' See Anon. (2010).

[67]   Cf. the arguments recorded by Sung (2010) that lawyers should not be
gatekeepers because auditors are gatekeepers.

counter that the difficulty of testing legal prototypes makes criticism of lawyers for this kind of outcome somewhat unfair, but engineers also face situations in which prototype testing is not practical, to which they react by exercising great caution in the deployment phase, looking for any signs of problems as they go ahead. Indeed, there is much in common between the problems of risk multiplication produced by lawyers in the years before the financial crisis and one of the typical situations in which engineers find themselves unable to test thoroughly, namely where there is a product that works well on a small scale, but it is proposed to deploy it at a much larger scale, a scale so large that testing before deployment is not feasible. Engineers would be looking for signs during deployment of cumulative problems that testing of the individual products would not pick up. Did lawyers exercise similar caution and vigilance as risk-multiplying financial devices were deployed at scale? One suspects not.

Another version of the same defence is that even in questions of feed-back during deployment, lawyers were dependent on economists, and economists failed. Turner argues that the ultimate causes of the crisis were intellectual – a naïve faith in the rationality of markets that led to, among other mistakes, a belief that all financial innovations adopted in the market were beneficial.[68] How could lawyers, it might be argued, withstand an intellectual consensus that encompassed not just their own clients in the financial world but also governments, academic economists and even the IMF?[69] But that is to assume that lawyers have nothing of their own to contribute to such intellectual debates. Just as Walter Vincenti objected to the idea that engineers are merely appliers of science, lawyers should object to the idea that they merely apply other people's economic dogma. Engineers realise that the problem with science is that it has to simplify the world and isolate effects to understand them. In contrast, engineers have to deal with the world as it really is, in all of its complexity. Equally lawyers should realise that economists' models, and above all the grossly simplifying and sometimes ideologically-driven assumptions they make, cannot necessarily withstand the pressure created by the complexity of the real world. One might even question whether economics is yet fit for engineering purposes, since it has largely been driven by its own intel-lectual interests and not by the interests of those who need it to build and create working devices. [70]

---

[68]　Turner (2009) at 47–49.
[69]　Turner (2009) at 85.
[70]　Some economists seem to be of the opinion that economics is fit for some engineering purposes as it stands. See Ken Binmore and Paul Klemperer, 'The Biggest Auction Ever: the Sale of the British 3G Telecom Licences' (2002)

A variation on the blame economists defence is the argument that lawyers are not the ultimate designers of the system, but they themselves are merely non-designers within someone else's system. The argument relies on the third argument in favour of professionals having broader responsibilities than non-professionals, the argument from the position of designers, but turns it on its head. Instead of accepting that the 'many-hands' argument is of limited application to lawyers because of their role as designers, it claims that lawyers hold the status of non-designers with a system designed by others.

One version of this variation is that bankers are designers of these transactions and that lawyers merely carry out their instructions. That version, however, fails to recognise that lawyers are not merely supplying a component for a device put together by bankers, (in which case the bankers might count as the designer of the device) but design the whole device from a brief given to them by bankers. Lawyers take an idea from bankers about how a transaction might work and put it into a form in which it does work. In such circumstances, responsibility for safety and sustainability for the whole device remains with lawyers.

Another version, perhaps more plausible, treats the regulators as responsible for the design of the whole system and in particular responsible for safety engineering at the level of the market. The argument is, effectively, that lawyers should be seen as the objects of safety engineering rather than safety engineers themselves. But, even laying aside the point that, especially in the US, many of the regulators were themselves lawyers, even this version of the defence of lawyers is ultimately unconvincing. Engineers are also subject to safety standards imposed by regulation, but merely complying with those standards does not relieve engineers of thinking about safety (or sustainability). Equally lawyers have an obligation to comply with regulations but they also have obligations about safety

---

112(478) Economic Journal C74–C96 and Harold Kincaid and Don Ross, *The Oxford Handbook of Philosophy of Economics* (Oxford: Oxford U.P., 2009) at 334 for an example of economic design driven by practical concerns. But the design of one-off devices with well-defined objectives is a much more tractable problem than predicting the effects of the mass production of devices. On the other side of the debate, see Trivers (2011) chapter 13. Trivers, whose thesis is that the more social an area of study is the more it is vulnerable to self-deception, asks 'Is economics a science?' and answers with a blunt 'No', although he welcomes the development of psychology-grounded behavioural economics. But, as Trivers points out, self-deception is related not just to sociality but also to power, and so one might expect disciplines associated with high prestige and political access, such as economics, to be more attractive to the self-deceptive than lower prestige, lower access disciplines such as sociology.

that go beyond mere compliance that flow from their own responsibilities as designers.

The Repo 105 example is particularly clear, since the effect of the device itself was to interfere with regulatory oversight, but even in the Goldman example, one might question whether lawyers thought enough about market level safety. The underlying problem was not only Goldman's Big Short strategy but also the fact, regardless of whether Goldman's own position was short or long, that devices such as the synthetic CDOs were multiplying risk to an extraordinary degree. No doubt there is a version of the many hands problem here, that the level of risk in the market was the work of many lawyers, and that (perhaps with the exception of Goldman's lawyers) no law firm created enough risk by itself to destabilise the market. But the third counter-argument to the many hands problem still applies in its original direction. Lawyers, as designers, should take into account the actions of others in thinking about the safety of what they make. When those others are themselves lawyers, the responsibility is even clearer. Effectively, responsibility for safety at the level of the market lies with the legal profession as a whole, not only in the sense that the profession should lay down ethical rules for all lawyers (though it should), but also in the sense that each lawyer should think about the effects of their actions on the market on the assumption that other lawyers are doing the same thing. The point is particularly important where, as in both the Repo 105 and ABACUS CDO incidents, the work involves creating results in different jurisdictions and arbitraging between different legal systems. In those circumstances, in the absence of global regulation of legal ethics, lawyers will be able to arbitrage between different formal systems of ethical regulation. But that is precisely what lawyers should not do. The obligation to go beyond compliance applies with particular force at the global level.

WIDER LESSONS – PRACTICES AND ACTIONS

The comparison of lawyers and engineers puts the ethical responsibilities of lawyers in a new light, and helps to identify, and to broaden, their responsibility for the use of the devices they create. There is, however, a further point. Could we use the law-as-engineering perspective to alter the starting point for legal ethics, so that it automatically incorporates the problems faced by transactions lawyers?

One characteristic of the discussion of lawyers' professional ethics, especially in the US literature, is an almost invariable assumption that a lawyer's main job is to represent clients in some kind of litigation – whether civil or criminal.[71] The nature of the system, for example the adversary nature of the US legal system, is then used to justify acts by lawyers that in other forms of life might be considered reprehensible. For example, in ordinary life, consciously taking advantage of someone else's error is unacceptable, but for lawyers engaged in litigation, letting pass another party's erroneous assumption that happens to favour one's own side is often considered permissible, as long as the lawyer takes no active steps to encourage the misapprehension.[72] In another area of life, such behaviour would be frowned upon, for example in science, where the object of the exercise is gaining a better understanding of the subject matter. But writers often assume that the purpose of the lawyering is 'winning' for one's client, a goal that can only be subordinated to specific prohibitions (and even those prohibitions are to be construed narrowly).

An appeal to the adversarial nature of the US legal system and to the image of the lawyer as litigator has provided US lawyers with their main defence against the imposition on them, by regulators such as the SEC, of legal duties to blow the whistle on clients whose activities threaten the interests of others or the stability of the market.[73] Even after Enron, the American Bar Association insisted that lawyers should be under no obligation to 'exit noisily' from relationships with clients whose activities were a risk to the interests of others.[74]

The conventional argument uses a distinction developed by John Rawls between judging actions at large and judging actions within practices that are themselves justified.[75] If we accept that a whole practice (for example, the adversary system) is justified, acts of individuals within that practice need no further justification.[76] The only question that needs to be asked, in this view, is whether the act fell within the practice. There is no need to justify them from the ground up, as isolated acts. The result for lawyers is that, although there is a long tradition of saying that the professional status of lawyers rests on their pursuit of the public interest,[77] the requirements of the public interest are taken to be fulfilled by pursuing the adversarial

---

[71]　See e.g. W. Bradley Wendel, 'Institutional and Individual Justification in Legal Ethics: The Problem of Client Selection' (2005–2006) 34 Hofstra Law Review 987–1042.

[72]　Wendel (2005) at 1003.

[73]　Sung (2010). See also Humbach (2009) at 1001–12.

[74]　Sung (2010).

[75]　John Rawls, 'Two Concepts of Rules' (1955) 64(1) Philosophical Review 3–32.

[76]　Rawls (1955) at 27.

[77]　See e.g. Roscoe Pound, *The Lawyer from Antiquity to Modern Times* (St Paul, MN: West, 1953) at 5.

system and so become redefined as actions which can be characterised as the 'zealous' pursuit of the client's interest.[78]

Perhaps the most important aspect of the point that litigation as a practice treats as acceptable conduct that would otherwise be seen as reprehensible is that litigation involves doing other people harm – forcing them to

---

[78]   See e.g. David Luban, *Lawyers and Justice: An Ethical Study* (Princeton: Princeton U.P., 1988) at 10. One might remark in passing that the philosophical distinction between actions judged at large and actions within justified practices might itself benefit from some systems engineering analysis. One way of putting the distinction is that if an action counts as an action within a practice and the practice is itself justified, moral considerations from outside the practice are not relevant to assessing the action. Hence if the legal system requires defendants, no matter how obnoxious, to be represented, a lawyer who takes the case should not be criticised for the 'external' sin of helping an obnoxious person. The fact that the action was within the practice is thus said to be 'exclusionary' because it excludes consideration of matters outside the practice.

But considered as an engineering system, this would mean that legal ethics is treated as sub-system within the legal system. The legal system is judged only in terms of how it fits into its super-systems (the social world with its own ethical sub-system). The inputs and outputs are information about conduct and statements about whether conduct was proper, and the processes ones of coming to judgments about the inputs. There is no output from the legal ethics sub-system directly to the super-system. All statements of proper conduct about lawyers must go through the legal system itself.

But notice that the systems analysis immediately reveals that the outputs of the legal ethics sub-system must affect the output of the legal system as a whole, via its output to the legal system. One cannot ask sensible questions about the functioning of a system if one has omitted to consider the effects of some of the sub-systems. In other words, any debate about whether the 'adversary system' is a justified practice should include the consequences of using the norms of that practice as a basis for legal ethics. It makes no sense to approve of the adversary system in advance of considering all the effects of doing so.

More generally, philosophers might want to consider whether the generalised use of Rawls' distinction might be accused either of jumping too quickly to the approval of the more general practice, or of being tautologous, of making an assessment of a practice that has already included an assessment of the action to be assessed.

Similar problems seem to abound in theoretical speculations about law. For example, the enormous literature on private law emanating from the work of Ernest Weinrib, which claims that private law is a closed system within which all issues can be decided by reference to some internally generated standard such as 'rectificatory justice', seems to suffer from the same kind of systems level error. What justifies the existence of such a system as private law? It can only be how it fits into its super-systems. But the internally-generated standard does not by itself establish that the 'private law' system is justified at that higher level. In crude terms, it does not resolve the question of why any social (or more particularly state) resources should be expended on 'private law'.

part with their money, or to refrain from doing something they want to do or even, in criminal law, taking away their liberty in more radical ways. Sometimes the harm works the other way, so that the defendant is permitted to continue to harm the claimant, or it operates by frustrating another person's purposes, as when defence lawyers frustrate the purposes of prosecution lawyers. But in all these cases, the common theme is that litigation is inherently capable of doing harm.

If, however, we start with the thought that the characteristic lawyer is not a litigator but a transactions lawyer, it soon becomes apparent that a different approach is required. As a preliminary point, many transactions lawyers deal with multiple legal systems, trying to build devices that will work across jurisdictional boundaries. The peculiar practices of specific legal systems are incapable of generating ethical standards for lawyers who work in many different systems. The accident of a lawyer's home system is an arbitrary basis for a global standard and a recipe for irreconcilable conflicts between lawyers originating from different systems. A parallel point can be made for legislative lawyers. Although they generally work within specific national systems, it makes no sense to tie them to norms that generalise from a particular procedural system when they themselves might be asked to draft statutes that entirely replace that system with a different one.

How might we go about constructing an ethic for lawyers-as-engineers from their practices? One starting point might be to notice that the essence of law-as-engineering is the relationship between the lawyer and the client. Lawyers deliver what clients want, whether that is the benefit of a deal, a will or politically-desired changes in the law. But delivering what other people want, although it has an immediate wealth-maximising appeal, always raises the ethical question of whether those other people are justified in wanting what they want. If I am helping someone else to do X, it seems inescapable that whether I am justified in doing so depends to some extent on what X is.

There is a minimalist approach that says that as long as X is itself not unlawful, lawyers are permitted to help bring it about. But there are serious objections to that approach. For legislative lawyers, it cannot work at all. In the UK, the doctrine of parliamentary supremacy means that whatever Parliament does is lawful. Ultimately, Parliament can ignore all restraints, whether domestic or international. In states with legally binding constitutions, legislative lawyers can be asked to draft constitutional amendments. But even for transactions lawyers, the legality criterion is inadequate. If transactions lawyers offer advice about matters beyond the law, it seems odd to restrict the ethical criteria they use to what is lawful or unlawful. And if non-lawyers can be held morally responsible for harm even where causing that harm is lawful (for example causing types of harm that are not actionable), why should we grant lawyers special protection?

Legality might then be taken as an absolute minimum requirement. But what other requirements exist that are inherent in transactional practice? The most obvious is consent. Transactions lawyers work most typically on deals. Deals that are consensual deliver benefits for all the parties to them, at least as the parties see the situation at the time of the deal. Deals that lack consent might in some circumstances end up delivering benefits to the non-consenting parties, but there is a high risk that they will not. Ethical standards based on 'zealous representation' concentrate on the consent of the lawyer's own client. But for a deal to be justifiable in itself, that is for it to constitute a justifiable 'X', the consent is required not just of one party, but of all the parties. Without that consent, the benefit of the deal itself, and not just the benefit of the deal to the lawyer's own client, remains in doubt. The likelihood of effective consent by the other parties to a deal, depends, for example, on the likelihood that the other parties understand the deal, or at a minimum understand the risk they are taking if they agree to the deal without fully understanding its contents. That in turn depends on the nature of the other parties, the quality of the advice they are receiving and their ability to understand that advice. It also depends on the complexity of the deal itself and the other parties' familiarity with its subject matter.

As we have seen, the ethical position derived from litigation maintains that if the other side is legally represented, there is no obligation to consider whether the other parties understand what is happening. On this view, the whole of the responsibility to ensure that consent is effective falls on the other parties' lawyers. But the objection to this position is that one party's lack of effective consent undermines the justification for what all of the lawyers are doing, and so it is a problem for all the lawyers working on a deal. It is possible that it is reasonable, as an empirical matter, in the particular circumstances, to expect the other parties' lawyers to ensure that their clients give effective consent. That is not, however, the same as an invariable rule that legal representation equals consent. Where there is reason to believe that lawyers for one of the parties do not themselves understand the deal and so will be unable to protect their client's interests, an ethical problem arises for all the lawyers involved in the deal. It is not enough to take the trial lawyer's easy way out of resolving doubts in favour of one's own client and pressing on, since the problem lies not with one's own client but with the other lawyers' clients.

Different considerations apply in the legislative context but the underlying problems are similar. The legislature does not have to consent to a government bill (although in Britain it almost invariably does so), and there is an argument that members of the legislature are responsible for obtaining their own advice about what a bill means and that the gaining of sufficient consent is a political process for ministers to achieve after the bill has been drafted. In the same way that parties to a deal who do not fully understand its terms may nevertheless fully consent if they at least understand the risks of giving consent without full understanding, members of the legislature who, for example, vote in favour of bills that they have failed to comprehend but about which they trust the judgment of others can be counted as having consented. But a number of factors might come together to bring about a situation to which legislative lawyers might legitimately object. Emergency legislation, for example, rarely receives detailed consideration.[79] The sheer size of a bill might also reduce the degree of scrutiny it receives. Complexity – the degree to which a bill's clauses are interlocking and mutually dependent – creates a barrier to understanding in itself, quite separate from size. All these factors increase the degree to which legislators will be placing trust in others, which is to say, in the British system, in the government, as a substitute for their own judgment. If legislative lawyers in any of these circumstances come reasonably to suspect that their governmental clients intend to abuse that trust by misleading members of the legislature about the meaning of parts, or the whole, of a bill, one might argue that a serious ethical issue arises.[80]

Another requirement that arises largely from legislative legal practice, but which has resonance for transactions lawyers, is that it cannot be right for lawyers to undermine the very institutions of the law itself. A legislative lawyer asked to create a statute or a constitutional amendment that frees the executive from any obligation to obey the law or to be limited by the law might wonder whether it is the kind of device that should be designed by lawyers. Legislative lawyers might object that the rule of law is not an exact concept and that maintaining it is a political rather than legal task.

---

[79]   See e.g. House of Lords Select Committee on the Constitution, *Fast-Track Legislation: Constitutional Implications and Safeguards* (London: TSO, 2009).

[80]   A leading legislative lawyer comments on this passage there is a legitimate role in this kind of situation for legislative lawyers to endeavour to make sure that the legislature at least has adequate information for its decision. For that reason, a principle of the utmost good faith (uberrimae fidei) should apply in the dealings between government lawyers and officials of the legislature. The same lawyer also comments that the best way to persuade ministers to do the right thing might not be an ethical argument but a prudential one – for example, the most effective argument against a ministerial request to hide a controversial point in a schedule might not be to say that doing so would be wrong, but that experience shows that such devices rarely work and when they fail, the political damage is greater than that which would have flowed from facing the issue openly.

It is true that defining the exact point at which the line is crossed might require more discussion. Does the exclusion of judicial review of certain administrative actions suffice, or what about violations of Lon Fuller's inner moral principles of law, such as the introduction of secret laws?[81] But there has to be some limit, because otherwise legislative lawyers would end up undermining the very tools with which they work. There will also be some anxiety that placing ethical burdens on the government's lawyers might somehow let their political masters off the hook – that some form of novus actus interveniens argument might take hold under which blame might shift from those who ask for statutes that undermine the law to those who draft them. This is, however, not a situation in which such arguments work. Those who ask for bad laws remain responsible for them regardless of what their lawyers do. The ethical responsibility on the state to maintain legality applies to the whole state and not just to state officials who happen to be legally trained.

The problem of undermining the law itself does not arise in the same form for transactions lawyers, whose powers do not extend so far. Tax lawyers, however, might wonder about tax avoidance schemes so large that they undermine the viability of the state and all lawyers might ask whether ethical limits to jurisdictional arbitrage might appear at the point where legal systems are chosen not on the basis of the content of their law but on the basis of their lack of content.

There is further resonance from the problem for legislative lawyers of bills that undermine the law itself in another aspect of transactional practice. Lawyers should be concerned about devices that have been designed to fail. For example, some of the Goldman CDOs seem to have been intended from the start not to work. They were designed with the intention they would end up worthless and be wound up, with Goldman profiting from that failure.[82] Admittedly, those devices might be thought to be deceptive and so unethical for other reasons, but there are devices that are designed to fail for reasons other than obtaining a financial benefit from an unsuspecting third party. An example might be a will deliberately designed to fail – perhaps because of a mistake in formality or because it violates a substantive rule of law[83] – where the testator is fully aware of the defect but wants to avoid posthumous blame for leaving the property to

---

[81]   See Lon Fuller, *The Morality of Law* (New Haven: Yale U.P., 1969).

[82]   See e.g. Levin (2011) at 392 (the 'Hudson' deal, in which Goldman delayed liquidation to maximise the return on its short position) and 395 (the 'Timberwolf' CDO, which was liquidated in 2008).

[83]   For a fictional example of a will designed to fall foul of the rule against perpetuities, see the film *Body Heat*. http://www.imsdb.com/scripts/Body-Heat.

the person who ultimately inherits on intestacy. Should a lawyer take part in such a scheme?[84] One might say that, as in existing legal professional ethics, the issue is merely one of professional pride rather than ethics – that lawyers should not involve themselves in deliberately shoddy work. There is, however, an ethical dimension to the issue. Even though it might be difficult to identify the net social loss to non-lawyers from such a device, the problem with it is that it reduces trust in the law as an effective way of fulfilling expectations. Rather as the market for second-hand goods might disappear completely if there were no credible guarantees of quality – because consumers would offer too little to induce sellers of better goods into the market leaving only defective goods for which the prices offered would be seen as too high[85] – a legal system that offers no guarantees of minimum quality and in which appearances cannot be trusted is likely to be one that no one uses. The problem is not merely respect for the existing boundaries of the law, or protection of the dignity of the profession, but maintenance of the social conditions that make the rule of law possible.

More generally, unlike litigation, transactional law as a practice does not carry with it any assumption that lawyers are allowed to harm other people. No doubt it is possible, as we have seen, for deals to harm third parties – that is the essence of the idea of an economic externality – but the imposition of such harm is not inherent in the concept of a deal.[86] The result is that ethical debate about harm founded on transactional legal practice is not limited to the modalities of harm, as in the case of litigation, but can extend, as we have seen, to the fact and degree of harm.

Perhaps the position of legislative lawyers is different. After all,

---

html at 83. Sadly, in England, the Perpetuities and Accumulations Act 2009 makes this plot difficult to replicate convincingly.

[84] There is a risk that the lawyer might be liable in tort to the disappointed legatees (see *White v Jones* [1995] AC 207), but this only happens if the lawyer has 'assumed responsibility' to the legatees and such an assumption can be cut off by the terms of engagement between the testator and the lawyer. See Lord Goff at [1995] AC 207 at 268.

[85] See George Akerlof, 'The Market for "Lemons": Quality Uncertainty and the Market Mechanism' (1970) 84(3) Quarterly Journal of Economics 488–500.

[86] Some might argue that by agreeing to contract with one person rather than another, a form of harm is imposed on the latter – that, in effect, all competition involves harm. They might also claim that the harm is similar to that imposed by a successful defendant frustrating the purposes of a claimant or a prosecutor. But the denial of a single opportunity when other opportunities remain does not leave anyone worse off in any significant way. It differs from the frustration of losing claimants in two ways: there is no other opportunity for this claimant or prosecutor to win in this action or prosecution; and the purpose of the claimant and the prosecutor was to harm the defendant, not to provide a benefit by another route.

legislation, although not inevitably harmful to anyone and perhaps always claimed by its promoters to be in the public interest at some collective level, in practice often benefits one set of people at the expense of another, thus arguably harming the latter. There can be no assumption that legislation, unlike consensual transactions, always benefits more than one person, or one type of person. Perhaps that is why legislative lawyers, especially in the Office of Parliamentary Counsel, are particularly reluctant to assess the consequences of legislative proposals at any level beyond the legal, since they have no professional standpoint, as opposed to their own personal political views, from which they could conclude that the benefits to one group outweigh the costs to another.

But that acceptance of harm gives rise to a problem for legislative lawyers, especially in the UK with its fundamental constitutional rule of parliamentary supremacy and thus a lack of constitutional boundaries. The problem is that legislative lawyers might come to look like the ultimate hired guns, even more lacking in critical distance and a sense of responsibility than US litigators operating under the 'zeal' standard. Possible responses include the adoption of human rights standards as providing limits to what legislative lawyers will do,[87] although even in the UK that might count as a 'legal' minimum standard rather than an ethical one. Another response, as we have mentioned, is the adoption of an ethical standard that rules out working on measures too confusing to generate real consent or measures that free the government from legal restraint. But even with those constraints in place, the ethical standards for legislative lawyers about third party harm seem thin.

Perhaps the fact that legislative lawyers are also civil servants whose first duty is to serve a democratically-elected government makes their position particularly weak.[88] The more powerful and independent position of the French Conseil d'État, however, demonstrates that other types of relationship are possible, and suggests that the degree to which legislative lawyers might exercise judgment about the proposals on which they work

---

[87] Procedures exist to allow UK legislative lawyers who believe that proposed legislation is fundamentally wrong, especially on human rights grounds, to complain to the Attorney-General. See e.g. Edward Garnier, 'The Law Officers and Legislative Procedure', Speech to ALBA Summer Conference 17 July 2010 (http://www.adminlaw.org.uk/docs/sc%202010%20by%20Edward%20Garnier.pdf) at 7.

Since the Attorney-General is also a government minister, it might be thought unlikely that such complaints will be effective against deliberate and considered government policy, but at least the Attorney-General is a lawyer, albeit usually a barrister brought up on litigation-based ethical standards.

[88] See e.g. UK Civil Service Code s. 10.

is sensitive to institutional arrangements. British legislative lawyers might baulk at the French system, pointing out that it tends to dilute the responsibility of ministers for the product that reaches the legislative assembly, but in many ways all the French system does is to bring the interaction between the ministers and drafters more into the open. The independence of the Conseil d'État is created and guaranteed by transparency as much as by law.

CONSEQUENCES

Drawing these themes together we can see the possibility of basing legal ethics on three principles that arise out of the practice of transactional and legislative law – a principle of consent, a principle of maintaining confidence in the rule of law and a principle of avoiding harm. A question that might immediately suggest itself is where those principles would leave litigators? They would claim that in litigation the principle of consent could apply only to the relationship between lawyers and their own clients, the principle of maintaining confidence in the rule of law should be interpreted narrowly to allow for zealous representation and the principle of avoiding harm should not apply at all. But starting with the ethics of lawyer-engineers suggests that we might ask some challenging questions of litigators. Is it really necessary for the practice of litigation that we should permit conduct that arguably undermines both the principle of consent and the principle of maintaining confidence in the rule of law? For example, is it really necessary that litigators should be permitted to engage in sharp practice such as taking advantage of the other side's misapprehensions?[89] More generally, do not standards encouraging 'zeal' or its equivalent tend to produce conduct that undermines confidence in the rule of law, particularly by tending to treat law not as a search for justice but as a competitive game? Similarly, if we begin with the principle of avoiding harm, we might ask whether litigators need complete exemption from it, or only an exemption solely in terms of the remedy or sanction potentially to be imposed by

---

[89] One government lawyer remarked, on an earlier draft of this chapter, that it was, and still should be, a principle for government lawyers that where they had a clear view of the law, they should act on that view even where it was possible that another party, especially another party to litigation, might mistakenly concede a view more favourable to the government. That view, which can be justified as arising from the government's obligation to act congruently with the law, seems incomprehensible to ordinary litigators, for whom the authority of the law as a whole is unimportant.

the court. We might question whether there should be any exemption in respect of other forms of harm, including tactics designed to put pressure on the other side by increasing costs.

Other aspects of the current litigation-based system of legal ethics might need to be reconsidered. One is the primacy given, at least in the exaggeratedly adversarial US ethical code, to client confidentiality. For the most part, compliance with the ethical principles we have developed here can be achieved by lawyers simply refusing to carry out offending work, but what if the client already possesses the device, warning the client has not worked and there is nothing more the lawyer alone can do to prevent its misuse. Should the lawyer alert other parties or the regulatory authorities of the danger? Adversarial ethics has hesitated over such questions,[90] but a transactional-based ethic should not hesitate for one moment. Lawyers will no doubt object that even the possibility of such a course of action on their part will seriously damage their relationship with their client, which will in turn interfere with their ability to understand the client's requirements, but the situations we are considering are those in which, if the lawyers had properly understood the client's requirements in the first place, they should have refused to act. The clients lost would be those they should never have had.

Another related issue is the cab-rank rule, the (admittedly easily evaded)[91] rule that lawyers should not pick and choose between clients and should act for anyone who asks for their services. Solicitors have never been formally subject to the rule, but sometimes act, or at least talk, as if they are.[92] The question is whether we should conceive of solicitors as being 'exempt' from the rule or of the rule itself as the exception. The basis of the rule is access to justice – that no one should be denied the assistance of counsel regardless of their character or previous conduct. The rule itself, at least in principle, assists lawyers to provide services to unpopular litigants by breaking any link between those with whom the lawyer personally identifies and those the lawyer takes on as clients. In the context of the work of transactions lawyers, however, the issue becomes a different one, in two respects. On the one hand, the identity of a client might be relevant to the issue of third party harm. For example, the risk of misuse of an otherwise innocent legal device can depend on who is to use it, a matter Goldman's lawyers might usefully have taken into account. On the other hand, lawyers should recognise that their transactional activities

---

[90]   See Humbach (2009) at 1001–12.
[91]   See e.g. Andrew Boon, 'Cause Lawyering and the Alternative Ethical Paradigm: Ideology and Transgression' (2004) 7 Legal Ethics 250–68, 256.
[92]   Boon (2004) at 256–57.

make those for whom they act more powerful – legal devices help clients to fulfil their objectives and those with access to legal design services will be more able to fulfil their objectives than those without that access. The former factor points against the cab-rank rule: denying access to legal design services to those likely to misuse them seems entirely to be in the public interest. The latter factor, however, points, if not in the direction of the rule itself, at least in the direction of a principle that lawyers should consider the adverse effects of refusing their services to particular types of people. Each factor is in play at all times, but in certain circumstances the balance might clearly fall on one side. For example, in the field of criminal defence, the risk of misuse should, if lawyers are competent and ethical, be relatively low, but the harm done to unrepresented defendants will be high. The balance should therefore fall consistently on the side of providing services regardless of prior conduct or character. The balance, however, will be different in the case of the provision of financial services.

Some firms might already be moving in this direction. One solicitor reported to the author, 'The Magic Circle currently obsesses about its new client acceptance criteria, wanting only to act for the perceived good guys, not least because junior lawyers want both the penny and the bun i.e. to earn lots whilst sleeping well at night.' Passing judgment on clients' reputation for ethical behaviour before deciding whether to act for them is an important departure. Client acceptance criteria until now have largely concerned possible conflicts of interest – technically in England solely conflicts between clients in the same matter, although stricter firms have included 'business' conflicts, namely situations in which confidential information gleaned from one client might be relevant to the interests of other clients. The use of substantive criteria seems to be new. The same solicitor added, however, 'I am not sure it can be done', pointing to difficulties such as 'what happens when a "good" client goes "bad"? Does it make a difference if the badness is institutional or that of a lone wolf? Can't a "bad" client become "good", not least through the agency of a lawyer?' One might also mention a question raised by a legislative lawyer, namely how do lawyers avoid, in the process of trying to persuade a 'bad' client to act in a better way, the outcome that they have merely helped the client to cover their wrongdoing in an ethical wrapping paper? All these are good questions, but they are not incapable of being answered by the profession following sufficient open debate. They are precisely the kind of questions that a code of legal ethics that starts with the engineering functions of lawyers' work, and not with litigation, should be asking and answering.

A further issue that arises from consideration of the question of to whom lawyers should offer their services is equality. Should lawyers consider as matter of professional ethics the problem that if they provide their services principally to those who are already wealthy and powerful, they will in effect reinforce existing inequalities? The problem is not just the effect lawyers have on their clients. It is also the effect working for wealthy and powerful clients has on lawyers. As Karl Llewellyn remarked:

> [T]he activity of most skilful lawyers will be upon the side of the Haves and not upon the side of the Have-nots; conscience-sturdy activity, too, impassioned skill; one cannot live with the Haves for twenty years without contagion.[93]

One might interpret existing professional obligations to take part in pro bono activities as at least recognising the problem,[94] albeit perhaps at a limited scale. Should they go further and recognise a duty to provide transactional services at lower fees to the general public? Some writers now advocate the wider provision of transactional legal services as a way of reinventing the financial system in a popular direction,[95] so that arguments are gathering momentum that such a professional obligation might not only help the profession but might also count as in the broader public interest. No doubt law firms would complain that their revenues and profits would fall, but lawyers, of all people, should be able to take seriously the point that the pursuit of profit outside a moral framework is capable of undermining itself by destabilising the social relationships that make markets possible.[96]

THE FUTURE OF LEGAL ETHICS – LAWYERS AND PUBLIC WELFARE

That closes our discussion of the implications for lawyers' ethics of the law-as-engineering approach. It is, of necessity, merely a beginning. Legal

---

[93]　Karl Llewellyn, *The Bramble Bush* (New York: Oceana Publications, 1960) (1960a) at 144.

[94]　E.g. ABA Code of Professional Responsibility Ethical Consideration 2–25. Pro bono legal work normally takes the form of litigation is conventionally contentious, for example representing employees in disputes with employers, but transactional pro bono work is developing. See e.g. Thomas Morsch, 'Discovering Transactional Pro Bono' (2003–4) 72 UMKC Law Review 423–31. In a parallel development, engineers increasingly carry out pro bono work. See B. Moulton, 'Pro Bono in Engineering: Towards a Better Understanding' in Magued Iskander, Vikram Kapil and Mohammad A. Karim, *Technological Developments in Education and Automation* (Netherlands: Springer, 2010) at 333–37.

[95]　Robert Shiller, *Finance and the Good Society* (Princeton: Princeton U.P., 2012).

[96]　See e.g. Daniel Finn, *The Moral Ecology of Markets: Assessing Claims about Markets and Justice* (Cambridge: Cambridge U.P., 2006) especially at 72.

ethics has long been dominated by an approach deriving from an activity, litigation, in which only a minority of the profession engages. Much work remains to be done to generate ethical standards appropriate for the legal profession as it now exists.

In particular, lawyers should begin to ask themselves whether they, like engineers, should adopt as an overriding purpose of the profession the promotion of public welfare. The litigation model turns the minds of idealists in the legal profession in the direction of justice, that the overriding purpose of lawyers in an ideal world should be that courts come to just decisions. That ideal remains important, but it provides little useful guidance for lawyers whose main activity is making things for clients. What broader ideal might legal engineers adopt that, like the litigator's ideal of deciding cases justly, both justifies what they do and provides a criterion for evaluating it? Public welfare, in the broad, not exclusively economic, sense adopted by engineers fits the bill. It justifies legal activity and gives us a way of thinking about evaluating it.

At first hearing, a public welfare ideal for lawyers sounds odd, largely because we have become accustomed to think of lawyers as furthering very particular interests and because litigation is rarely assessed in terms of its public, as opposed to its private, benefits. But the ultimate ideal for any activity that involves design is to produce something of benefit, and the most general way to measure benefit is in terms of maximising public welfare.

Both transactions lawyers and legislative lawyers have reacted to a public welfare test for what lawyers do with a great deal of suspicion, if not downright opposition. One transactions lawyer, commenting on a previous draft of this chapter, declared 'profound disagreement' with its conclusions, and a legislative lawyer expressed great scepticism. The basis for this unease in both cases seems to be the inherent difficulty of assessing public welfare. There are two separate problems. First, there is a practical problem of specifying the consequences of a specific action in complex situations – the problems of complexity and chaos are particularly acute in the social world. How can we assess the public welfare consequences of a legal device if we cannot say precisely what its consequences are? Second, there is a normative problem – if the client's idea of what counts as a good outcome conflicts with that of the lawyer, why should the lawyer's idea prevail? The second problem is particularly difficult for legislative lawyers, where the client is a democratically elected government – one legislative lawyer commented that there was no test for public welfare that could be applied by a legislative lawyer in public service in a way that would be consistent with constitutionalism – but the problem arises for both.

There are, however, answers to both problems. On the practical question, although there might be situations in which unexpected results occur, both positive and negative, the precise question that arises for lawyers is not whether they can be blamed for any negative results that have ensued but whether, before the event, they should continue to create what a client wants to be created. At that time, there will be estimates of what the device might do, both in terms of its direct purposes and its side-effects, and although questions might later arise about whether those estimates were reasonable, it is more important that lawyers should take them into account as they were at the time. This is a matter of ethics rather than liability. It concerns the lawyer's actions at the time of creating the device more than the consequences as they turned out. As for the normative issue, the answer for the transactions lawyer is that lawyers who defer to their clients' view of what counts as the welfare of the public cannot then deny their complicity in that view. Only if they maintain their own view can they separate themselves from their clients. Lawyers' attempts to distance themselves from their clients' views lack credibility if lawyers claim to have no views of their own. The situation for legislative lawyers is more difficult – assessing the public welfare to be expected from a new law is precisely the kind of political function that legislative lawyers instinctively recoil from exercising. But without it, the spectre of the hired gun rises once more. Perhaps the way forward is to remember that we are not talking about requiring legislative lawyers to go out of their way to impose their own view of public welfare, or to deceive their clients about what is possible or impossible for the law to achieve, but about lawyers saying, to the point of resignation and beyond, that if the government wants to go ahead with a plainly harmful proposal, they should find someone else to do their drafting work.

Is this too utopian a standard to require of lawyer-engineers? The competitive pressures on transactions lawyers and the political pressures on legislative lawyers will remain great, and many will be tempted by the corollary of the many hands problem, namely the argument that 'if I don't do it, someone else will, so since I can do nothing to stop it, I may as well do it myself'. The answer to that argument is that ethical standards only work if they are shared, so that each lawyer has an obligation to uphold not only personal standards but also the standards of the profession. The situation in which 'someone else will' is one in which that someone else would also be in violation of the standard. That is also why, difficult as they might be to draft, ethical standards of this type need to be written down, in the way engineers have done, and not just left to individual consciences. The external existence of the standard gives courage and protection to those who want to follow it, and a legitimate expectation that others should also follow it. No doubt there is a problem that lawyers, unlike engineers, might be tempted to treat written down standards as legal rules, to be manipulated as other rules are, but that is why lawyers need to be educated in the difference between law and ethics and to be brought to an understanding that it makes no sense to look to the law for guidance about how the law should be used.[97]

Another objection might be that there is no practical way to ensure that standards of this type will be adhered to. The sheer mass and complexity of transactions makes enforcement by conventional means difficult in the absence of events as catastrophic as those of 2008, and since the object of the exercise might be thought to be the avoidance of any repetition of 2008, an insuperable problem arises. One response, however, to that scepticism is to think about the adoption of law-as-engineering standards as itself a type of legal engineering project. How does the system work now and what are the best points to affect it so that its outputs change? One might think about changing the flow of people who move into legal work so that those whose ethical outlook is deficient in the relevant sense have a lower chance of entering the profession. One might also look for the way decisions about transactions function and target specific types of lawyer for careful selection or training (for example in-house lawyers, who often appear as crucial intermediaries in the flow of transactional work). Or one might concentrate on the ethical training of all lawyers at a sufficiently early stage to make a difference, a topic taken up in the next chapter. A mixture of these various methods may well be required.

Litigators, Judges and Public Welfare

The public welfare standard is designed to operate for transactions and legislative lawyers. One might nevertheless ask how a public welfare ideal might apply to the minority of lawyers engaged in litigation? Perhaps for them, public welfare could not entirely replace justice in judicial decision as their ultimate ideal. Only if we could put a value on justice that we could easily compare with other aspects of public welfare could we integrate the two ideals. That might prove very difficult to do and might possibly be morally wrong in itself. Public welfare does, however, provide a second measure of success or failure even for lawyers concerned with litigation, one important enough that one should be able to say that if litigators cannot explain how what they have done promotes public welfare, they should perhaps reconsider their actions.

Finally, what about judges? It seems to follow that judges deciding cases in ramshackle bricolage-filled common law fields, such as tort law,

---

[97]   See the next chapter for further discussion of this point.

although they characteristically lack the means accurately to assess the consequences of their decisions, should at least be prepared to acknowledge that their decisions might have consequences for third parties and to explain the assumptions they are making about those consequences. We noted in Chapter 3 the dangers for judges inherent in constructing a client for themselves out of concepts such as the public interest, and we suggested that, as an empirical matter, the image of the judicial bricoleur without clear goals apart from keeping the structure standing was perhaps more accurate than any grander conception of judging. As a normative matter, however, even a bricoleur is engaged in a project that can be judged by the good bricolage does. Keeping the structure working can usually be judged a successful outcome in itself, but where the structure's effects are clearly harmful, judges who ignore those effects in circumstances in which they could prevent them should arguably be counted as acting unethically.

Some legal theorists have, of course, long objected to assessing judges' decisions in 'pragmatic' terms,[98] and some are anxious to shield judges from thinking about consequences at all, maintaining that, even though legal rights might have social, economic and political purposes, judges have no business thinking about those purposes, at least not in terms of their real world effects.[99] On this view, the only job of judges is to identify and enforce the parties' rights. But that form of analysis, itself a form of only-one-level-up thinking, risks mistaking solutions for problems. Rights are solutions to problems, not problems in themselves, and deliberately ignoring their functions is not likely to lead to clear thinking or successful design. It is one thing for designers to acknowledge that their brief is unclear, their options restricted, the resources available to them poor and their understanding of the system they are designing for weak – all of which should lead them to caution and circumspection – and quite another to pretend that they are not engaged in design at all but merely choosing between solutions on the basis of how well their components work together. Judges, like all lawyers, have responsibilities as engineers.

---

[98]   See especially Ronald Dworkin, *Law's Empire* (London: Fontana, 1986) chapter 5.
[99]   See e.g. Robert Stevens, *Torts and Rights* (Oxford: Oxford U.P., 2007) especially 308–29.

5. Implications (2) – Legal research and teaching

We now turn to the implications of the law-as-engineering approach for the smallest branch of the legal profession, but one through whose hands all prospective lawyers in many countries, including England and Wales, now pass, either at a university or during their professional formation – namely academic lawyers.

It is worth prefacing this chapter with an observation about legal academic life in general. Legal academics exist in two worlds, the world of the university and the world of the law. The world of the university, notwithstanding government efforts to the contrary, tends towards the self-consciously impractical, towards disdain for the merely useful and towards drawing sharp distinctions between education (what universities do) and training (what lesser institutions do). The world of the law, especially in common law countries, is the opposite – it is self-consciously practical, disdains the merely theoretical and cares less about whether lawyers have well-stocked minds than about whether they know what they are doing.

One of the fears of academic lawyers is that their academic colleagues in other disciplines regard them as tainted by practicality and engaged in training rather than education, in short as not real academics, whereas practising lawyers regard them as head-in-the-clouds theoreticians, or, worse, dilettantes with little of value to contribute, whose version of legal education produces no useful skills. Some academics resolve this tension by embracing the university world-view, by engaging in research programmes that treat law as merely a jumping off point or as subject-matter in the theoretical investigations of some other discipline and by teaching not law itself but about law. The methods they use are those of the other discipline – whether the equations of economists, the symbols of philosophers or the vocabulary of literary theorists. Law merely provides the object of analysis. Ultimately, law on this view ceases to be a discipline in its own right.[1] Legal philosophy becomes a branch of philosophy, not

---

[1]   Cf the process described in J.M. Balkin, 'Interdisciplinarity as Colonization' (1996) 53 Washington Lee Law Review 949–70.

of law, the economic analysis of law becomes dominated by professional economists to the exclusion of lawyers and legal history becomes a sub-category of history studied by historians rather than by lawyers. Some US legal academics survey the consequent wilderness that is left to them and conclude that the only role left for academic lawyers is as a kind of all-purpose interdisciplinary academic interpreter.[2] Other legal academics resolve the tension by becoming practitioners, retaining only tenuous links with the university, writing exclusively for practitioners and teaching through war stories and anecdotes. Most, however, (I include myself in this group) have failed to resolve the tension. We have largely unconsciously sought instead to reduce the tension by looking for research projects and teaching methods that concentrate on areas of least difference between the two worlds. Our teaching and research thus tends to identify with the role in the practical world of law that most closely resembles that of theoretician, namely the role of appellate judge. Our research projects study what appellate judges say and do, and make suggestions for what they might say or do in the future. Our teaching consists of expositions of the same kind of material. But the tension remains, albeit slightly hidden from sight. Judges are engaged in a practical activity, not a theoretical one. If we are really striving to offer judges advice, rather than just applying the methods of another discipline to what they say and do, we are stepping outside the world of the university as conceived by academic theoreticians.

Law-as-engineering offers a different way of resolving the tension. If academic lawyers look around the university, they will immediately see other academics in positions structurally equivalent to their own. The most obvious example is that of engineers themselves. Other examples include academics in clinical medicine, business schools and public policy schools. They might also think about the place of ethics in philosophy departments, especially those who are interested in applied ethics. Academics whose subject matter is decision, and whose students need to know not just how others make decisions but how to make decisions themselves, should see themselves as allies. They are all associated with activities the point of which is not just to understand the world but to change it.

Furthermore, all these academics have a common interest in the status of study as a basis for action rather merely for understanding. They should refuse to see themselves as inferior. As Walter Vincenti pointed out, scientists often misunderstand the relationship between engineering

[2] Stephen Matthew Feldman, 'The Transformation of an Academic Discipline: Law Professors in the Past and Future (or Toy Story Too)' (2004) 54 *Journal of Legal Education* 471–98.

and science. Engineers do not just apply science. Often engineering's need to understand is what drives science. The same is true of medicine (which drives much of bio-science), and public policy and business (which together drive more of economics than economists like to admit). It could become true of law.[3]

There is a case for pursuing the pure understanding of nature for its own sake, as an elevated form of human endeavour. Spinoza put the case at its highest when he argued that when we understand nature we come to share in eternity. The university can thus be seen as a modern monastery, a place designed to encourage and to protect contemplation. The university-as-monastery has other advantages, including a built-in ability to survive over very long periods of time.[4] But, despite its attractions, there are limits. Cloistered monks tend to generate resentment, even more so when they live in the midst of populations who do not share their faith. Universities cannot afford to be seen as, in the words of a French revolutionary lambasting the monasteries in February 1790, 'hors de la société . . . contraires à la société'.[5] The best way to preserve the universities' important role of protecting pure contemplation is unlikely to be the cultivation of a lofty disdain for all contact with the world of practical reason. To be allowed to continue to contemplate, contemplatives need intermediaries between themselves and the world, to act as buffers as well as advocates, and who better as intermediaries than those who understand the attractions of contemplation but whose aim is to use its results to make useful objects?

---

[3] The situation inside universities seems to have developed into the opposite of that Kant was writing about in *The Conflict of the Faculties*. Then, the problem was to free the purely academic disciplines ('philosophy' in Kant's usage) from the potentially domineering 'higher' faculties (Theology, Law and Medicine), which might illegitimately use their connection with authority, especially the authority of the state, to silence their academic inferiors. See David Evans, 'The Conflict of the Faculties and the Knowledge Industry: Kant's Diagnosis, in his Time and Ours' (2008) 83 Philosophy 483–95. Now the problem is that the internal status systems of universities, arguably built precisely to counteract the authority of the state, treats the previously 'higher' faculties with disdain, to the extent that law has arguably joined engineering in a new category of 'low' faculties. But neither law nor engineering can escape from their 'low' status by eliminating their essentially practical character, because that would be to undermine their whole purpose. What they need to do instead is to celebrate that character.
[4] Katja Rost, Emil Inauen, Margit Osterloh and Bruno S. Frey, 'The Corporate Governance of Benedictine Abbeys: What can Stock Corporations Learn from Monasteries?' (2010) 16(1) Journal of Management History 90–115.
[5] Antoine Barnave, Ass. Cont., 12 February 1790, in Guillaume Lallement, *Choix de Rapports, Opinions et Discours Prononcés à la Tribune Nationale* vol. 2 (Paris: A. Eymery et Corréard, 1818) at 42.

We return to these questions at the end of this chapter. We begin, however, with a more specific question. What should legal academic research be about?

LEGAL RESEARCH

It is an awkward fact that academics in other disciplines often find it difficult to grasp what academic research in law is about. Colleagues from scientific disciplines are usually puzzled by the idea that legal academics spend time discovering what the law is. Simply summarising what statutes say or what judges have decided does not seem all that difficult a task, and it certainly seems not to involve discovering facts that no one yet knows, since the people who drafted the statutes or who decided the cases clearly already knew what they were saying. On the other hand, taking what statutes and judges say and shaping it into a more coherent whole strikes them as an odd activity, at least unless it contributes to predicting how judges will behave in the future, something it rarely achieves. It is not open to scientists to tell nature that it is wrong.

Mathematicians, in contrast, might recognise the process of discovering connections already inherent in a system but not yet articulated, but lawyers' standards of proof strike mathematicians as loose, and the concept of authority – at least to the extent that it requires lawyers to accept and to incorporate results of previous cases that are themselves logically indefensible – strikes them as utterly alien. The purpose of mathematics is to find new consequences of what we already know to be correct. The consequences of what we know to be incorrect are not very interesting.

The idea of authority also creates a barrier between academic legal research and the research programmes of the humanities. The very idea of authority produces anxiety in literary studies, and in other fields, such as history, it is a phenomenon to be investigated, not a scholarly norm to be accepted. If, however, academic law were to eschew the concept of authority, it would look indistinguishable from political or moral advocacy.

Forms of Legal Research

What then, precisely, are we doing? A glance at the leading academic law journals reveals that legal research is not a single activity but a number of different activities. Some research is straightforward social science, with legal events – case results, expenditure on litigation, legislative activity and so on – as the object of study. A related type of research concerns the history of legal events, tracing their development or decline in terms either of the legal arguments that produced them or of the events or conditions beyond those arguments. But much legal research is aimed not at explaining or predicting behaviour that just happens in part to be classified into legal categories but rather at exposition or criticism of the law itself. Some articles lean more to exposition, some to criticism. The expository articles tend to take an area of human activity not previously treated as a legal category and proceed to summarise the statutes and court decisions about that activity, sometimes pointing out inconsistent approaches to the same factual problem in different areas of the law. For example, an article might take an environmental problem and describe both the private law and regulation relevant to it, pointing out the different assumptions about the value of the environment lying behind the different treatment of the problem in the two areas of the law. Critical articles tend to concentrate on legal rather than factual categories but also proceed by pointing out inconsistencies in assumptions and approach in different decisions (or, more rarely, different statutory provisions). They might also attempt a rational reconstruction of the law, cleaning up the inconsistencies in assumptions either by arguing that some of them should be abandoned in favour of others (a method that invariably takes the argument beyond the immediate legal material) or proposing a synthesis that reconciles the opposing positions. Sometimes, however, the author presents a naked critique, an argument that the legal material is incoherent either in assumptions or argumentation but without any attempt at reconciliation or reconstruction. The impression might even be given that, for historical, social or logical reasons, reconciliation is impossible. An important sub-category of naked critique is the article that claims that some area of the law, or indeed the whole of the law, is radically indeterminate, usually in the sense that legal texts do not and cannot lead 'courts' or 'judges' to specifically predictable answers in 'cases'.[6] Another type of article simply takes the subject matter of an area of the law and, without examining too closely the existing provisions or decisions about it, proposes a reform that arises out of a set of policies or principles that strike the writer as rational or attractive. Finally, there is a type of article that takes existing provisions and decisions and explains them in terms entirely different from those used by those who originally made them, but which, the author claims, provide a better guide for future decision or

---

[6] E.g. Mark Tushnet, 'Defending the Indeterminacy Thesis' (1996–97) 16 Quinnipiac Law Review 339–56. See also Gunther Teubner, '"And God Laughed . . .": Indeterminacy, Self-Reference and Paradox in Law' (2011) 12 German Law Journal 376–406.

law-making than the stated reasons (much of law and economics falls into this category).

A number of observations can be made about these types of research. First, at least in English law journals, the target audience of most articles appears to be judges, who are impliedly asked to interpret the law in the way the writer would prefer, or litigators looking for ammunition. Much more work concentrates on the decisions of courts than on the output of legislatures, and even work that looks at statutes tends to ask how judges interpret them, or should interpret them, rather than, for example, asking how they might be interpreted by those who behaviour is intended to be regulated by them.

Second, most journal articles rarely offer advice or assistance to transactions lawyers. Very few suggest new ways for producing useful legal results or more effective legal designs. Naked critique is for obvious reasons, of little interest to transactions lawyers but critique and reconstruction is also of limited use. Areas of the law in need of reconstruction are for that very reason unreliable for constructive purposes. More generally, the tendency of journal articles of all types to concentrate on disputed or difficult points of law limits the utility of academic research for transactions lawyers. No matter how interesting or persuasive such research, it ultimately consists of arguments at the edge of acceptability, and consequently cannot be well-enough established to make good building materials. Karl Llewellyn's employer, the counsel to a bank, would certainly find them too risky for everyday use.

Third, in the minority of articles that call for reforms to be made by statute (or occasionally for reforms not to be made), and which are thus impliedly addressed to legislators rather than to courts, one very rarely finds attempts at any legislative drafting. They are more like submissions to ministers from policy experts than either a set of instructions drafted by departments for parliamentary counsel to turn into legislation or, even less, the output of legislative lawyering. It is as if the distinctively legal part of the policy process – the complex interaction between policy and legislative drafting – is either uninteresting or too difficult for academic lawyers. One might contrast the output of academic journals with that of the UK Law Commissions, which seem to be the only legal research institutions in Britain whose job is to think about law and policy at the same time. The aim of the Law Commissions, after all the rounds of consultation and analysis through which they proceed, is to produce a fully-fledged draft bill.

The Relationship between Legal Research and the Judges

The picture that emerges from the law journals is that, at its most constructive, legal research is the servant of judges, litigators or politicians. That is
not to say that it is irrelevant to the engineering function of law. Judges at
least have a role in constructing legal devices that work, even if the role of
litigators in legal engineering is peripheral and the role of politicians more
like that of clients than designers. It also needs to be said that the relationship between academics and judges in England tends to be co-operative
and productive, unlike that sometimes alleged to obtain in the USA, where
academic lawyers are frequently accused of losing touch with the judiciary, citation of academic legal writing by judges is becoming less common
and academic disdain for judges has reached crisis proportions.[7] English
judges faced with novel points, especially in the higher courts where their
decisions will be taken as creating new law, will often turn to academic
writing or conversation for clues about what to do, and to the extent that
academics have consciously constructed systems of rules that are designed
to work together to produce desirable results for the society as a whole,
judicial adoption of academic solutions will tend to trace the same kinds
of path. Naked critique is, of course, of little use (although if the situation
really is one in which there is no perfect solution other than the overthrow
of capitalism, at least a judge knows not to seek one). Critique and reconstruction in contrast can be very useful for judges and even if obstacles of
authority and precedent present themselves, especially in the lower courts,
the identification of contradictions can help judges to overcome those
obstacles even if they cannot adopt the whole of a reconstruction all at
once.

A number of problems, however, arise out of the judge-academic relationship. Both judges and academics lack identifiable clients possessed of
their own interests, values and priorities for whom they are designing. That
means that both are forced to construct those interests, values and priorities for themselves. There is a danger for both that they will confuse their
own interests, values and priorities with those of society as a whole. The
structure of precedent and the authority of statute are supposed to limit
the extent to which judges can insert their personal views into the process
of legal decision. The whole idea of fidelity to law involves a degree of

---

[7] See e.g. Harry Edwards, 'The Growing Disjunction Between Legal
Education and the Legal Profession' (1992) 92 Michigan Law Review 34–78. See
also Brian Tamanaha, *Law as a Means to an End: A Threat to the Rule of Law*
(Cambridge: Cambridge U.P., 2006) at 152. But see also Robert Gordon, 'Lawyers,
Scholars and the "Middle Ground"' (1993) 91 Michigan Law Review 2079–119.

surrender by judges of their ability to follow their own lights. Academics, however, tend not to feel the constraints of authority in the same way, at least to the extent that they habitually write as if they were members of the highest possible court with the widest possible powers to ignore their own previous decisions. The interaction between judges and academics has the potential, therefore, to be liberating for judges, but it also raises the question of how academics choose their interests, values and priorities and how they relate to the ones encoded in the existing law. Much has been written about how ideal judges should decide cases – for example Ronald Dworkin's hypothetical perfect judge Hercules – but less has been written by academics in the same terms about themselves. If they are to see themselves as unacknowledged legislators for mankind, however, perhaps it is time they started to ask such questions.

Another problem is the relationship of common law decision-making to the concept of legal design. Because judges know that the facts available to them in individual cases rarely cover the whole ground desirable for broad policy decisions, and because they realise that broad policy decisions are in any case more legitimately the business of other branches of government, they tend to decide cases on the narrowest plausible grounds and to keep open as much as possible the options available to future courts when deciding related cases. Judges often see their role as to do justice in the immediate case without disturbing the existing structure of the law, and the challenge of the job is that sometimes doing both is not possible. In other words, they are reluctant engineers, worried that they do not fully understand how the systems in which they are intervening work and anxious to avoid making adjustments whose consequences they cannot predict. One can argue for such an approach, the bricoleur style, as we have identified it, as a general principle of design. For example Nassim Nicholas Taleb, who writes about the unfathomable complexity of financial markets recommends adopting modest 'organic' styles of decision-making as a way of building in resilience against the shocks caused by 'black swan' events (events that are highly unlikely but very significant if they do happen). But the inherent tendency of academic legal writing, because its topic is almost always a whole area of law or of human activity rather than a single case, is to look for and to offer broader solutions. The result is an unavoidable tension between judges and academics, often a creative tension but one never fully resolvable. Even though judges are involved in engineering, their approach will always strike academics as tinkering and adjusting rather than as full-scale design.

Legal Research and the Legislative Process

Legislation, on the other hand, is normally self-consciously designed. One might therefore expect legal academics to have well-developed relationships with those active in the legislative process, whether in government or in Parliament. The reality, however, is more mixed. One does find legal academics serving on government review committees, especially committees about topics considered to be 'technical', such as the company law review. Similarly, the constraints imposed by European law can impel government departments to draw upon academic expertise in EU-related topics such as competition law. But where the topic is considered politically sensitive, academic lawyers fade into the background, and perhaps out of the picture altogether. For example, none of the members of the Iraq Inquiry was a legal academic, and although the committee did belatedly appoint a legal adviser who had at one point been an academic, that academic experience was long ago. In the meantime she had practised as a barrister and acted as a judge. Similarly, only one of the eight members chosen to serve on the UK Commission on a Bill of Rights was a current legal academic, and he was also a practising barrister. Perhaps more surprisingly, a 2010 Ministry of Justice working party on libel law contained 17 members, only one of whom was a legal academic and he was more a specialist in human rights law than in defamation. The view in government seems to be that committees about controversial topics require one person with respectable academic credentials but usually no more than one and preferably someone who now does something else. In phases of the legislative process beyond reviews of policy, academic lawyers are less in evidence, especially during the drafting phases, when the interchange between departments and parliamentary counsel occurs entirely within government.

Given that academic commentaries on statutes often criticise their drafting, it might be surprising that so little interchange appears to occur, but two factors seem to contribute to the failure to engage. First, the culture of secrecy in British government is still very strong and there is great reluctance to allow outsiders into any part of the process in which ministerial indecision might be revealed. Second, academic lawyers show very little interest in drafting up their own policy proposals, preferring merely to criticise others' drafting after the event. Consequently, from the government's point of view, little evidence exists that academics have anything useful to contribute in advance. As the composer Sibelius said, no statue has ever been put up to a critic, and perhaps no statute should ever be drafted by one.

The relationship between academic lawyers and Parliament is, at least in the UK, if anything less strong than that with government. Legal academics do, of course, appear as witnesses before select committees, and some have served as special advisers to such committees. But select committees are, in the British system, investigatory not legislative. Academic lawyers also appear occasionally as witnesses before committees on draft bills, an optional stage of the process sometimes adopted for controversial or difficult topics. But if we turn to the main legislative process itself, legal academics disappear almost entirely. Witnesses are called to give evidence before legislative committees dealing with government bills that have originated in the Commons. If we look at such committees since the 2010 election, of the dozens of witnesses called, not one was a legal academic, unless we count a single professor of criminology appearing before the committee on the Police Reform Bill.[8] In some cases the absence of legal academics might follow from the topic of the bill, and in others the constitutional nature of the bill meant that it was taken on the floor of the House rather than in committee, but their absence is not so easily explained in the cases of bills on legal aid and civil procedure, control orders and civil liberties. Even a bill on the National Health Service might have benefited from impartial legal expertise as soon as it became clear that the central issues in contention included the scope of European Union competition law and the nature of the legal duties of Secretaries of State to provide services.

The distance between academic legal research and the parliamentary legislative process is at first sight puzzling. A number of factors, however, might explain it. First, the process by which witnesses are chosen – essentially a negotiation between government and opposition whips – assists those who might bolster a political point of view rather than those who might offer impartial advice. Second, reinforced by the first point, the process favours those who keep themselves at the forefront of parliamentarians' minds, which largely means those with a high media profile or resources to spend on lobbying activity. The role of legal expert is therefore usually taken not by academics but by the Law Society and the Bar Council – professional bodies dedicated to their members' interests. Third, it is an oddity of UK parliamentary procedure that although the committee stage of a bill is supposed to examine the detailed drafting of the bill, the witnesses tend to deal with the bill's overall policy – a matter which in legislative terms should already have been dealt with at the debate that precedes the committee stage, the second reading debate. A fourth factor, however, might well be that it is unclear precisely what legal academics are experts about. Those who write naked critique of legislation can hardly expect to

---

[8] See http://services.parliament.uk/bills/2010-12.html, from which there are links to information for each bill.

play a part in constructive activity, but, in a system in which Parliament is legislatively supreme, those who write critique and reconstruction of judicial decisions as advice to judges also largely exclude themselves from the legislative process. Judicial decisions, even rationally reconstructed, tell us what the law is or might be, but they tell us nothing about what it can be. Parliament is only interested in the current law to the extent that it poses a problem to be solved. Beyond that its attention is focussed on the future rather than the past.

That leaves those who formulate reform proposals, whether radical or incremental, with only incidental reference to existing law. The difficulty for that group is that it is not obvious what comparative advantage it has over academics in other disciplines (for example economists, psychologists, and sociologists) or over non-academic policy entrepreneurs. What skills or insights specific to academic lawyers but relevant to the process of formulating new policy do we bring into play? As policy analysts most academic lawyers are amateurs. They rarely have the quantitative skills or the feel for politics or the appreciation of the managerial problems of implementation necessary for professional policy formulation. The one undoubtedly relevant skill lawyers possess, drafting rules to meet clients' ends, legal academics either fail to use or perhaps simply lack.

One possible conclusion is that academic lawyers should stick to types of research that require no skills beyond the ability to spot (or perhaps to create) contradictions in legal texts and to leave it to others to think about what, if anything, should be done about them. That is the path of naked critique. Its attractions are that it looks a lot like research in the humanities, thus achieving a certain amount of academic respectability, and that it tends to create an aura of radicalism unencumbered by any specific proposals, which is useful for the purposes of appearing simultaneously both political and apolitical. The objection, however, to the path of naked critique is that it is deeply unsatisfying for anyone of a creative or constructive turn of mind, and an academic profession that rewards only naked critique will drive away creativity and constructiveness, leaving only a dry, negative scholastic husk that will be difficult to justify to the professions or to the state or to the public.

Engineering Research as a Template for Legal Research

If we look at academic engineering research, however, we can see a different way forward for legal research. A central activity for engineering research is the study of the process of design. Academic engineers study how practising engineers create new useful objects. Their objective is to take engineers' implicit, unspoken 'know-how' and to turn it into explicit knowledge. But they do so not for sociological purposes but for the purpose of improving the process itself. They systematise what engineers do and make it explicit, but they also study the existing processes' successes and failures, and on the basis of careful sorting of the evidence and analysis, so that they can suggest improvements to those processes. In effect, academic engineers engineer engineering.

There is a template here for legal research. The most important lesson for academic lawyers from what academic engineers do is that academic lawyers have largely ignored the most important thing that lawyers do, namely to design new legal devices.[9] The way lawyers go about designing contracts, companies, statutes and constitutions could be, and should be, an important object of legal academic research. As in engineering, the starting point is a profession that largely believes that the processes of design are a matter of implicit know-how, picked up through apprenticeship and experience. But there is enough that is explicit, in the writings of lawyers themselves, and in some existing studies to suggest that this is a field of inquiry ripe for development. But, as in engineering, the purpose of studying the process of design could be more than purely sociological. By studying systematically examples of successful and unsuccessful design we might be able to suggest improvements in the process.

Also instructive is the way engineering research works on all the various possible stages of an engineering project and across a range from concrete objects to abstract methods. Engineering research can concentrate on any part of the process of producing useful objects, from the development of new materials (or merely the better understanding of existing materials) through design and production to use, breakdown and disposal, and can look at both specific objects and devices and at whole systems. More abstractly it can look at measurement, methods and processes. As engineering deals increasingly with open systems, systems that constantly interact with their environments, engineers' research covers not just objects themselves but also their environments, which involves understanding not just the physical conditions within which they operate but also biological, psychological and social conditions.

Legal research would benefit from a similar attempt at classification, not least because doing so reveals more possible forms of research that are currently not much attempted or are underdeveloped because they are misclassified. One clear example is to think about the equivalent in law to materials science. There is such a field in legal research already. It is

---

[9] Honourable exceptions include the work of Gilson, Utset, Choi, Gulati and Schwarcz. See Chapters 2 and 3 above.

Law as engineering

the study of the properties of legal rules. Legal rules provide lawyers with the materials they use for making their devices and structures. What kinds of legal rule exist, how they interact and what new types there might be constitute a fundamental form of inquiry indispensible to all other types of legal research. The work of Wesley Newcomb Hohfeld is the core of the field, tracing logical relationships between claims, liberties, immunities and powers and their corresponding obligations and vulnerabilities.[10] But one could add Ronald Dworkin's distinction between 'rules' and 'principles'[11] and the distinction developed by several writers, including Roscoe Pound, Hart and Sacks, and Duncan Kennedy, between 'rules' and 'standards'.[12] These concepts have been separated out into the study of 'jurisprudence' or 'legal philosophy' or, slightly more practically, the economic analysis of law, but that is to misunderstand their role and importance. They are not 'philosophical' concepts in the sense of mildly interesting but ultimately useless abstractions but, rather, intensely practical ones. They are the building blocks of legal design. Anyone with a contract or a statute to draft uses them everyday, and if robustly useable new ones were developed, the effect would be the legal equivalent of the invention of plastics or semiconductors.

Another example is the relative under-development of legal research about the use and formation of legal rules by anyone other than judges, including the self-application of law.[13] Even less work appears on the formation of rules by legislatures.[14] Indeed, in some ways it is positively discouraged. One major English journal, for example, routinely rejects manuscripts about bills rather than Acts, on the ground that bills are of no interest to lawyers until they have 'become law'. The equivalent of that position in case law research would be, absurdly, to reject reconstructive studies unless the reconstructed law had already been accepted by a court.

---

[10] See especially Wesley Newcomb Hohfeld, *Fundamental Legal Conceptions as Applied to Legal Reasoning* (New Haven: Yale U.P., 1919).

[11] Ronald Dworkin, *Taking Rights Seriously* (Cambridge, MA: Harvard U.P., 1977).

[12] See e.g. Pierre Schlag 'Rules and Standards' (1989) 33 UCLA Law Review 379–430.

[13] But see, for an example of a study of the application of rules by non-judicial officials, Simon Halliday, Jonathan Ilan and Colin Scott, 'Street-Level Torts: The Bureaucratic Justice of Liability Decision-Making' (2012) 75 Modern Law Review 347–67.

[14] For an example, however, see Daniel Greenberg, *Laying Down the Law: A Discussion of the People, Processes and Problems that Shape Acts of Parliament* (London: Sweet and Maxwell, 2011), which provides a useful, though often autobiographical, tour d'horizon.

The difference between the two is an arbitrary distinction between 'legal' rule formation in the courts and 'political' rule formation in the legislature. Another apparent gap is bringing together such histories of rule formation, whether by courts or legislatures or private actors, into comparative studies of legal design. That is, for example, what Vincenti achieved for engineering in his pioneering historical studies on aircraft design. One can see the introductory classic Twining and Miers' *How To Do Things With Rules*[15] as a version of such a study, but the field has not developed much beyond its initial pedagogic purposes (important though they are).

The engineering comparison also brings into focus an important distinction between materials and design. Academic legal research often confuses the two and seems silently to assume that new designs require new materials, so that bringing about change is assumed to be a matter of discovering or developing at least a rule with new content if not a new form of rule. In engineering, that is not so. A new design can be innovative and useful in itself, without having to incorporate new materials or new uses for old materials. Legal research might develop in new ways if it incorporated the same insight. Such a development could also produce important changes in the way purely expository studies are viewed. Currently, as far as journal reviewers and editors are concerned, 'descriptive' is a term of abuse. But, especially for Llewellyn's counsel to a bank and his myriad equivalents, accurate exposition of the existing law, without speculation, boundary-pushing or hidden advocacy of reform, is indispensable for the successful construction of new legal devices, and the same ought to be true for academic researchers who set themselves equivalent tasks.

One might go on to complete the entire mapping of engineering research onto legal research (for example, there seems to be an entirely undeveloped field of how lawyers should measure success), but the fundamental point has been made: current legal research concentrates on a very narrow band.

Naked Critique and Resilience Engineering

The engineering template also allows us to find a place for naked critique, albeit one its practitioners might not appreciate. Showing that a legal project is self-contradictory or otherwise impossible is an important practical result and studies that aim at such findings are to be encouraged, just as showing that a proposed design violates known physical principles is an important part of engineering. In fact, when lawyers in the Office

---

[15]   William Twining and David Miers, *How To Do Things With Rules: A Primer of Interpretation*, 5th edition (Cambridge: Cambridge U.P., 2010).

of Parliamentary Counsel subject policy proposals to detailed analysis, looking for contradiction and incoherence, that is what they are doing. Critics, of course, believe that they are doing more, either establishing that the materials the law uses are themselves indeterminate, or demonstrating that the whole society within which law works is incoherent. The engineering template, however, throws a different light on those claims.

On the issue of indeterminacy, it seems reasonably clear that many legal devices do in fact work, in the sense that the objectives of those who designed them are achieved. In some cases, it is possible to believe that those objectives might have been achieved anyway, without the legal device having been made. For example, it is entirely possible that it makes no difference at all to what the parties do to draw up contractual documents for very simple transactions. But that is presumably why such transactions rarely attract lawyers' attention. In very complex deals where the contract acts as a plan (the Heathrow Terminal 5 contract for example) and in statutes authorising officials to act in ways in which they would otherwise have refused to act, it is difficult to deny that the creation of the legal device was a necessary condition of the end result. One can conclude that, whatever the degree of indeterminacy from which the legal system suffers, it is not sufficient in many circumstances to prevent the achievement of practical results. The question is then, from an engineering perspective, under what conditions does indeterminacy become a problem? One might posit, for example, that if contractual or statutory rules conveyed no information at all, it is difficult to see how they could have any effect. They must, therefore, convey some degree of determinate meaning to be successful. The question is what degree of play or tolerance can there be before a legal device becomes ineffective? One might speculate about the answer to that question, but it is ultimately an empirical one. It is, in fact, an example of a scientific project that legal engineering might generate.

There is also the question of how one might allow for the effects of such problems in the design of devices and how to design the device to control the effects of any variance. What if, for example, we include in a document some mechanism for deciding the meaning of unclear words and phrases? Does that increase or decrease the variance? Theorists of indeterminacy might say that it makes no difference, since if a word is of indeterminate meaning, a third party decider would have no more or less reason for saying what it meant than the parties themselves.[16] But the question is an empirical one, not one of literary theory. How much variance would

---

[16]   See e.g. Brian Leiter, 'Legal Indeterminacy' (1995) 1 Legal Theory 481–92, 482–83.

there be? How would that degree of variance affect the functioning of the device? And what if the decider was restricted to a set of kinds of reason that could be applied to the problem? Or what if the decider was someone who was chosen as someone likely to further the success of the deal or the policy aims of the legislature? One could not perhaps say that any of these methods would guarantee that the decider would always arrive at a single answer, and so might not count as 'determinate' for the purposes of the theorists, but they might reduce the variance and thus increase the useful-ness of the device. Furthermore, these empirical matters about which we presently know little also qualify as a scientific question that we, as legal engineers, would like answered.

Those brought up in the tradition of the Critical Legal Studies move-ment might at this point be protesting that there is no such thing as 'solid' or 'clear' law, that all legal rules are inherently contradictory and can only be stabilised by a political process that suppresses one possible set of meanings.[17] Critics argue that even the most fundamental legal concepts – 'property', 'obligation', even 'rule' itself – lack coherence because they are committed simultaneously to conflicting visions of society. But if the suppression of possible meanings happens in the same way for all those who apply them, including those who apply them to themselves, the practi-cal effect of the rules is still solid enough for design purposes. No doubt circumstances can arise in which the other possibilities are not suppressed and fundamental contradictions lead to instability in interpretation. In such cases, legal constructions built out of material will at that point fail. That makes legal constructions more vulnerable to failure than physical constructions, but, since those circumstances need not arise, it does not make them useless. Perfect theoretical coherence is not a necessary condi-tion of effectiveness, in law as much as in engineering.

In any case, even physical constructions eventually fail, and might fail earlier than expected if exposed to conditions more extreme than antici-pated or if their functioning depends on a flawed understanding of physi-cal processes, or, perhaps just as important, on a flawed understanding of human behaviour. Neither law nor engineering deals in the eternal. Even the very long term is rarely at stake. The most long term of legal construc-tions, the constitutions of states and international treaties, often include provisions for their own amendment or abrogation, and even when they contain no such provisions and so pretend on their face to be eternal, those who operate them know that ultimately their existence can be terminated,

---

[17]   See e.g. Mark Kelman, *A Guide to Critical Legal Studies* (Cambridge, MA: Harvard U.P., 1990) 12–13.

by political events if not by legal ones. Both engineers and lawyers build for purposes limited in time and space, and it is no disgrace if at some point their constructions need to be repaired or replaced.[18]

The critics' claim amounts to saying that the whole of the society in which the law operates is incoherent and somehow bound to fail, so that all legal devices are also bound to fail, whereas the engineering template would lead us to see the issue largely as one of the relationship between a device and its environment in an open system. If we take the claim that the whole of society is incoherent to be a claim that social conditions, including the most basic political and economic relationships, are unstable and might reconfigure radically without warning, the critics' claim amounts to saying that a legal device might fail if the environment within which it was designed to operate fundamentally changes. That is undoubtedly true. Contracts could not cope with the nationalisation of all economic resources. Constitutions rarely survive violent revolution.

But that is not the end of the story. The relationship between system and environment has more states than either perfect harmony or complete collapse. One of the lessons of the new and developing field of resilience engineering is that systems differ in their ability to adapt to external change and to return to previous levels of functioning.[19] Some systems are brittle, some resilient. Resilient systems have buffers against unexpected change, build in flexibility to adapt to change, maintain vigilance and openness to information about change in their environment and learn quickly from experience.[20] Brittle systems exhibit the opposite

---

[18]   This also applies to the constructions of the courts, in the form of case law – even though the doctrine of stare decisis seems to give the impression that the courts pronounce for all time. Cf. Alexander Bickel's remark in *The Least Dangerous Branch* that 'what one means by the ultimate, final judgment of the Court is quite frequently a judgment ultimate and final for a generation or two' (2nd edition (New Haven: Yale U.P., 1986) at 244).

[19]   See e.g. Erik Hollnagel, David Woods and Nancy Leveson (eds), *Resilience Engineering: Concepts and Precepts* (Aldershot: Ashgate, 2006), Scott Jackson, *Architecting Resilient Systems: Accident Avoidance and Survival and Recovery from Disruptions* (Hoboken, NJ: Wiley, 2010), Azad Madni and Scott Jackson, 'Towards a Conceptual Framework for Resilience Engineering' (2009) 3(2) IEEE Systems Journal 181–91, Erik Hollnagel, Christopher Nemeth and Sidney Dekker, *Resilience Engineering Perspectives, Volume 1: Remaining Sensitive to the Possibility of Failure* (Aldershot: Ashgate, 2008), Christopher Nemeth, Erik Hollnagel and Sidney Dekker, *Resilience Engineering Perspectives, Volume 2: Preparation and Restoration* (Aldershot: Ashgate, 2009).

[20]   See e.g. David Wood, 'The Essential Characteristics of Resilience' chapter 2 in Hollnagel, Woods and Leveson (2006), Madni and Jackson (2009), Christopher Nemeth, 'The Ability to Adapt', in Nemeth, Hollnagel and Dekker (2009).

characteristics. Many contracts may well be relatively brittle with regard to major political and economic change, largely because the timescale over which they are designed to work is too short to justify diverting resources to building in resilience against that sort of event (though they might well build in resilience about other types of change). But one would expect legal devices designed to work over long periods of time, for example constitutions, international treaties and some very long-term contracts, to be more resilient, and many of them are. For example, one can see the possibility of legal enforcement of constitutional provisions against political actors who violate them as a form of monitoring and early warning system that alerts the population to the fact that the system is being steered out of its safe area. In addition, constitutional amendment procedures build in a degree of flexibility that might allow constitutions to survive and even to incorporate and domesticate major political change. We are thus led into treating alleged incoherence in broader social, economic and political systems not as a refutation of the possibility of coherent, effective law but as a design challenge. It is also an opportunity for empirical research. In what circumstances have contracts and constitutions failed to recover from external shocks? In what circumstances and to what extent have they proved resilient? What can we learn from these failures and successes in terms of design principles? If such studies prove successful, given that resilience engineering itself is concerned with the role of humans in systems (for example as the sources both of accident precipitating errors and of the adaptability needed to recover from them) and thus ultimately with regulation and policy-making, there is every possibility that law and engineering might interconnect at this point in ways that go beyond analogy.

Law and the Social Sciences

The engineering template also provides legal researchers with a clear and stable view of what their relationship should be to other fields of knowledge, especially to the social sciences.

That relationship is currently hampered by a conception of legal research that fails to recognise that law is a design discipline and conceives of legal research as merely offering some kind of explanation of legal phenomena. Some, for example, hold that we should distinguish between 'internal' and 'external' explanations of the law. 'Internal' explanations of the law, whether of its current state or of its historical development, are explanations in legal terms, which usually means restricting the explanatory material to that which would itself be acceptable in argument before a judge (or, even more strictly, which would have been acceptable to a judge at the time of the event being explained). 'External' explanation is any other kind of explanation, including explanations which incorporate political, social, economic, psychological or biographical material. According to those who make the 'internal/external' distinction, it is entirely possible to do social science about law, but it is a different activity from the study of law itself from the 'internal' point of view.

Another 'explanatory' position holds, in sharp contrast, that law is itself one of the social sciences, with its own methodology and characteristic modes of explanation and fields of study, so that just as economics offers an economic explanation of events and sociology a sociological explanation, law offers a legal explanation. Just as economics studies the economy and sociology studies society, law studies the law.

Neither position is very satisfactory. The 'internal/external' distinction is inherently unstable. It depends on what counts as a legal argument, but the boundary between the acceptable and the non-acceptable differs not only from legal system to legal system but also across time in the same legal system. For example, economic argument is more acceptable in the USA than in England, but comparative law is more acceptable in England than in the USA. Academic research used to be unacceptable in England, except for the works of the great and dead, but now is routinely referred to. As a result, it is perfectly possible for an 'external' work 'about' law itself to become part of an 'internal' legal debate 'within' law. The 'law is a social science' position, however, seems inherently to confuse what people ought to do and what they in fact do. Legal rules are attempts to guide behaviour, but an attempt is different from a success, just as making a plan is different from carrying it out. The point of the exercise is certainly to change behaviour, but one cannot just assume that change will happen, or that when it does happen, law was the cause.

It makes more sense to think about the relationship between engineering and the fields of knowledge engineers use – originally the physical sciences, but now, as engineers have moved into thinking about sociotechnical systems, fields such as physiology, psychology and the social sciences. Engineers need to understand the systems into which they are inserting their designed object, as well as understanding the object itself. That understanding comes from the other disciplines. That is not to say, however, that engineering can be equated with those disciplines. As we described in Chapter 3, engineering has its own field of knowledge and, as a design discipline, has a distinct orientation to the world.

Legal researchers similarly need to understand the systems into which lawyers insert their devices. Better understanding of those systems should lead to better design. For the most part, better understanding of those systems is to be found in the social sciences – at least if those sciences can reach what might be called engineering standards of rigour and accuracy. But understanding those systems is not the same as legal design. That is the error made by Lasswell and McDougal in their equation of law with social science. Lawyers crucially also need to understand the material that they characteristically use, namely legal rules, and to be able to design with them. The need for the former means that research sometimes dismissed as merely 'descriptive' or 'black-letter' is, as we have seen, rather more important than it is currently given credit for. The need for the latter brings in the study of the lawyer's equivalent of sociotechnical systems, which requires understanding of many other fields, but it also requires an understanding of the processes and techniques of design itself, and, crucially, the interaction between the process of design and effects, or non-effects, in the world.

In this respect research programmes that take law-as-engineering as their starting point have much in common with 'New Legal Realism', an attempt to reconnect legal research with empirical social science research but in a way that retains a place for doctrine to be studied in its own right and an awareness that translating the social sciences into legal categories is far from straightforward.[21] New Legal Realism also places itself between pessimism about the effects of law, the view that law 'always fails', and over-optimism that assumes that legal change implies social change. But there are some differences (or since New Legal Realism is still a work-in-progress and is determinedly inclusive, perhaps it would be more accurate to say that law-as-engineering is a specific kind of New Legal Realism). In particular, New Legal Realism often operates at a grander level than law-as-engineering. New Legal Realism wants to understand law better through social science and to use that understanding to assist in implementing programmes of social reform. Law-as-engineering does not claim that interdisciplinary study leads to a better understanding of law itself, but merely to better lawyering. Moreover, that better lawyering will not necessarily be deployed in promoting programmes of social reform. It might lead only to better service for very specific clients in a very narrow set of circumstances. Some might attempt law-as-engineering at the grander levels of social reform, and legislative lawyers are often faced with clients who operate at those levels, but the law-as-engineering perspective also works in more modest, and less self-consciously progressive, ways than those favoured by many New Legal Realists.

---

[21]   See e.g. Howard Erlanger, Bryant Garth, Jane Larson, Elizabeth Mertz, Victoria Nourse and David Wilkins, 'Is it Time for a New Legal Realism?' [2005] Wisconsin Law Review 335–63 and the New Legal Realism website http://newlegalrealism.org/index.html.

The Normative Orientation of Legal Research

That is not to say, however, that the law-as-engineering perspective lacks the capacity to operate from a normative perspective. Like the engineering profession itself, academic engineering often assumes that its purpose is to benefit society.[22] Could there be an equivalent for academic lawyers? One difficulty academic lawyers face is that a professional code of ethics planted in the soil of the adversary system, bearing fruit marked 'justice', but tasting more of gladiatorial combat seems very ill-suited to the work of academics. But, as we saw in the previous chapter, a form of professional ethics for lawyers based on transactional practice, which would have much more in common with engineering ethics, produces very different results. If academic lawyers were to orientate their work to that form of ethics, namely the three principles of consent, maintaining the conditions for the rule of law and the avoidance of harm, together with the overarching principle of public welfare, we might have an equivalent place from which to start.

Academic lawyers might still object that 'public welfare' is, like 'justice', a politically contested term too dangerous to incorporate into the basic orientation of their research. But that danger already exists, obviously so in work that recommends statutory reform, but also more subtly in work that reconstructs existing law. In reconstructive work, the analyst can always say 'this is the law as it *really* is, not my view of what it ought to be', but in practice it is rare for an analyst to carry out a reconstructive exercise but at the end of it declare that the resulting position is so unsatisfactory that it should be rejected. Indeed, the purpose of reconstructive work is often to find ways of achieving reform without having to bother or rely on the legislature. It would be better to face the danger straightforwardly and to make one's assumptions explicit rather than, consciously or inadvertently, to smuggle conceptions of public welfare or justice into one's work surreptitiously.

Another instructive aspect of engineering research is its ability to work with outside partners, especially partners who are not governmental bodies, such as commercial interests and NGOs. Why should not academic lawyers work on using existing law to construct legal devices that achieve socially beneficial ends for private actors? Work on charities law, for example, might include inventing new structures for charities that allow them to

---

[22]   See e.g. 'The Department of Engineering seeks to benefit society by creating world-leading engineering knowledge that fosters sustainability, prosperity and resilience.' http://www.eng.cam.ac.uk/research/.

achieve their purposes more effectively. Work on company law might include designing new company structures in which certain principles of effective co-operation (for example fairness in remuneration) are built into the structure. Work on commercial contracts might include developing model contracts or contractual terms that better reflect the parties' current conceptions of their deals than the existing boilerplate terms and so will tend to reduce disputes. Indeed, some such work already takes place in the guise of consultancy, but it is treated as slightly shameful and not real academic work. It should rather be treated as a core legal academic activity. As with academic engineering's relationship with industry, tensions might arise between the requirements of commercial confidentiality and the requirements of academic publication, specifically around intellectual property rights, but those tensions can be managed satisfactorily much of the time.

The Future Law School

Using engineering as a template for academic legal research to some extent merely reclassifies what legal academics already do, albeit encouraging a redistribution of effort to currently neglected corners. But it also suggests a more radical new concept of a law faculty which sees itself as solving legal problems rather than just offering commentaries on them. Academic engineers not only study the design process for new useful objects, they can also take on the process itself and design their own useful objects. Applying that to law, the concept would be of a law school that takes on the task of generating new legal devices. It would operate as a kind of freelance Law Commission, except that it would not restrict itself to projects suggested by the government or to drafting statutes.

Like an engineering department, such a law school would aim at innovation based on developing an understanding both of problems and of solutions superior to that currently in use in practice, which would mean not only using existing social scientific knowledge but also driving advances in that knowledge. It would mean using the best systematic approaches to designing solutions drawn from the other design disciplines.

Also like an engineering department, such a law school might encourage research that requires teams of academics with different interests and skills to work together to solve design problems and create new devices. It would encourage work with external partners (governmental and non-governmental) but also work on academics' own initiatives. Indeed, given the modest costs of legal research, it could probably do much more of the latter than engineers can usually afford.

Such a law school could also develop new research methods. One difference between engineering and legal design we have come across repeatedly is that engineers can often more readily test their inventions before they are released into circulation, whereas lawyers simply have to hope that their ideas work. When Wachtell Lipton invented the poison pill, they had no wind tunnel or testbed to try it out on first. But law schools devoted to legal engineering might develop techniques for improving the chances that a new legal device might work in the wild – for example asking those expected to interpret new rules for themselves to test out new doctrines or statutory drafts, or developing simulation techniques that capture more systematically what lawyers do already, for example challenging assumptions by playing devil's advocate and thinking through possible future scenarios.[23] Ultimately we might even be able to create models of how new rules are interpreted and carry out virtual testing, a development which would, of course, have other valuable uses.

Such a law school might also reconsider its relationship with the profession. One minor point is that, currently, English law faculties tend to treat visiting judges, even junior ones, as minor deities, their every word assumed to contain deep insight into the law. Visiting barristers are treated with only a little less reverence. In sharp contrast, visiting partners of major law firms are often assumed merely to be recruiting students and are treated as opportunities for fundraising. That is a misunderstanding of how the law works and of who has interesting and important information about it. A more substantial point is that a law faculty with a more systematic approach to the analysis of problems and to the generation of solutions than the profession itself should be able not only to maintain better relations with the profession than those that currently obtain, but eventually to drive up standards in the profession.

TEACHING LAW

Law-as-engineering also has implications for legal education. The failure of law schools in the United States to prepare students for practice as transactions lawyers has frequently been noted, and some attempts have been made to improve the situation.[24] In England, there are fewer such

---

[23]   These techniques can be grouped into what is known in some circles as 'alternative analysis', and can include exercises such as 'red teaming', which involves setting up internal games to attack or defend a proposal. See e.g. Gregory Treverton, *Making Sense of Transnational Threats: Workshop Reports* (Santa Monica: RAND, 2005).

[24]   E.g. Daniel B. Bogart, 'The Right Way to Teach Transactional Lawyers:

complaints, but the big law firms still recruit large numbers of non-law graduates, as many as 30–40 per cent of their annual entry,[25] then push them through a one year 'graduate conversion' course to give them the basics, followed by a compressed seven-month legal practice course designed with the needs of the specific firm in mind.[26] Thereafter they rely on their own in-house training programmes. One can interpret that practice as itself indicating that English law firms see no great advantage for legal practice in studying for an English law degree.

The seven-month legal practice courses the big English law firms have devised for themselves are particularly interesting. The conventional legal practice course taken by prospective English solicitors consisted of a combination of elementary law (taught in a recipe-book fashion), instruction on how to fill in forms (those relevant to property transactions and litigation, for example), and some practical skills, such as how to maintain accounts. The courses influenced by the big firms are very different. They typically revolve around case-studies of transactions, attempting to familiarise students with the materials needed to make the transaction work and the problems that might arise. They teach the law through transactions rather than teaching the law abstractly and then 'applying' it to a dispute. These courses approach law essentially from an engineering perspective.

It seems clear that university law degrees are failing to satisfy law-firm demand for training in transactional law. How should universities react? In the US, some law schools, notably Columbia, building on Ronald Gilson's idea of lawyers as transactions costs engineers, have responded by attempting to incorporate into the curriculum the knowledge and skills necessary for making deals.[27] In England, however, no major university law faculty

---

Commercial Leasing and the Forgotten "Dirt Lawyer"' (2000) 62 University of Pittsburgh Law Review 335–66, Tina Stark, 'Thinking Like a Deal Lawyer' (2004) 54 Journal of Legal Education 223–34, David Snyder, 'Closing the Deal in Contracts – Introducing Transactional Skills in the First Year' (2002–2003) 34 University of Toledo Law Review 689–97. See also Roger Dennis, 'Commentary: The Epistemology of Corporate Securities Lawyering: Beliefs, Biases and Organizational Behavior' (1997) 63 Brooklyn Law Review 677–84.

[25] E.g., according to a survey in *The Lawyer* in 2008, Linklaters (40 per cent) (http://www.thelawyer.com/linklaters/128777.article) Freshfields (35 per cent), (http://www.thelawyer.com/freshfields-bruckhaus-deringer/128739.article), Clifford Chance (30 per cent) http://www.thelawyer.com/clifford-chance/128706.article, and Eversheds (40 per cent) (http://www.thelawyer.com/eversheds/128726.article). The OPC also takes a considerable proportion of non-law graduates.

[26] See e.g. Allen & Overy, *Becoming a Lawyer at Allen & Overy,* (http://www.allenovery.com/AOWeb/binaries/28904.pdf).

[27] Victor Fleischer, 'Deals: Bringing Corporate Transactions into the Law School Classroom' (2002) 2 Columbia Business Law Review 475–97.

seems to have adopted the idea.[28] Moreover, even in the US, no law school seems to have applied the approach beyond the confines of contract and corporate law. No one seems to have instituted an engineering approach to, for example, public and constitutional law.[29] An approach to legal education that assumed from its start, and not just near its end, that lawyers in all fields need to be able to construct and to draft effective legal devices would, perhaps surprisingly, break new ground.[30]

Why might there be resistance to making law-as-engineering the starting point for university education in law? There are some practical problems, as Columbia experienced – appropriate materials are scarce, students need to learn not just about the law but also about business, and, most of all, existing teaching staff often lack relevant skills and experience – but they are not insuperable. In England there might be a further problem that the Bar, which has less of a stake in transactional law than the solicitors' profession, has equal representation with solicitors on the body that controls the recognition of law degrees, but the situation is far from hopeless since the combined total of lay and academic members outnumbers each profession.[31] The main barrier, however, is ideological. In particular, the dominant view, even in England, seems to be that it is no bad thing that academic law degrees are distant from legal practice. Academic law, the conventional view holds, should be autonomous of the profession and that autonomy is enhanced if university courses in law are not controlled by the profession.[32]

---

[28]   An honourable mention, however, might be made of the School of Law at the University of Northumbria, which runs an innovative programme combining the academic and professional stages of English legal education and incorporating a student law office in which students work for real clients across the normal range of solicitors' work.

[29]   Though one should note the existence of an LLM in legislative drafting at Institute for Advanced Legal Studies, taught largely by UK practitioners (http://ials.sas.ac.uk/postgrad/courses/cls_MA.htm).

[30]   It might also be more interesting for students – it would involve a more active style of learning and might easily incorporate new technology. For an approach that might be developed in this direction, see Gregory Silverman, 'Law Games: the Importance of Virtual Worlds and Serious Video Games for the Future of Legal Education' in Edward Rubin (ed.), *Legal Education in the Digital Age* (Cambridge: Cambridge U.P., 2012).

[31]   http://www.barstandardsboard.org.uk/qualifying-as-a-barrister/academic-stage/joint-academic-stage-board/jasb-membership/.

[32]   For a fleeting glimpse of this view, see e.g. Fiona Cownie, 'The Academic Stage of Training for Entry into the Legal Profession in England and Wales: Response by the Society of Legal Scholars to a Consultation by the Law Society of England and Wales and the General Council of the Bar of England and Wales with

There is a version of the autonomy thesis that maintains that 'Law professors are not paid to train lawyers, but to study the law and to teach their students what they happen to find'.[33] Somewhat less committed to methodological anarchy, but still committed to the autonomy of academic law is the view one hears frequently in law faculty common rooms that law students study an academic discipline in the same way that history students study history or philosophy students study philosophy.[34] The point of courses in academic law is claimed to be the same as that of all courses in academic disciplines at degree level, namely to give instruction in the methods of thought characteristic of those disciplines. Ultimately, according to this view, what matters is mastery of a method, rather than knowledge of any specific set of facts, for what is valuable about mastery of an academic method is that it shows that one can direct and control one's thinking, not that one has acquired specific knowledge. Law as an academic discipline, on this view, should concentrate not on the place law degrees have in the education and training of lawyers, but on cultivating and refining its own distinctive method.

There are several problems with this academic purist response. One, which might be thought merely tactical but which is serious nonetheless, is that if one holds that law is just another academic discipline, and it turns out to be true that as a preparation for the practical world of lawyering, studying law as an academic discipline is no better than studying any other discipline, student demand for law degrees will ultimately depend solely on the inherent interest of the subject matter. It is difficult to believe that, if students choose purely on the basis of intellectual interest, law will have many takers. Furthermore, if government funding is involved (which in

---

Law Faculties offering Qualifying Law Degrees'http://www.legalscholars.ac.uk/ documents/SLS%20Reply%20HoDs.doc, which robustly asserts: 'Law is funded [by the Higher Education Funding Council for England] to provide a general tertiary level education. It is not funded to provide for the training needs of specific legal or other professions' (at 1); 'Members of the Society of Legal Scholars [the association of UK legal academics] are, as the name of the Society suggests, expert academic lawyers whose realm of expertise encompasses making judgements about the appropriate content of curricula. . . . The Society regards the detail of the Law curriculum in institutions of higher education as lying squarely within the expertise of its members' (at 2); and 'The Society of Legal Scholars is firmly of the view that it would be extremely undesirable for the professional bodies to specify more detail in relation to the knowledge content of qualifying law degrees' (at 3).

[33] Owen Fiss, quoted in Tamanaha (2006) at 152.

[34] See e.g. Fiona Cownie and Alan Paterson, 'Evidence Submitted by the Society of Legal Scholars to the Review of the Regulatory Framework for Legal Services in England and Wales' p 2 (http://www1.legalscholars.ac.uk/education/ clementi.pdf).

England at least used to be the case), and law is no better than English, history or chemistry in producing employable lawyers, it is also difficult to see why university law teaching should receive public support.

But there is a more fundamental objection. If one attempts to understand a person, a society or a state using only law, one comes across the insuperable problem that the law's requirements are not automatically mirrored by human behaviour. Legal duties might or might not be fulfilled, legal powers might or might not be used. One cannot read off social or political facts from legal facts. That means that if one treats law as a method of understanding the world, the only aspect of the world it can help one understand is the law itself. For some, this result is a matter of comfort and even pride, but it gives rise to a sharp difference between law and other disciplines. In other disciplines, the methods employed are designed to achieve knowledge about subject matter that goes beyond knowledge about the discipline itself. A physicist is not trying to find out more about 'physics' but more about the physical universe. A historian is trained to find out about the past, not just about historical writing. Even economists, who sometimes give the impression that their only task is to expand their understanding of mathematics, sometimes remember that their real purpose is to understand aspects of human behaviour.[35] 'The economy' and 'society' might be constructs of the disciplines of economics and sociology, but those constructs themselves are ultimately aimed at understanding human behaviour beyond the disciplines themselves. By comparison, the conception of law as a pure academic discipline seems exceptionally inward-looking and self-referential. It cannot expand our understanding of ourselves or of the universe. On that conception law becomes a kind of radically inapplicable mathematics, interested only in itself and determined to separate itself from any use, even scientific use.

The mistake, of course, is to assume that law is a discipline concerned with understanding the world. It is concerned instead with affecting the world. It is fundamentally a design discipline. But the world it seeks, not always successfully, to affect is not the legal world – indeed there are interesting difficulties raised by trying to understand the law itself as an

---

[35] See the collection of essays in Uskai Maki (ed.), *Fact and Fiction in Economics: Models, Realism and Social Construction* (Cambridge: Cambridge U.P., 2002) for the state of debate in economics even before the traumas of the Crash. It might not be too much of a caricature to describe the debate in that collection as one between Partha Dasgupta, whose essay claims that 90 per cent of the articles published in the major economics journals are about 'the real world' and Maki, whose contribution is to question whether economists have a grip on what counts as 'reality'.

attempt to change the law – but the world of human behaviour. Others have observed that the methods of law as a discipline, especially doctrinal analysis, have always themselves arisen from central concerns of the legal profession.[36] Even more important, however, is the fact that the legal profession itself exists only because of the purposes of its clients, whether individuals or the state, purposes that are intrinsically practical. To cut the study of law off from the world of human behaviour is therefore perverse. It denatures the subject. Medicine makes no sense except in the context of human health. Engineering makes no sense except in the context of the physical tasks humans want to accomplish. So law makes no sense outside the context of the human purposes it attempts to fulfil. Those purposes inevitably take the study of law outside the narrow bounds of the law itself.

There is an intellectual tradition, including for example, the autopoiesis theory of law,[37] that maintains that the social world outside the law can only become active within the law if it undergoes a form of translation that tames it and corrals it into legal categories. That might be true of the characterisation of facts for the purpose of the application of rules – which must always be reshaped, at least by the suppression of many details, to fit the requirements of legal analysis. But it is not true of the purposes people have in wanting to use the law. Those purposes, which are crucial to understanding what law is for, need no translation into legal language to be relevant to the task of legal construction. It might be that certain types of purpose are very difficult or even impossible to satisfy in certain legal systems – for example, it is very difficult in the English legal system to draft a statutory power completely immune to judicial review (though that did not prevent an attempt at just that in 2004)[38] – but the purpose itself remains relevant to the task of design.

The problem, however, is that for the most part legal education as currently delivered, at least in England, takes into account human purposes in a haphazard and essentially undisciplined way. Purposes can be invoked in almost any course – the purposes of legislators, contractors, or litigants, for example – but without any attempt at systematically studying what purposes people are likely to have in reality. English textbooks aimed at students are not as hostile as they used to be to incorporating material

---

[36] See Douglas Vick, 'Interdisciplinarity and the Discipline of Law' (2004) 31 *Journal of Law and Society* 163–93.

[37] See e.g. Gunther Teubner (ed.), *Autopoietic Law: A New Approach to Law and Society* (Berlin/ New York: de Gruyter/ EUI, 1987).

[38] Clause 11 of the Asylum and Immigration Bill 2004.

from the social sciences,[39] but students are generally not invited to think about the social sciences in a systematic way, to consider, for example, the limitations of their methods and results. The relationship between law and the social sciences in England is still at the 'bricoleur' stage reached by American Legal Realism many decades ago.[40] It is here that legal education could develop. Just as engineers need to be familiar with the physical sciences they rely on, lawyers should be familiar with economics, politics, sociology and psychology, not in a spirit of pure curiosity but with conscious attention to the relevance to legal design of the types of knowledge these disciplines might be capable of, and, just as important, might not be capable of, producing. There might also be a place in legal education for more particularistic attempts at understanding human purposes, such as history.

But the analogy with engineering education goes deeper. Engineering education is not merely scientific education. Engineering students learn science to use it, for which purpose they need to learn about specifically engineering tasks, such as design. Similarly, the disciplines that help lawyers to understand the purposes of their clients are not the same as law itself. Legal techniques are important in themselves and there is legal knowledge entirely separate from social scientific or historical knowledge. The object of the exercise is not to produce policy analysts with no conception of the law itself, but rather to produce better educated lawyers, who can do better than common-sense or guesswork in understanding what clients and their counterparties want and what can and cannot be achieved through law. But how to achieve those purposes through legal design is a distinct and separate task for which specifically legal education is required.

The law-as-engineering perspective does not, therefore, require doctrinal studies to be abandoned, which is what the Lasswell–McDougal approach seemed to require. On the contrary, it provides a good reason for continuing with them, since doctrine lies at the heart of legal design. Even devices that are deliberately designed not to be legally binding can only be made by those who know what is and what is not legally enforceable. It might be that knowledge of whether a structure is binding is not enough to know what practical effect it will have, since not only might non-binding structures nevertheless have real world effects but also binding structures might

---

[39] For a good example of an eclectic approach, see Jonathan Herring, *Family Law* (London: Pearson, 2007) especially 8–44.

[40] See e.g. N.E.H. Hull, *Roscoe Pound and Karl Llewellyn: Searching for an American Jurisprudence* (Chicago: University of Chicago Press, 1997) at 10–11.

have no effects because of real world considerations about, for example, the costs of enforcement or the reputational or relational consequences of attempting to enforce. But that knowledge is always relevant to the question of the structure's practical effects and attempting to devise a structure without it is like attempting to build a brick wall without knowing about cement: it might work, but only with enormous amounts of luck.

One aspect of doctrine needs further consideration. The real world effectiveness of legal doctrine depends in large part on the common understanding of lawyers about what the law says. That common understanding – what one lawyer can expect another lawyer will advise someone else the law says – is not necessarily the same as advanced academic opinion about what the law says (or ought to say). As Karl Llewellyn's principal, the counsel to a bank, might have said, what matters is not what a lawyer as brilliant as Karl Llewellyn might persuade a judge the law means, but what other lawyers who are counsel to banks take the law to mean. A consequence of that for legal education, no doubt unwelcome to many academic lawyers, is that students are best served by learning about conventional interpretations of the law, no matter how unsatisfactory those interpretations may be. 'Better' interpretations need to come with a warning that they might not work in practice. In other words, a certain lack of adventure in teaching is neither to be disparaged nor despised.

Another probably unwelcome point should be made. There is a tendency currently for law teachers to highlight the difficult and the uncertain aspects of their subject-matter. Such an approach adds to the interest of lectures and sets up challenging examination questions. For a law school that seeks to teach law as litigation, its ultimate justification is that difficult and uncertain issues are central to law conceived of as litigation. They provide the raw material out of which disputes are made and provide perfect practice materials for future litigators. But if one is interested in constructing working legal devices, the difficult and the uncertain are the opposite of perfect practice materials. They are, ex hypothesi, unreliable materials the use of which has uncertain results. The principal reason a legal engineer would want to know anything at all about the uncertain and the difficult is to be able to identify such unreliable materials and avoid them. Engineering courses on materials teach what is known about existing materials, not speculation about the properties of materials not yet developed.[41] Similarly, legal engineers need to know principally

---

41   See e.g. http://www.eng.cam.ac.uk/teaching/courses/y1/P2-M.html http://www.eng.cam.ac.uk/teaching/courses/y2/P3-Mat.html and http://www.eng.cam.ac.uk/teaching/courses/y3/3c1.html.

about the properties of existing doctrines, not those of doctrines yet to be developed. The problem for legal education is that, currently, teaching the aspects of the law about which we are most certain is far from a high status activity. Just as legal research aimed at the accurate exposition of solid law has been unjustly condemned as 'descriptive', so teaching solid law has been unjustly characterised as the equivalent of 'service' teaching, close to teaching easy law for non-lawyers. But if one takes as the test of a good lawyer not to be the advocate's ability to persuade a court but the transactions lawyer's ability to construct a successful device, what matters is less the ability of lawyers to speculate about the uncertain and more their ability to create solutions with what they have. It follows that what makes a course interesting should not be the marginality of what is taught but the difficulty of the problems it offers for solution.

One further consequence might be that instead of tacking on to the end of basic courses some speculation about uncertain and difficult questions arising out of the material just taught, we might teach additional solid, even if dull, material about further topics. For example, English courses in the law of obligations now often end with academically rarefied discussions about the law of restitution, a practice now validated by the profession, which has been persuaded that the law of restitution forms a part of the law of obligations as important as that of contract and tort. But, given the uncertainty and difficulty of the law of restitution in England, its usefulness as material in legal construction remains relatively low. One wonders whether it might be better instead to introduce students to some solid, even if elementary, information about materials of more immediate use, such as intellectual property rights.

Teaching Legal Ethics

An even more important implication of the law-as-engineering perspective for legal education concerns ethics. The ethical formation of lawyers should take into account what lawyers actually do. That means more emphasis on questions of consent, the conditions for maintaining the rule of law, harm avoidance and public benefit and less on the peculiar conditions of litigation. The central conflicts of lawyers' lives, beyond the obvious one between their own interests and those of their clients, are, as we saw in Chapter 4, not so much between the claims of their clients and the claims of their clients' opponents as between the claims of their clients and claims of the rest of the world.

At its most basic level, the law-as-engineering perspective teaches that lawyers bestow power on their clients. Consequently, the nearest parallel for the kind of ethical education law students should be exposed to is, perhaps, that offered at the best Schools of Government or Public Policy. At the Kennedy School at Harvard, for example, Masters in Public Policy students are required to take a course on 'The Responsibilities of Public Action' that includes elements law students could usefully study – for example taking responsibility for the consequences of one's actions, the problem of diluting responsibility by involving many hands in a decision and whistleblowing – all of which were relevant to the decisions lawyers made in the City of London and Wall Street in the early years of the 21st century.

Moreover, the most familiar problem of legal ethics – the extent to which lawyers should invoke their special role in society as a defence against the demands of ordinary morality[42] – is itself a special case of the problem of the extent to which different moral standards apply to those involved in making public decisions,[43] and law students might usefully consider it both from their own point of view and that of one of their most important clients, the state. Indeed there is a case for lawyers to have some insight into the ethical problems that face, or perhaps ought to face, all of their clients – including businesses and banks. It is an ethical problem in itself whether one should help someone else to breach their own moral duties.

In passing, we might note a specifically English issue. Currently, unlike students in many other jurisdictions, English law students are not required to receive any teaching about ethics in their undergraduate law degrees, and virtually no ethical education of any kind happens in practice.[44] It is sometimes assumed that this omission results from English legal academics' acceptance of the view that the role of a law faculty is solely to teach knowledge of the law and skill in manipulating legal rules.[45] It is certainly the case that the dominant mode of legal thought in English law schools is a form of positivism, which aims to separate legal and ethical judgment. But positivism, far from obstructing the teaching of legal ethics,

---

[42] See e.g. Deborah Rhode, 'Ethical Perspectives on Legal Practice' (1985) 37 Stanford Law Review 589–652, James Fleming, 'The Lawyer as Citizen' (2000–2001) 70 Fordham Law Review 1699–716, Thomas Huff, 'The Temptations of Creon: Philosophical Reflections on the Ethics of the Lawyer's Professional Role' (1985) 46 Montana Law Review 47–77.

[43] See e.g. Thomas Nagel, 'Ruthlessness in Public Life', in *Mortal Questions* (Cambridge: Cambridge U.P., 1991).

[44] See Kim Economides and Justine Rogers, *Preparatory Ethics Training for Future Solicitors* (London: Law Society, 2009) at 19.

[45] Economides and Rogers at 11. For a more radical version of this position, see Stanley Fish, *Save the World on Your Own Time* (Oxford: Oxford U.P., 2008). See also Anthony Bradney, *Conversations, Choices and Chances: the Liberal Law School in the Twenty-first Century* (Oxford: Hart, 2003) 53–56.

arguably assists it, because it allows ethics about law to stand as a subject separate from identification of the law. Another possible explanation is that academics in England might be peculiarly attached to the idea that virtue cannot be taught,[46] but there is no particular evidence for that hypothesis. On the contrary, English universities readily teach medical ethics to medical students and engineering ethics to engineering students.[47] Another possibility is that English legal academics lack the confidence of their medical and engineering counterparts to discuss the ethical problems of practice precisely because they have distanced themselves from practice more than academics in those other disciplines. The problem with that as a complete explanation is that ethics was not taught even when large numbers of academic posts were held by current practitioners, although it might be a partial explanation of the situation now. A fuller explanation, however, might be that at the time the legal professions first intervened to standardise law degree courses neither they nor legal academics considered ethics to be a problem, but by the time the omission began to be remarked on, legal academics, resenting further constraints on the curriculum, and perhaps at that time conscious of their increasing distance from practitioners, found it convenient to argue that there was no space in the timetable for additional required courses.[48]

The post-graduate legal practice element of English legal education does insist on some study of legal ethics, but only in the form of understanding existing professional standards.[49] It consists of what some researchers have called 'ethics as law' or 'the law of lawyering', namely the teaching of ethics not as reflection on what one ought to do or as meta-ethics (what are the

---

[46] Debate on the view that values cannot be taught goes back to Plato, of course (especially in *Meno*), but its influence on legal ethics continues. See e.g. Vittorio Olgiati, 'Can Legal Ethics Become a Matter of Academic Teaching? Critical Observations from a Late-Modern Perspective', in Kim Economides *Ethical Challenges to Legal Education and Conduct* (Oxford: Hart, 1998). Cf. in a business context, Wesley Cragg, 'Teaching Business Ethics: The Role of Ethics in Business and in Business Education' (1997) 16 Journal of Business Ethics 231–45. But see generally, Thomas Ryan and Jeremy Bisson, 'Can Ethics be Taught?' (2011) 2 International Journal of Business and Social Science 12–52, which provides some interesting empirical evidence.

[47] Ethics education is required for UK medical students at undergraduate level. See General Medical Council, *Tomorrow's Doctors* (2009) at 25–26. Ethics teaching to UK engineering undergraduate students is not yet universal, but it has at least started. See the survey conducted by the Royal Academy of Engineering (http://www.raeng.org.uk/news/releases/pdf/Teaching_of_Ethics.pdf).

[48] See Nick Wikeley 'The Law Degree and the BVC' (2004) The Reporter – The Newsletter of the Society of Legal Scholars 23–24.

[49] Economides and Rogers (2009) at 25–28.

theories about what one ought to do?) but as learning the rules of professional codes as if they were legal rules.[50] Some writers favour the 'law of
lawyering' approach as a way of holding lawyers' attention to ethical issues.
But the law-as-engineering approach leads one away from that approach.
In a transactions or legislative context, to treat ethical codes merely as
another set of rules to be used for particular ends – the lawyers' ends or
perhaps the clients' ends – seems to miss the point that the public interest
needs to be constructed and respected. Moreover, in those contexts, the
'ethics as law' approach is self-defeating. The question of how one should
use one's power to manipulate rules cannot be answered by further instruction in the manipulation of rules. That infinite regress can only be avoided
by adopting a different approach at some stage.

Leaving ethics until the professional stage of a lawyer's education is also
a problem in itself. It gives the impression that ethics is merely a technical
matter to be dealt with at the last minute, rather than something integral
to the lives of those who will work in the law.[51] If we are to inculcate a
new professional ethic of public welfare in the law, and to embed it in how
lawyers react to the tasks they take on, we need to start earlier, to begin as
soon as young lawyers come into contact with the law. One might add that
a single course, or even a series of courses in each year of study, might not
be enough to establish a new ethical principle and that it might be necessary to incorporate ethical questioning of the role of lawyers in furthering
public welfare into every substantive course.[52] Some of the most ethically
aware university teachers of law do this already, for example raising with
students of commercial law the question of what they would do if their
client asked them to carry out a transaction highly damaging to the interests of third parties, but for the most part these issues remain unexplored.

A 'Liberal Legal Education'

Much of the discussion about legal education in UK universities has
centred on the concept of a 'liberal legal education'.[53] 'Liberal' here is not

---

[50] For discussion see e.g. Alice Woolley and Sara Bagg, 'Ethics Teaching in Law
School' (2007) 1 Canadian Legal Education Annual Review 85–114.
[51] It might be noted that the same problem arises if ethics is taken only
as a third year requirement. See David Luban and Michael Milleman, 'Good
Judgment: Ethics Teaching in Dark Times' (1995–96) 9 Georgetown Journal of
Legal Ethics 31–87, 37–38.
[52] D. Richard O'Dair, 'Ethics by the Pervasive Method: the Case of Contract'
(1997) 17 Legal Studies 305–22.
[53] The literature is extensive. One might cite in particular W.T. Stallybrass,

meant in a political sense (although some writers seem to have confused it with various meanings of political liberalism)[54] but rather in the sense that pervades John Henry Newman's *The Idea of a University*, namely the imparting of 'liberal knowledge' defined thus:

> [T]hat alone is liberal knowledge, which stands on its own pretensions, which is independent of sequel, expects no complement, refuses to be *informed* (as it is called) by any end, or absorbed into any art, in order duly to present itself to our contemplation. The most ordinary pursuits have this specific character, if they are self-sufficient and complete; the highest lose it, when they minister to something beyond them.[55]

Although liberal knowledge in this sense has no utility apart from its own inherent value, a liberal education itself has a purpose, namely to inculcate a 'habit of mind', which Newman describes in these terms:

'Law in the Universities' (1948) [N.S.1] Journal of the Society of the Public Teachers of Law 157–69, Bob Hepple, 'The Liberal Law Degree' (1996) 55 Cambridge Law Journal 470–87, Roger Brownsword, 'Teaching Contract: A Liberal Agenda', in Peter Birks (ed.) *Examining the Law Syllabus: The Core* (Oxford: Oxford U.P., 1992) and Bradney (2003).

[54]   E.g. Fiona Cownie, 'Alternative Values in Legal Education' (2003) 6 Legal Ethics 159:

> 'A central tenet of the traditional version of liberalism, as applied in higher education, was that the focus was exclusively on intellectual, rather than moral development. Newman suggested that it was not only naive, but also misguided, to expect that intellectual development would of necessity be accompanied by a corollary moral development. For Newman, the development of the intellect is the concern of the academy, the development of a moral sense the domain of the Church. Liberal education itself was morally neutral, a view which persists to the present time.'

(See also Bradney (2003) at 53 and Fiona Cownie, 'Exploring Values in Legal Education' (2011) Web Journal of Current Legal Issues).

As an account of Newman's views, this leaves much to be desired. He certainly thought that a liberal education was no guarantee of virtue. It produced, he claimed, neither a Christian nor a Catholic but a 'gentleman' (*The Idea of a University* (London: Longmans, 1907) at 120). But Newman's main purpose in writing *The Idea of a University* was to justify the inclusion of theology as a university subject, against those, including the founders of University College London, who maintained that it was not a suitable subject for university study. Newman contended that theology was just as much a science as astronomy (at 42), for it was the science of the knowledge of God. Since he also believed that there is moral truth (e.g. at 193) and that theology was essential in the apprehension of such moral truth, it is difficult to classify him as a relativistic liberal who wanted to separate moral and scientific education.

[55]   Newman (1907) Discourse 5.

A habit of mind is formed which lasts through life, of which the attributes are, freedom, equitableness, calmness, moderation, and wisdom.[56]

Beyond that, Newman claims that if one needs to assign a purpose to a liberal education outside its value to individuals, it is 'the training of good members of society', 'the art of social life' and 'fitness for the world'.[57] Newman maintains that his version of a liberal education aims at 'raising the intellectual tone of society, at cultivating the public mind, at purifying the national taste, at supplying true principles to popular enthusiasm and fixed aims to popular aspiration, at giving enlargement and sobriety to the ideas of the age, at facilitating the exercise of political power, and refining the intercourse of private life'.[58]

In short, a liberal education is one fit for life as, and makes one fit to be, a free person, a gentleman, someone who is in no sense 'servile'.[59]

For many British legal academics, these ideas are a cause of great anxiety. The wide acceptance within the English universities of Newmanesque views of what universities do presents a constant threat to the legitimacy of legal academics' presence in the universities.[60] As recently as 2012, Stefan Collini, a leading British intellectual historian, although himself acutely aware of the limitations of Newman's views, described universities as institutions engaged in 'post-secondary school education, where "education" signals something more than professional training' and 'advanced scholarship or research whose character is not wholly dictated by the need to solve immediate practical problems'.[61] The problem for legal academics is that legal education is always in danger of being accused of being, in Newman's terms, dependent on sequel, informed by an end and absorbed into an art, namely that of the practising lawyer or the judge.

Newman himself conceded that he was not arguing that universities should not teach law or medicine,[62] but only that those subjects should be

---

[56]   Newman (1907) Discourse 5.
[57]   Newman (1907) at 177.
[58]   Newman (1907) at 177–78.
[59]   Newman (1907) at 106.
[60]   See Bradney (2003) at 3–6.
[61]   Stefan Collini, *What are Universities for?* (London: Penguin, 2012) chapter 1 part 2. For his well-balanced account of Newman and Newman's relevance now, see chapter 3. It is worth mentioning that although teaching and research remain central to what universities do, their internal functioning has become immensely more complex than in Newman's time and they have a number of subsidiary outputs, many of which revolve around intellectual property – traditionally publishing but now patents.
[62]   Newman (1907) at 166.

taught for the higher purposes of liberal education and not for the sake of their usefulness in any 'low, mechanical, [or] mercantile sense'. But that is little comfort for academic lawyers. All it means is that the spectre of being accused of conducting a trade school constantly hangs over them and that they have to make strenuous efforts to persuade their colleagues that legal education can be 'liberal' in Newman's sense, or, using Collini's slightly easier test, as providing 'more than professional training' and engaging in research 'not wholly dictated' by practical concerns. Calling law a form of engineering, of course, will only make things worse, because many academic lawyers, like many scientists and others in academia, see engineering itself as the essence of the 'low, mechanical [and] mercantile'. Worse, as C.P. Snow put it, since some scientists in particular see engineering as fit only for 'second-rate minds',[63] academic lawyers might see the comparison as a threat to their standing as intellectuals.

But, at least if one strips away the snobbish rhetoric about the 'low' nature of the 'mechanical' and the 'mercantile', not an unusual theme in Newman's 19th century England,[64] there is nothing in Newman's desired 'habit of mind' that one would not hope for in a lawyer or an engineer. What better description could there be of the best senior partners of large law firms and of senior Parliamentary Counsel than 'freedom, equitableness, calmness, moderation, and wisdom'. One might also require some technical skill, especially of the latter, but possessing that skill seems to pose no obvious threat to the habit of mind itself. Where is the contradiction between them?

Newman's position, however, seems to be that his desired habit of mind needs to be inculcated before taking on a profession. His liberal education 'prepares [one] to fill any post with credit, and to master any subject with facility',[65] but to take on professional training first, he implies, leads to a narrowing, just as teaching professional subjects outside a university narrows teachers.[66] Especially in England, where law is taught to

---

[63]   C.P. Snow, *The Two Cultures* (Cambridge: Cambridge U.P., 1998) 32. Snow was referring to 'applied science' rather than engineering, but he consistently made the error of equating the two.

[64]   See Martin Wiener, *English Culture and the Decline of the Industrial Spirit* (Cambridge, Cambridge U.P., 2004) especially at 177. One does not have to assent to Wiener's controversial claims about the effects of anti-commercial culture on Britain's economic performance to accept his points about its existence.

[65]   Newman (1907) at 178.

[66]   Newman (1907) at 166–68. One might very much doubt Newman's contention that university teaching is broadened by the presence of other disciplines. Since Newman's time, the opposite has happened. University research and teaching has become increasingly specialised and compartmentalised.

undergraduates and not just to graduates, the question arises for the follower of Newman of how it might be possible to teach a professional subject such as law without narrowing the student and preventing the development of his desired habit of mind.

The conventional answer to the question of how to teach law without narrowing the students is to teach it as much as possible without reference to the concerns of the legal profession, to teach it as an academic discipline in itself. But we have already seen the drawbacks of that position. Law cannot be understood without considering broader human purposes, but as soon as one considers those purposes, one moves into the concerns of the profession, at least the majority of the profession.

A different answer might lie in doing the exact opposite of attempting to insulate the universities from the profession. If students encounter the law from the start as the material out of which useful devices are made, it will be easier, not harder, for them to understand why good lawyers approach the law with Newman's habit of mind, and why studying the law requires objectivity and intellectual honesty. Honing one's intellectual skills in a field apparently without consequences for other people is not obviously better for coming to realise the value of self-criticism and self-discipline than doing so in a field in which the wider consequences should be obvious from the start. One can see how an emphasis on litigation and deciding cases might bring about a very different conclusion – that excessive attention to the immediate consequences of judicial decisions (joy on one side, misery on the other) might lead teachers of law to want their students to distance themselves from the emotional content of the situation (a process arguably necessary for students to understand the difference between being a lawyer and being a politician, but once accurately described as stealing students' souls.)[67] The time-honoured practice of teaching using hypotheticals whose cast of characters have unreal or even jokey names is a good example of dehumanising abstraction. But teaching law from a legal engineering perspective changes the relevance and effects of using the perspective of the profession. The problems under scrutiny are no longer zero-sum conflicts, whose emotional elements constitute a threat to objective judgment, but potentially positive-sum situations in which the role being adopted requires from the start an integration of empathy with the client's purposes and objectivity about how they might be achieved.

---

[67] Peter Goodrich 'Of Blackstone's Tower: Metaphors of Distance and Histories of English Law Schools' in Peter Birks (ed.) *Pressing Problems in the Law (2): What Are Law Schools For?* (Oxford: Oxford U.P. 1987).

Freedom

One anxiety about whether a legal engineering education would count as
liberal in Newman's sense might be that, although it is clear how 'equitableness, calmness, moderation, and wisdom' are desirable traits of professional advisers, it might be less clear how legal education might promote
'freedom'. 'Freedom' in Newman's sense seems to be connected with the
Ciceronian notion of leisure – 'free from necessary duties or cares'.[68] His
point seems to be that the search for truth requires a state of mind free
from worldly constraints. Given that the state of mind of a lawyer in a
major firm is rarely free from worldly constraints, a follower of Newman
might fear that to import the profession's point of view into legal education would be to accept too freely that the quality of legal work can be
limited by considerations of time and money. The same objection might
apply to engineering at the point engineering students are taught that
cost is a legitimate factor in design. But one might respond in two ways
to that anxiety. First, the constraints of cost in design are not freedom-
denying emotions but facts about the world that one can assess in a spirit
of calmness, moderation and wisdom. Second, although universities also
experience limits imposed by the availability of money and people, the
relative leisure of academic research can provide opportunities to create
legal devices that can serve as exemplars for students in their later life –
establishing work done in close to ideal conditions as a standard against
which students can later judge their own work, made in less than ideal
conditions.

The relative freedom of the university also explains why law (and engineering, and medicine) might meet Stefan Collini's rather easier tests for
what counts as university work. Collini himself goes on to propose a
defence of universities essentially in terms of timescales – that they are
repositories of modes of understanding and values that, although possibly
of no immediate use or relevance, need to be preserved and passed on as
part of a larger project of humanity understanding itself.[69] University
lawyers and engineers, both students and teachers, should be able to work
to much longer timescales than their counterparts in the professions, to

---

[68] Newman (1907) at 105. I presume this is a reference to De Officiis 1.13
('Itaque cum sumus necessariis negotiis curisque vacui, tum avemus aliquid videre,
audire, addiscere cognitionemque rerum aut occultarum aut admirabilium ad
beate vivendum necessariam ducimus') and therefore connected with the notion of
otium, or leisure, (negotium, or 'business', is the opposite of otium) rather than to
duty in the moral sense, from which Cicero says we are never free (ibid 1.4).
[69] Collini (2012) Epilogue.

think about projects whose realisation might never happen and to preserve projects whose immediate relevance might seem to have gone.

The Artificial

The most direct assault on the contention that engineering forms no part of a liberal education came from Herbert Simon. He declared that the idea of design was so important that 'the proper study of mankind is the science of design, not only as the professional component of a technical education but as a core discipline for every liberally educated person'.[70] Simon's claim is that to understand humanity requires one to understand the drive to design as one of humanity's most important and constant features. It is an unequivocal challenge to those who think that the best of human culture is embodied in uselessness.

Some would take fundamental objection to Simon's proposal. Simon placed human purposes, and human purposiveness at the centre of what is worth studying. Simon ultimately celebrates the artificial, that is objects, or configurations of objects, that would not exist in nature. Law fits into Simon's view because lawyers also create something that does not exist in nature, namely artificial social structure. Those who see only danger or disappointment in human attempts to control their environment, whether Oakeshottian conservatives or deep greens, will instinctively reject Simon's position.[71] From a conservative point of view, the deliberate creation of new social structure is particularly objectionable. If law is to exist at all, many conservatives say, let it be created not by deliberate design but by a slow accretion of small decisions, and if it is to change, let it change only to reflect changes that have already happened in behaviour.

Ultimately the choice between Simon and Oakeshott might come down to what Oakeshott himself described as a 'disposition', a tendency to think and behave in characteristic ways and to make certain characteristic choices. The conservative disposition, said Oakeshott, 'centres upon a propensity to use and to enjoy what is available rather than to wish for or to look for something else; to delight in what is present rather than what was or what may be.'[72] Simon's designers look to what might be and delight instead in making available what has not been available. It is probably no coincidence that conventional legal education in the English-speaking

---

[70] Herbert Simon, *Sciences of the Artificial* (Cambridge, MA: MIT Press, 1996) at 138.

[71] See e.g. Michael Oakeshott, *Rationalism in Politics and Other Essays* (London: Methuen, 1962) at 5, 120, 128, 189–91.

[72] Oakeshott (1962) at 168.

world has emphasised the activities of the common law judges, whose characteristic method is precisely 'to use what is available rather than to . . . look for something else'. It is an education that suits very well those of a conservative disposition, including those whose radicalism is so thorough-going that they end up denying that any change is possible. An education as a legal engineer would suit those of quite a different disposition.

6. Conclusion

We began with the question of how we should characterise what lawyers do. We have made the claim that characterising what lawyers do as engineering is both accurate and useful. It is accurate because it captures more of what lawyers do, both in private practice and in public service, than characterisations based on assuming that lawyers are engaged in litigation or on those that proceed from some form of evaluation, whether positive (lawyer-as-hero, lawyer-as-statesman) or negative (lawyer-as-trickster, lawyer-as-hired-gun). It is useful because it provides a sound starting point for appraising what lawyers do, through the application of engineering ethics to their activities, and for improving their performance, through searching for principles of effective design. Accuracy and utility might be thought to be enough, but we should consider some possible objections to thinking about law in engineering terms, and this chapter takes on that task. It also speculates on some possible further benefits of the approach and closes with a reflection on how seeing lawyers as engineers might save them from a repetition of the part they played in the Great Crash of 2008.

OBJECTIONS TO LAW-AS-ENGINEERING

We will consider four possible objections to treating law as a form of engineering. One is that, although it might be true in quantitative terms that lawyers mainly engage in activity that can be described in terms of engineering, in some other, qualitative, sense, those activities are not as important as litigation and adjudication. The second, related, objection is that law-as-engineering is merely the latest in a line of instrumentalist conceptions of law, and that it is a mistake, a dangerous political mistake, to treat law as a means to an end. The third, a more focused version of the second, is that treating law as a form of engineering encourages manipulative behaviour that fails to respect human autonomy. The fourth is that law-as-engineering breaks the link between law and justice and replaces it with a technocratic view imbued with the worst aspects of legal positivism.

Insisting on the Centrality of Adjudication

Vast amounts of intellectual effort, especially in common law countries, has been expended, both at the bar and in the universities, in activities associated with understanding, predicting or assisting judges. Law-as-engineering shifts attention away from judges and those who argue in front of them, to those who make law and those who apply it to themselves. One can understand resistance to such a shift. It threatens investments made, especially in the universities, over lifetimes, or at least over entire careers. But are there substantive reasons for maintaining the centrality of adjudication despite the small number of lawyers engaged in it?

The argument is that, especially in common law systems, but in reality in all modern legal systems, keeping track of judicial decision is indispensable for understanding the law, and, as legal engineers appreciate, understanding the law is as important to a lawyer as understanding materials is to an engineer. One often hears solicitors declare that they never open a law-book or read a case, but that is only because someone else is doing that job for them – professional support lawyers in the big firms, barristers for the rest. Moreover, the decisions of the courts can alter the terms of existing deals and throw them into doubt. Decisions on the meaning of widely used terms can affect arrangements that have already used them. Decisions on tort law can change the relative position of millions of insurance contracts. No individual deal can have the influence that a court decision can have. The number of lawyers involved in litigation thus fails to reflect the number of people that can be affected by its results.

The issue is, however, one of proportionality. Clearly, legal certainty requires some understanding of judges' decisions, and so one cannot dispense with that understanding entirely. But the question is how much attention to pay to what judges do. In reality very few cases have wide consequences for existing or future arrangements. Even those that do seem to have less effect on subsequent deals than those involved in the litigation might have expected. As we have seen, what appeared to be a major decision on the way sovereign bonds worked had next to no effect on the way those bonds were drafted for several years, and when change came, it came in an unexpected way not immediately related to the court's judgment.[1] For the most part, judicial decisions affect as few people as individual deals, perhaps fewer.

In any case, following the minutiae of the case law is becoming increasingly arduous. The electronic reporting of more and more cases is already

---

[1]   See above, Chapter 3.

straining the processing capacity, patience and eyesight of those, including many academic lawyers, who still believe that their duties include mastering the case law as it emerges.[2] English lawyers, perhaps a hundred years after their American counterparts, are about to reach the moment when the sheer number of cases will force them to admit that their view of the law as the product of judicial decision has to change. As Grant Gilmore pointed out, 'When the number of printed cases becomes like the number of grains of sand on the beach, the precedent-based case-law system cannot work and cannot be made to work.'[3] In England, there is the added factor that the long-term effect of abolishing the civil jury, combined subsequently with the great ease with which judges can now generate text, is that judgments have grown extraordinarily in length. Judgments of a hundred pages, once very rare, are now common. The intensity with which English academics follow the decisions of the judges must sooner or later collapse under its own weight. It would be prudent to make a virtue out of that necessity and turn our attention to other aspects of the legal system as soon as we can.

We should also take into account the benefits of relegating the judiciary to a more peripheral place in thinking about law. We would gain a more accurate view of the balance between the law's role in dealing with conflict and its role in promoting co-operation. We would spend more time on rules significant for economic and political life and less time on minor disputes about detail. Above all, we obtain a more accurate and balanced view of the role of the judiciary itself. Judges really are better seen as bricoleurs, patching up a structure designed, or at least built, by others, than as great architects of public policy or as distant God-like defenders of abstract rights based on a timeless morality. There might be moments of grand design or deontology, but most judges, most of the time, are carrying out a humbler, though often difficult task.

Perhaps in some constitutional structures, especially in that of the United States, judges have acquired power to such a degree that treating them as peripheral seems unrealistic, even eccentric. But the centrality of judges in the United States is not a matter of their importance in the legal system. Judges are not significantly more important in the United States

---

[2] If one takes a random year a generation ago, say 1964, about 400 cases would be reported in the All England Law Reports, covering all legal topics, and perhaps about another 100 might appear in other sources. For 2011, a Lexis search finds reports of 60 Supreme Court cases, 994 Court of Appeal cases and 1439 High Court cases, and that is only a start.

[3] Grant Gilmore, 'Legal Realism: Its Causes and Cure' (1961) 70 Yale Law Journal 1037–48 at 1041.

than anywhere else when it comes to the everyday uses of law – the use of contracts for planning commercial relationships, the use of wills and trusts for transferring property or the use of companies for both. It is rather a matter of American judges' importance in the political system. American judges have acquired practical and symbolic power in politics to an extent reproduced in few other systems. Frequent, and arguably partisan, intervention in core political decisions, from who wins presidential elections to what kind of health care policy is permissible, have, from the point of view of an outside observer, turned the US Supreme Court into a third legislative chamber, carrying out two of the functions of parliaments in the rest of world, namely the creation of governments and the formation of the main lines of public policy. But none of that should require lawyers more generally to remain obsessed with courts.

Objecting to Instrumentalism

A more fundamental attack on law-as-engineering might come from those who object to the whole idea of law being conceived of as a means to an end or as an instrument for human purposes. That objection has been most recently and comprehensively expressed by Brian Tamanaha.[4] Tamanaha's view is that a purely instrumental view of law is a recent invention, the result of the Enlightenment and the rise of utilitarianism. He claims that in the 20th century instrumentalism combined with moral relativism to produce a situation in which law came to be conceived of purely as a means by which individuals can enforce their will against other individuals. In the process, Tamanaha fears, all ideas of the law as standing for the common good or for the public interest beyond the desires of individuals have disappeared.

One might contest Tamanaha's heavily schematic history, in which until the late 18th century the law was conceived exclusively either as a reflection of the Divine Will or as emanating directly from society in the form of 'custom', so that deliberate legislation was not just rare but also could only be justified as merely confirming what already existed. Members of Henry VIII's Parliaments called upon to legislate for the break with Rome would have been surprised to be informed that they were only confirming the existing custom of the realm, and the argument that it was God's will to defy the Pope might have been made, but it would have be very difficult for many at the time sincerely to believe. Moreover, the fact that Mary

---

[4]   Brian Tamanaha, *Law as a Means to an End: Threat to the Rule of Law* (Cambridge: Cambridge U.P., 2006).

I induced Parliament to repeal most of Henry's legislation shows that it was accepted even by Catholics that English law really had been changed by Parliament. Admittedly, Henry VIII was not a 20th century moral relativist, but it is unlikely that he failed to realise that putting his political programme into legislative form was helpful for him or that his opponents would deny that what he was doing was for the common good. Moreover, Tamanaha seriously underestimates conscious or half-conscious instrumentality in pre-1800 politics. Even in the 17th and 18th centuries, disputes about the relationship between, for example, the common law and legislation were deeply political. The right of Parliament to sweep away customary rights would not have struck a country gentleman with an Enclosure Bill to promote as at all objectionable, but the excluded peasantry might well have thought otherwise. But even if Tamanaha's history is a little suspect (and even if, as one might surmise, he has deeper objections to what Henry VIII did in the 1530s), he does have a point. Attempts to divert public power into the channels of private interest (18th century Enclosure Bills included) are always potentially obnoxious and require justification in terms of the interests of others, and a conception of law that excluded any notion of the public interest, so that the law is simply a prize to be contested by competing forces, would have lost something important and valuable.

Does law-as-engineering condone or encourage the faults Tamanaha points to, the diversion of public power into private interests and the exclusion of the notion of the public interest from law? Law-as-engineering is certainly an instrumentalist view of law. It treats law as a means to achieve ends that are set consciously by human beings, not by God (at least directly) or by impersonal forces such as 'custom' or 'society'. It nevertheless could defend itself against Tamanaha's charges. It would reject the first accusation, that it encourages the diversion of public power into private interests, on the ground that any diversion it involves is an intended consequence of the legal structure itself. Contracts and companies are permitted by the law and the process by which statutes are generated is a legitimate one.

Law-as-engineering would also reject the second accusation, that it implies the exclusion of the idea of public interest or the common good from the law, leaving only a clash of competing interests. It would point to the fact that transactional law is inherently co-operative and agreement-seeking, and that legislative lawyering, although not consensual in the same way, is at least constructive. In transactional law, what is being engineered is usually the bringing together of different interests for mutual benefit. That mutual benefit might not always be in the public interest (for example an agreement to fix prices) but lawyers who attempt to design agreements that contravene the public interest face the problem that if the law supports the form of public interest in question, one of its usual effects will be that such designs will fail. Tamanaha himself illustrates the point. Although he usually thinks of lawyering exclusively in terms of litigation and so often misses the point of what lawyers do, when he does turn to examples of ethically indefensible transactional lawyering (for example the creation of fake transactions for Enron or the selling of fraudulent opinion letters to support tax shelters)[5] one cannot help but notice that in every case the device failed in its purpose. In practice, to design legal instruments using materials that will fail on the grounds of illegality is usually to have designed not just unethically but also ineffectively. In legal systems where the content of the law generally reflects ethical standards, even unethical lawyers would be prudent to assume that unethical designs will fail. Indeed, lawyers with sound ethical instincts will have a distinct advantage over those who lack them, not just as more trustworthy advisers but also as better-equipped technical lawyers.

Much of Tamanaha's attack on legal instrumentalism is specifically directed against litigators rather than against transactions lawyers. For example, he bemoans the way lawyers look not for the most reasonable interpretation of the law seen from the perspective of the common good, but for arguments that bolster the position of their clients.[6] But law-as-engineering is the cure for this sickness, not its cause or something that exacerbates it. Such an attitude might be the natural position of litigators, in both the civil and the criminal courts, but for a transactions lawyer it would be disastrous. Lawyers, like engineers, prefer to build within tolerances, within margins of safety. For a transactions lawyer in the tradition of Mr W.W. Lancaster, a deal that ends up in the courts is a failure even if the litigation ends in success. The device will have failed to work properly and has had to be patched up in a way that tends to undermine the clients' future dealings. The invention of new transactions, the Wachtell poison pill, for example, is something of an exception, because successful litigation might be necessary to confirm that the device works, but even then the best route is the one that least relies on litigation. Moreover, from the point of view of a transactions lawyer, when taking into account the risks of litigation (or regulatory decision) the result that should be contemplated is not the one that brilliant or twisted advocacy might produce but the reasonable result an ordinary judge following the rules and keeping the public interest in mind is most likely to come to. One final story from David Caruth's memoir will illustrate these points:

---

[5] E.g. Tamanaha (2006) at 146–47.
[6] Tamanaha (2006) at 145–50.

> At one point we faced a rather obscure point of Peruvian law and we were advised by our local lawyer that there was one particular professor, who lived in the mountains, who would be the authority to advise on this particular point. We therefore sent an emissary to him to find out whether or not he could give us an opinion. The reply came back that he could have done but unfortunately he had already advised the Government. Nevertheless he said he would be delighted to give us an opinion (giving the precisely opposite view from that expressed to the Government) if we were prepared to pay him rather more for the privilege. In the circumstances we thought it right to decline.[7]

The Peruvian professor was confusing the need of litigators for plausible points to fire at the opposition with the need of transactions lawyers to find a solid, reckonable view of the law from which they can proceed with confidence. Taking unreasonable points not only fails to advance the common good of society, it also fails to advance the common good of the parties.

Tamanaha further objects that those who seek to change the content of the law often ignore the common good and pursue only their own private ends. That is a complaint, however, no matter how justified, about politics in general rather than specifically about the law. The two admittedly sometimes intersect in some forms of litigation designed to change the law, and so also in the person of the judge, but that is again a problem for litigation-centred views of the law, not for law-as-engineering. It is perhaps revealing that Tamanaha attributes to the combination of instrumentalism and moral relativism the exceptionally harsh atmosphere in both legal and political life in the USA. But from outside the US, one wonders whether the real problem might be an exceptional lack of concern about inequalities of power and wealth. Few Europeans, for example, read without bewilderment the opinion of the US Supreme Court in *Buckley v Valeo*,[8] which holds that legal restrictions on election campaign expenditure, including restrictions on total spending and on the amounts candidates can spend from their own wealth, are unconstitutional. The Supreme Court asserted that spending one's own money on one's own election campaign was protected by the First Amendment guarantee of freedom of speech, equating speech with money in a way startling to Europeans, and that there is no legitimate public interest in attempting to equalise the chances of rich and poor candidates for public office.[9] The Court's remark, 'But the concept

---

[7] David Caruth, *A Life of Three Strands: A City Lawyer's Memoir* (London: Avon Books, 1998) at 45.

[8] 424 U.S. 1 (1975).

[9] Cf. *Bowman v UK* (1998) 26 EHRR 1, where, although the Court agreed that a third party expenditure of £5 was so low that it amounted to an unnecessary

that government may restrict the speech of some elements of our society in order to enhance the relative voice of others is wholly foreign to the First Amendment', which assumes that stopping a billionaire spending more money on an election campaign than a pauper somehow restricts the billionaire's freedom of speech, represents a very specifically American view of how the interaction between wealth and power should work.[10]

Tamanaha worries that US legal instrumentalism has produced a kind of Hobbesian war of all against all. An alternative explanation is that a political war of all against all has produced a very crude version of legal instrumentalism.

Admittedly, some lawyers on both sides of the Atlantic engage in lobbying (or in what is called 'public policy' or 'legislative' practice), and are thus involved in a form of legal engineering that might well be described as diverting public power to private ends. But the question then is what types of ethical standards apply to these lawyers? There are undoubtedly problems here. For example, there is some suspicion that City of London lawyers are inappropriately using arguments drawn from the armoury of litigation ethics to resist regulation of their lobbying activities.[11] But ethical standards that derive from engineering ethics, especially standards about harm and public welfare, should point lawyer-lobbyists in directions that do not ignore broader social interests. In legislative practice as much as in transactional practice, lawyers should be considering the client's usage plan and their part in it. Again, law-as-engineering is not the cause of the problem but an accurate description of what lawyers do and a way of helping them to do it better.

One suspects that the underlying objection raised by Tamanaha's work is not to instrumentalism but to artificiality. Tamanaha harks back to a world where law seemed to arise naturally, without human intervention, from God or custom. The problem is that, as we discussed at the end of Chapter 5, law is a human invention. It is the deliberate creation of artificial social structure. Herbert Simon noted a widespread hostility to the artificial,

---

restriction on freedom of expression during an election, it was legitimate for the state to put in place measures designed to maintain equality among election candidates.

[10]   See further *Citizens United v Federal Election Commission* 558 U. S. ____ (2010), 130 S.Ct. 876, which declares unconstitutional any limit on corporate spending on elections – a logical development of *Buckley* for those who accept the questionable idea that corporations 'speak', but a further blow to any notion of a republic of equals.

[11]   See e.g. City of London Law Society, *CLLS Response to HMG Consultation on Introducing a Statutory Register of Lobbyists* (London: CLLS, 2012) (http://www.citysolicitors.org.uk/FileServer.aspx?oID=1168&lID=0).

referring to standard dictionary definitions of 'artificial' that equate it with the fake or the affected.[12] In a culture that values the 'natural' over the 'artificial', it would not be surprising to find latent hostility to what lawyers do, especially in the form of a sense that we should be able to get by without lawyers, that our forms of social organisation should be spontaneous and 'natural'. The situation is worse for lawyers than for engineers since few people expect engineering to be anything but artificial, whereas law deals with social life and language, fields in which non-lawyers regard themselves as fully competent. As Karl Llewellyn noted:

> [T]he [legal] profession is charged with being what any profession should hope to be; expert enough to develop a black art of its own. All that makes law grotesque and dubious is that any man thinks that he has adequate knowledge by his common sense to judge of 'rights' and 'wrongs'. What lawyers do must be the diabolical cozenages of Cepola. The common man does not arrogate such knowledge to himself in engineering. The art of engineers is thus more white magic more than black.[13]

Lawyers themselves are not immune to this romanticism. It might, for example, in part explain the obsession of lawyers in English-speaking countries with the common law at the expense of statutes. It might even partially explain lawyers' attachment to disputes. The common law can be seen as a 'natural' form of law, arising without deliberate intent. Similarly disputes can be seen as arising 'naturally' and spontaneously from social interaction. In contrast, statutes are artificial law par excellence, and planning to prevent disputes requires unnatural forethought and can seem a cold and calculating business compared to the passions of litigation.

But romanticism is a refusal to engage with reality. It is reverie. As for passion, it denotes a state in which we no longer act on the world, but it acts on us. Humans are, admittedly, part of the natural world and whatever they invent for themselves cannot work unless it takes into account their nature as humans. But that nature, as Simon insisted, includes the urge to design, the urge to create the artificial. The distinction between the natural and the artificial is ultimately one of cause and effect rather than one between two different universes. To cut ourselves off from our own inventions and to treat them as the products of gods or of impersonal abstractions is the ultimate in alienation.

---

[12] Herbert Simon, *Sciences of the Artificial* (Cambridge, MA: MIT Press, 1996) at 4.

[13] Karl Llewellyn, *The Bramble Bush* (New York: Oceana Publications, 1960) (1960a) at 145. For 'the diabolical cozenages of Cepola' see Rabelais, *Pantagruel* chapter 10. Bartolomeo Cepola (or Cippola) of Verona was a 15th century jurist.

Law, Engineering and Manipulation

The issue of manipulation is more difficult. Law-as-engineering seems to fail the Kantian test that people should be treated as ends not means. The difficulty of the problem is in no way reduced by the fact that the same problem is constantly ignored in the discussion of public policy. One might ask of every technique at the disposal of the state, except for attempting to engage the citizenry in rational conversation, whether it treats people as means rather than ends. The question can be asked no less of the threat of punishment as of the creation of economic incentives, and no less of the selective use of information as of the now fashionable 'nudge' techniques built on the insights of behavioural economics.

There are two ways of meeting the accusation against law-as-engineering that it fails the test that people should be treated as ends. One is to argue that the state must always fail such a test, especially if strictly applied, so that we need to develop a different test or set of tests for judging the morality of politics and government. The other is to distinguish between different sociotechnical methods, and different ways of applying those methods, in a search for distinctions between ethical and unethical practice. Ultimately, it might be possible to combine these two approaches.

The first route is a version of the argument that ordinary moral standards drawn from personal life do not necessarily apply to political (or more accurately, governmental) action. The philosopher Thomas Nagel noticed that people in official roles were subject to duties that did not apply to personal life and that could not be derived from the duties applicable to personal life.[14] Those duties included a duty to consider the interests of the relevant political unit as a whole and a duty to act impersonally in those interests. The result is that those wielding governmental power find themselves obliged to consider the consequences of their actions rather more often and more intensively than those who need to think only about the morality of the way they interact personally with other people. For Nagel, the extra duties of those in public life explained why they were permitted (indeed sometimes obliged) to act in ways that in personal life would not be permitted, including 'coercive, manipulative, or obstructive methods that would not be allowable to individuals'.[15] Thus, governments may use coercion in the collective interest to collect taxes, even though on no plausible version of real personal consent by individuals can it be said that every

---

[14] Thomas Nagel, 'Ruthlessness in Public Life' in *Mortal Questions* (Cambridge: Cambridge U.P., 1991 [1979]).

[15] Nagel (1991) at 84.

individual consents to being taxed. (Nagel rejects as excessively strained any attempt to attribute consent to people who do not in fact give it, for example by falling back on indirect means such as consent to the constitution under which laws are made.) The morality of decisions to impose taxation cannot be judged by the standards of inter-personal morality.

Nevertheless, as Nagel himself points out, the additional emphasis allowable to consequentialist arguments in public life does not mean that every public decision is potentially justifiable by arguing that the ends justified the means. Otherwise all public actions would be potentially justifiable. It does mean, however, that even when we address the question of where the limits are to the governmental use of means that individuals should not use in their personal lives, we might give extra weight to consequentialist arguments. For example, in considering the limits to governmental use of deception, although it would be absurd to criticise a government for failing to tell the truth where the results would be disastrous or self-defeating (for instance where governments in a fixed exchange-rate system lie about their intention to devalue their currency), there must be an internal limit where the effects of repeated deception on the government's credibility are so severe that any gains in terms of the government's ability to implement its current plans are outweighed by the costs of impairing its ability to implement any of its future plans. In addition one might also want to limit the distance between ordinary morality and public morality for the purpose of ensuring that public life does not become so rebarbative to those of ordinary moral sensibility that they will refuse to serve, a process that would have the eventual effect of abandoning public life to sociopaths and sadists.

How does this argument work out in the case of manipulation? It is at this point that we need to turn to the second strategy, that of distinguishing between acceptable and unacceptable manipulation. Manipulation, we may suppose, is where a person is caused to do something without it being explained to them what is happening to them or why. A successful manipulation occurs where the object of the manipulation behaves in the desired way regardless of the reasons he or she had for acting that way. Manipulation differs from deception because in deception the target of deception is intentionally caused to form false beliefs and those false beliefs form part of the target's reasons for acting in the way desired by the deceiver. In manipulation, the manipulator does not set out to create false beliefs, but simply does not care what beliefs the target forms. (This is not to say that deception is always impermissible – it is not, as the devaluation example shows – but it is a different question.)

To what extent, then, are legal methods unacceptably manipulative? We might start by specifying how law achieves its effects, the methods by which it causes behaviour change. It works by direct prospects of loss or gain (punishment or reward), indirect prospects of loss or gain (for example facilitating co-ordination by settling the expectations of a number of different people) and self-application without prospect of gain or loss of any kind except the satisfaction of knowing that one has acted in accordance with the law – that is through loyalty to the law itself. Applying the definition of manipulation we have stipulated, it might be argued that none of the methods used by law is manipulative, since they all seem to involve giving their targets relevant information and leave it to them whether to comply. Individuals are told that there is a punishment or reward for particular behaviour, that there is a convention that we all do a particular thing, or that the law asks us to act in a particular way. The information about punishments, and perhaps about rewards, is intended to be, and sometimes is coercive. But coercive is not the same as manipulative. Manipulation depends not on whether incentives are so strong as to amount to coercion, but whether the incentives are out in the open.

Reality, however, is not so simple. There is a way in which two, or perhaps three, of the methods of the law might be manipulative. That is because it is possible for them to work through other people. The law might be known to person A, who as a consequence changes the incentives for person B. The behaviour of person B can be changed without person B having any knowledge of the law. An example is the insurance market. If the law says that a person is liable to pay another person compensation if they act in a particular way, insurers will set premiums, or will determine coverage, on the basis of that rule. Insurers' customers will face incentives to act as the law desires even if they are unaware of the law's content. In principle, the law's rewards can operate in the same way. Even convention can work by setting a social norm that others follow because it looks convenient to do so, or dangerous not to do so, without many of those acting in accordance with the convention knowing that its origin lies in the law.

Are these indirect methods of causing people to behave in particular ways objectionable manipulation? They certainly cause people to behave differently without full disclosure to them of what is happening. But two points can be made in their favour. First, they would still work even if full disclosure were made about the law and how it operates. Indeed they might even work better, because they might benefit from purely self-applying compliance. Second, at least one person in the chain of causation is induced to change their behaviour with full knowledge of the law – in the insurance example the insurer is caused to act in full knowledge of the law's threats and rewards. One might argue that the first point goes to deception rather than to manipulation – or at least to the kind of deception that arises from not disclosing the full truth. But it also mitigates the manipulative nature of the act that what happened would have been no different if the incentive had been accompanied by a note informing all the people affected of the relevant law. Manipulation is about causing behaviour, and it is arguable that the omission of the extra information was not itself causative in the sense of a being a necessary condition for the final result. One might also argue that the second point shows only that the intermediary was not manipulated, and says nothing about the ultimate target. But there is a difference between a course of action designed to bring about results in ways in which no one else knows how it is done, and those in which there is in principle no secret about the method.

These points, it is important to note, apply in terms only to legal methods of changing behaviour. Other means might not come out as well. Take, for instance, 'nudge' techniques. Many of them rely on quirks of human psychology that induce people to act irrationally. For example, people have a tendency to choose the middle option of three or to decide differently about the balance between certainty and risk if the choice is framed in terms of certainty of gains rather than in terms of certainty of losses.[16] What would happen if people whose behaviour was being targeted were told about these effects before they were asked to decide? It would seem likely that at least some of them might decide differently. These techniques look unacceptably manipulative in ways that law is not.

Justice

Finally, there will be objections from those for whom law-as-engineering makes too little of the connection between law and justice. We have already seen in Chapter 4 that the move from litigation-based ethics to engineering-based ethics implies a shift away from procedural concepts of justice. In its place come moral concepts centring on harm and public benefit. We also saw, however, that engineering-based ethics encourage consideration of justice in broader, distributive, terms, for example to consider equality of access to legal services. Law-as-engineering changes the focus of the way in which law intersects with justice, but it does not eliminate it. There might, however, be more theoretical objections.

Law-as-engineering is intended as an orientation towards law and lawyering, as a starting point for further work, and not as a 'school' of jurisprudence or as legal philosophy, but one can imagine the criticism being levelled at it that it is just another form of legal positivism, that it accepts too readily the separation thesis (that law and morality are distinct, so that

---

[16] Amos Tversky and Daniel Kahneman, 'The Framing of Decisions and the Psychology of Choice' (1981) 211 (4481) Science 453–58.

legal validity depends in no way on moral acceptability) and so underplays
the inherent connections between what counts as law and what counts as
just, a connection that exists not only in the more traditional forms of
natural law but in modern conceptions of human rights. That in turn leads
to an argument that law-as-engineering diverts lawyers' attention from the
forms of justice encoded in the concept of law itself – law's 'inner morality'
in Lon Fuller's terms – to justice, fairness and morality in the world outside
the law, a world into which lawyers have no special insight and in which
they have no privileged standing.

It would be unwise, especially for a non-philosopher, to deny that there
is anything in these criticisms. The German social democratic politician
and legal philosopher Gustav Radbruch insisted that law had to be seen
from three points of view – the point of view of utility or effectiveness, the
point of view of legal certainty and the point of view of justice.[17] Law-as-
engineering undeniably emphasises the role of the first two – utility and
certainty – rather than the third. Its basic orientation is to take the parts
of the law that are more certain and ask what of use can be made out of
them.

One important point to make, however, is that neither utility nor legal
certainty is an entirely morally neutral idea. Utility, even if conceived of
in very basic terms, is still inherently a normative idea in the sense that it
is an ideal to be pursued. Legal certainty contains within it the idea that
the purpose of law is to allow people to act freely, in the sense that they
are not subject to arbitrary power.[18] But the normativity of utility and
legal certainty does not settle the question of whether law-as-engineering
inherently assumes the positivist idea that 'the law is the law' regardless of
its moral standing. The issue is not, however, whether law-as-engineering
is compatible with a positivist approach, which it plainly is, but merely
whether it is incompatible with a non-positivist approach. The question
comes down to this. Is it possible to see lawyers as engineers if one also
believes that unjust law (using 'unjust' for some, perhaps very high, value
of injustice) is to be denied the quality of 'law'? The answer seems to be
that it is possible. Lawyers who believe, to put it crudely, that laws can be
so unjust that they do not count as laws at all, can still make legal devices
and useful legal structures out of aspects of the law they believe to be just.
A positivist legal engineer might worry only about the morality of the

<hr>

[17]   Gustav Radbruch, *Rechtsphilosophie* (Ralf Dreier and Stanley Paulson eds)
(Heidelberg: Müller, 2011 [originally 1932]) at 73ff.
[18]   For a forceful new version of the view that the very idea of law is based on
creating freedom, see Nigel Simmonds, *Law as a Moral Idea* (Oxford: Oxford U.P.,
2008).

eventual use of the device being developed. A non-positivist might worry additionally about the morality of the materials to be used to make it. One might add that a realist legal engineer would worry about the possibility that, regardless of whether positivism is true or false, if other lawyers are non-positivists, using unjust legal materials might prove risky. But they are all still engaged in making useful devices.

THE BENEFITS OF LAW-AS-ENGINEERING

What are the benefits of the law-as-engineering perspective? The most obvious benefit of the analogy is that it provides a more accurate description of what lawyers do than existing descriptions. Descriptions of lawyers that assume, for example, that lawyers are litigators, constantly fighting partisan battles in the courts, constantly engaging in persuasive rhetoric or even theatrics, are simply inaccurate.

But the benefits of a more accurate description are not just the satisfactions of attaining a better theoretical understanding of a phenomenon. They also include practical benefits for the profession and for the wider public. The most obvious kind of benefit is that if non-lawyers better understand what lawyers do, they will be in a better position to make use of lawyers' skills. From medicine to the military and from politics to engineers themselves, there are, as we have seen, professionals, especially those who come across lawyers either very rarely or only in the context of litigation, who might find collaboration with lawyers easier once they understand the connections and commonalities between what lawyers and what they do. But there are other benefits. In particular, we might consider what kind of person is initially attracted to take up the law as a profession. If the predominant image of lawyering in society is that of the courtroom advocate, it would not be surprising if young people thought that they would be suited to legal work if they were good at oral debate, thinking on their feet and drama. In fact, anyone who has read university application forms will know that large numbers of young people do believe that such skills and attributes, especially ability in oral debate, are essential qualities for lawyers. Student applications also reveal that young people believe, or at least their teachers and parents believe, that another quality is essential for lawyers, namely having an 'analytical' mind. That sometimes turns out to mean merely that they are pernickety or even a little pedantic, both of which might eventually prove very useful in some legal jobs, or at least so some Parliamentary Counsel allege. But being 'analytical' often refers instead, as subsequent interviews reveal, to a tendency to deploy a style of oral argument characterised by the ability to make points of the form 'how can you say X when you just said Y?' – in other words a forensic ad hominem style.

The characteristics of a good transactional or legislative lawyer are very different. Skill at oral argument, nimbleness of expression and the ability to make rapid ad hominem points are rarely relevant. In fact, at times they might be a positive hindrance to the success of a deal or the cogency of a draft statute. Transactions lawyers and legislative lawyers need to be analytical, but in a different sense. They need to be able to reduce the complexity of the world to essentials, to be able to break problems down into manageable parts and to see the logical structure that brings the parts together. But analytical ability by itself is not enough. Transactions lawyers also need to be able to see the world from the point of view of other people (especially those of their clients and of the people their clients are dealing with), but in a way that leaves them free to think through the consequences of seeing the world in that way. In other words they need empathy but also to be able to distance themselves from the subjects of their empathy. Analytical ability and controlled empathy, however, make only half a lawyer, the half that understands problems. The other half needs to be able to solve problems. That requires creativity and imagination, but also persistence in asking questions and in looking systematically for solutions, together with self-awareness and scepticism, especially the ability to see weak points or omissions in one's own designs. Linguistic ability is important, but not to the extent that it allows people to hide their own weaknesses from themselves. Numeracy – or at least an ability to think schematically and comprehensively – is just as important.

Even if universities and law firms filter perfectly those who apply to them, so that, regardless of what applicants think, the subset who eventually succeed are those most suited to the real work of lawyers, two forms of detriment will nevertheless persist. First, large numbers of young people will be disappointed because they will have made the wrong choice of degree or career. Second, there will presumably exist a large number of young people who would be just as well suited, or even better suited, to a legal career than those who apply. To the extent that the task of filtering is not perfect, we will end up with lawyers not suited to the task.

Another type of benefit of the law-engineering analogy is perhaps more controversial. Lawyers' self-image is not necessarily a sensible place to start if one wants to understand what lawyers do, but their self-image is important in other ways. It is at least plausible – one should go no further – that law-as-engineering is a better image for lawyers to hold of themselves than the alternatives. A self-image should be a normative standard grounded in reality, an image of what the role of lawyer entails both factually and normatively. It should be accurate both about the content of the role and about its importance, avoiding both delusions of grandeur and excessive modesty.[19] Above all, it should offer a reasonable normative standard – one that it is possible for ordinary professionals to reach in their daily lives but not overly permissive or indulgent.

We mentioned in Chapter 1 some of the options lawyers have developed for themselves. Tony Kronman, for example, called for the return of the ideal of the 'lawyer-statesman', a lawyer 'possessed of great practical wisdom and exceptional persuasive powers, devoted to the public good but keenly aware of the limitations of human beings and their political arrangements',[20] a paragon rather similar to the ideal product of a liberal legal education identified several decades earlier by Bill Twining and dubbed by him, in a spirit more of satire than aspiration, 'Pericles'.[21] Others have put forward, either as ideal or as stereotype, the 'lawyer-as-hero', the lawyer who fights injustice through the courts, taking on the rich and powerful to win cases for the poor and oppressed.[22] At the other end of the spectrum there is the lawyer as 'trickster' or 'hired gun', who, for a suitable fee, will bamboozle the other side or take them out completely.[23] Tricksters and hired guns, in sharp contrast to heroes, mainly work for the rich and powerful and take pleasure in grinding the faces of the poor, but they will work for anyone who pays them. In between the two is the lawyer as technician (Twining's 'Plumber' to contrast with 'Pericles'), whose work is necessary but dull, consisting mainly of knowing which forms to fill in and how to fill them in. A slightly warmer, more human version of the technician is the lawyer as 'helper' or 'social worker', the client's friend and protector.[24]

These images fail on one or more of the dimensions of accuracy or moral pertinence. Some are far too lofty (for example Tony Kronman's 'lawyer-statesman' or 'Pericles') for most mortals to reach. The 'lawyer as hero', more a literary figure than a real one, is no less lofty, and although

---

[19] It is interesting that, possibly as a consequence of centuries of Christian celebration of humility in all of its forms, 'excessive modesty' has struck some readers as an odd concept. Cf., however, Aristotle's 'μικροψυχία' (Nich. Eth. II.7 (1107b)).

[20] Kronman (1995) at 12.

[21] William Twining, 'Pericles and the Plumber' (1967) 83 Law Quarterly Review 396.

[22] Marvin Mindes and Alan Acock, 'Trickster, Hero, Helper: A Report on the Lawyer Image' (1982) 7 Law & Social Inquiry 177–233.

[23] Mindes and Acock (1982), Stephen Nathanson, *What Lawyers Do* (London: Sweet and Maxwell, 1997).

[24] E.g. Edward Dauer and Arthur Leff, 'The Lawyer as Friend' (1977) 86 Yale Law Journal 573, Nathanson (1997).

it might be possible for lawyers to engage in some part-time heroism in the form of pro-bono work, for the vast majority, heroics are not, and cannot be, their daily bread. As for the images on the dark side (the 'hired gun' or the 'trickster'), they are morally indulgent, setting no obvious limits to lawyers' conduct. The images in the middle (the technician, the helper or the social worker) are inaccurate either by underestimating the complexity of lawyers' work ('technician') or over-emphasising its personal aspects at the expense of the technical ('helper' or 'social worker').

The lawyer-as-engineer avoids these pitfalls. It is neither grandiose nor unduly humble. It recognises lawyers' technical skills, but in a way that goes beyond the humdrum and the straightforward. It emphasises usefulness as opposed to trickery or verbal violence, and professionalism without denying the obvious truth that the practice of law is usually a paid occupation, not a mode of aristocratic charity. It also implies a particular sort of professional ethic, not a free-for-all. Engineers are sensible reliable people who do what they say. They obtain results by solid work and they accept responsibility both for completing tasks and for whatever might go wrong. As we have seen, that ethic includes preventing harm to others and potentially promoting public welfare.

Perhaps the most obvious source of objection to law-as-engineering as a plausible self-image for lawyers is the suspicion by lawyers themselves that engineers are of lower social status than lawyers. There might be something in this as a factual claim. In Britain in the 1960s engineers ranked below lawyers in prestige even according to engineers themselves.[25] Whether that is still the case, however, is less clear, and some commentators have contended that engineers' complaints that they are treated with less respect than they deserve is not supported by the evidence.[26] Moreover, in other countries, at least according to some measures, engineers have more prestige than lawyers.[27]

---

[25] Joel Gerstl and Lois Cohen, 'Dissensus, Situs and Egocentrism in Occupational Ranking' (1964) 15(3) British Journal of Sociology 254–61.

[26] K. McCormick, 'Prestige versus Practicality – a Dilemma for the Engineering Profession' IMechE Proc B (1985) 199 B3 139–44.

[27] Some US polling shows engineers enjoying higher prestige than lawyers (see http://www.harrisinteractive.com/vault/Harris-Interactive-Poll-Research-Pres-Occupations-2009-08.pdf, although the definition of prestige used seems to confuse social standing and usefulness to society. On other measures US lawyers usually have came out as higher status than US engineers, or at least they did several decades ago. See Edward McDonagh, Sven Wermlund and John Crowther, 'Relative Professional Status As Perceived By American And Swedish University Students' (1959) 38(1) Social Forces 65–69 (the two professions were rated close together in status terms in Sweden, although in both countries engineers were

But even if the evidence supported the claim that engineers were less respected than lawyers, would that claim support the rejection of law-as-engineering as a self-image lawyers should adopt? Lawyers, we might say, should not be so snobbish. To the extent that any low estimation of engineering (if it exists) is related to the notion we glanced at in Chapter 5 that engineering is somehow 'ungentlemanly' because of its connection with commerce ('trade'), the obvious response is that law is intimately connected with the same thing. Transactions lawyers are commercial lawyers. If lawyers really do take such reasoning seriously, one might start to suspect that the court-centred misunderstanding of lawyers' work is a product of lawyers' own desire to hide the 'ungentlemanly' nature of much of their own work. To the extent that any underestimation of engineering is related to a disdain for industry as opposed to commerce – to the view that somehow manufacturing and creating physical infra-structure are less honourable than banking and stockbroking – the events of the early 21st century mentioned in Chapter 4 might well soon reverse the position. And the extent to which underestimation of engineering results from confusion between professional engineers and technicians or mechanics (a confusion that the decline of manufacturing employment has if anything made less likely), it is simply erroneous and not to be encouraged by acquiescence.

Admittedly, not even engineers understand what lawyers do, and some-times claim that engineers and lawyers differ because engineers are judged on whether they 'succeed' in every piece of work they do, whereas lawyers might be expected to 'lose' half of their cases (and doctors eventually to 'lose' us all).[28] But that is merely another example of wrongly equating lawyers with litigators. Transactional and legislative lawyers are expected to 'succeed' every time.

Yet another type of benefit of the law-as-engineering perspective relates to the development of public policy. Political interaction with the legal profession, especially in the UK, seems to be in long-term decline,[29] and

---

thought to be more useful to society than lawyers – narrowly in the US, decisively in Sweden). See also Alex Inkeles and Peter Rossi, 'National Comparisons of Occupational Prestige' (1956) 61(4) American Journal of Sociology 329–39 (lawyers marginally ahead of civil engineers in the 1950s). Perhaps counter-intuitively, lawyers also come out ahead of engineers in Japan. See Tetsuji Iseda, 'How should we Foster the Professional Integrity of Engineers in Japan: A Pride-based Approach' (2008) 13 Science and Engineering Ethics 165–76.

[28] Alastair Gunn, 'Integrity and the Ethical Responsibility of Engineers' in Ibo van de Poel, David Goldberg and Michael Davis (eds) *Philosophy and Engineering: An Emerging Agenda* (London: Springer, 2010) at 128.

[29] My own work on this topic is in preparation. The percentage of lawyers

concentrates around a small number of policy areas, none of which give government a rounded picture of what lawyers are doing and can do. Those areas either involve significant public expenditure on lawyers (in the UK that means legal aid and negligence actions against public authorities, especially organisations in the National Health Service) or they involve the interests of the most powerful political interest groups, most especially the media. Understanding the central task of lawyers as engineering, as making useful and successful devices for their clients (including their public sector clients) might lead public policy makers to see the effects of their interventions in a more accurate way.

For example, much of the debate on legal aid and on the regulation of litigation costs seems to assume that lawyers have no other work to go to outside the courts, so that reducing legal aid rates or making representation of claimants in litigation less attractive can lead only to a reduction in lawyers' incomes, not to a reduction in access to justice. But the reality is that most lawyers make their living in other fields. The issue is how easily lawyers can switch out of legally aided or regulated work if rates fall. It might be difficult for a longstanding criminal legal aid practitioner to move to writing wills or conveyances, and even harder to move into writing commercial contracts, but for young lawyers to move from helping a partner with a medical malpractice case to helping a different partner with a commercial property transaction might not be so difficult. Policy-makers need to know this kind of thing.

Seeing lawyers as engineers might also be helpful in thinking about other aspects of public policy. For example, instead of thinking in a stereotypical way about lawyers 'having field days', policy-makers might instead think about what lawyers might be able do at the behest of their clients with the legal rules that policy-makers cause to be created. There are important trade-offs for policy-makers that treating all legal costs as wasted conceals from view. For example, proposals for new rights that cannot safely be used without legal advice often start at a disadvantage. But no one would reject a new machine simply because it cannot be used by do-it-yourself enthusiasts. The need for legal advice might add to the cost of implementing a new right, but the benefits might outweigh the costs. Distributional issues might also cause concern, but if technical innovations were suppressed

---

in the House of Commons is in long-term decline, peaking at over 25 per cent just after the First World War, but dropping to about half that now. The fall is, interestingly, entirely on the side of barristers rather than solicitors. On the other side, there is currently only one judge of High Court rank or higher who has served as a Member of Parliament.

until everyone could afford them, the mobile phone, the personal computer and even electricity would have been strangled at birth.

Understanding the creative, useful role of lawyers might even help government use its own lawyers better. The higher civil service in Britain seems to contain very few lawyers. Accurate figures are not easy to obtain, but it is striking that of the nearly 50 fast-stream civil servants mentioned in the Civil Service's own elite recruitment website,[30] not one mentions having a law degree or any other legal qualification. At the highest possible level, only one of the six most recent Cabinet Secretaries had a higher law degree,[31] and that was thought very unusual. Many civil servants in policy-advising roles have very little contact with lawyers except when threatened with judicial review (that is with the 'Judge over Your Shoulder'),[32] or when dealing with the Office of Parliamentary Counsel about the drafting of a bill, a process Parliamentary Counsel themselves believe works better at arm's length.[33] A few might have experienced working at close quarters with highly skilled and creative transactions lawyers from the City of London firms during the era of large scale privatisations in the 1980s and 1990s, but the later equivalent of privatisation, the creation of private finance initiative deals, seems to have been carried out by a large set of smaller commercial firms at a more local level, away from the providers of policy advice. Some senior transactions lawyers appear in regulatory roles, especially regulation of the types of transaction they previously engineered – for example a mergers and acquisitions lawyer might sit on the Competition Commission or a corporate finance lawyer on the body responsible for managing bank assets guaranteed by the government in the wake of the banking crisis. But transactions lawyers' expertise has not been much used, at least openly, in designing regulation in the first place.

A final benefit of seeing lawyers as engineers is that it provides a clearer role for university law faculties and indicates to academic lawyers where they are most likely to find allies within their institutions. Law, like engineering, is about changing the state of the world more than just understanding it. Engineers, both inside and outside academia, prefer making something useful to discovering something new. It would not be surprising

---

[30] Data collected from http://faststream.civilservice.gov.uk/.

[31] The law degrees belong to Richard Wilson (Lord Wilson of Dinton). Two immediate past post-holders were economists (Lord O'Donnell and Lord Turnbull) and two classicists (Lord Armstrong and Lord Butler). The current incumbent (Jeremy Heywood) is another economist.

[32] See http://www.tsol.gov.uk/Publications/Scheme_Publications/judge.pdf for the latest edition of this celebrated pamphlet.

[33] See Chapter 2.

to find that practising lawyers have a similar preference. Legal academics, however, seem more torn. Many seek out opportunities to be useful – for example by advising governments or Parliaments, making submissions to reform bodies or seeking to influence policy debate through the media. But others seem deliberately to seek out opportunities to be less than useful. Part of the problem is that academic respectability seems to flow from claiming to understand the world rather than from claiming to be able to change it. Those disciplines whose central concern is design or decision – business, medicine, engineering and architecture – generally suffer from lower prestige than their 'pure' counterparts – economics, biology, physics and aesthetics. Even philosophers have been known to belittle ethics and to extol 'purer' topics such as logic. Academic lawyers would understandably wish to avoid being classified with these lower status disciplines of design and decision and would prefer to find themselves in the more elegant company of the disciplines of appreciation. But that would be to deny part of the fundamental orientation of lawyers. Academic lawyers would be happier, and more creative, if they stopped trying exclusively to associate, and even compete, with philosophers, economists and literary critics and gave in to their practical selves.

A FINAL WORD – LAWYERS AND THE CRASH

It is not unusual for world events to shake lawyers' views of themselves and to give birth to new perspectives. The New Deal in the US brought many lawyers not only to Washington, but also to see themselves as legal realists. In 1946, Gustav Radbruch, surveying the smoking ruins of his country and the genocide it had wrought, abandoned what last remnants of legal positivism he might have held in favour of a form of natural law that helped to create modern human rights jurisprudence.[34] The question now is whether lawyers will scan the wreckage of the world financial system they helped to create in 2008 and ask themselves once more who they are.

---

[34] Gustav Radbruch, 'Fünf Minuten Rechtsphilosophie' Rhein-Neckar Zeitung 12 September 1945, and 'Gesetzliches Unrecht und übergesetzliches Recht', Süddeutsche Juristenzeitung (1946) I 105-8, translated by Bonnie Litschewski-Paulson and Stanley Paulson, (2006) 26 Legal Studies 1–15. Whether Radbruch had ever been a fully-fledged positivist is disputed by Paulson ('On the background and significance of Gustav Radbruch's Post-War Papers' (2006) 26 Legal Studies 17–40), who interprets Radbruch's earlier position as fundamentally non-positivist but with the addition of not allowing the judiciary any room for implementing a non-positivist view.

Like the engineers who created the space shuttle, or even like the physicists who helped to create the atomic bomb, lawyers are now in a position to understand their own destructive power. Lawyers have been acting as engineers for centuries, but their ability to construct devices that empower or enrich their clients has grown only recently to the point that if they go wrong, they affect not just the lives of a few, but the lives of people around the world. The closed world of the litigator and the advocate, in which justice or injustice could be doled out in small doses, has been replaced by the open world of the transactions lawyer and the legislative lawyer, in which lawyers can bring pleasure or pain to millions.

Moreover, the era has gone when lawyers could tell themselves that the institution of the market ensures that, as if by an invisible hand, all they had to do to serve the public interest was to serve their clients. Sophisticated economists and legal theorists always knew that the relationship between the market and the law, and thus between commercial and legal behaviour, is complex. Many markets, especially the most abstract, depend for their very existence on legal structures, without which there would be no buyers or sellers and nothing to buy or sell. Lawyers were not just part of a system of regulation of commercial activity from outside those activities. Lawyers were intimately involved in creating the regulated devices and the market in them. Their responsibility should have extended to the whole market, and beyond it to the whole financial system. Instead, at best they adopted the Wernher von Braun theory of lawyering ('where it comes down, that's not my department') and at worst treated the world they helped to create as an aspect of nature, as a brute fact unconnected with their own actions.

Viewing lawyers, and lawyers viewing themselves, as engineers simultaneously captures both lawyers' power and their responsibilities, the power both to build and to destroy and the responsibility that when they exercise their power they should do so for the public good. It offers a way out of the adversarial, litigation-based self-image that lies at the heart of why lawyers thought, and perhaps still think, that the events of 2008 were nothing to do with them. Indeed, if there is one thing lawyers should learn from engineers it is that one should always learn from failure, and that one can learn even more from disasters.

One might still object that this is a theory only of elite lawyers, of the City of London or Wall Street firms and their mighty (or overmighty) clients in finance. But although the theory works most clearly for those lawyers, it also describes well what other lawyers do and what their responsibilities are. The government lawyer who helps to design secret courts and who purports to create authority for physical mistreatment of prisoners is also engaged in engineering, and risks disaster of a different kind. The media lawyer who advises a newspaper about how it might successfully profit from the destruction of someone's reputation is helping to create a machine as deadly, if not more deadly, than the Repo 105. All these lawyers need to ask themselves about the effects they are having not only on potential claimants in litigation but also on the culture and the mores of the society in which they live. Can they really say that their work is for the public benefit? Admittedly, most lawyers – those who specialise in commercial leases or contracts – rarely do anything that might trouble their consciences at this kind of level. But, potentially, even they might be faced with serious problems connected with the consequences of what they do. After all, what were the synthetic CDOs that Goldman marketed than the sum of thousands, even millions, of small property deals? Playing a small role in a big event brings its own responsibilities.

There might be some lawyers who are happy to be described as engineers, but not happy with the ethical baggage suggested here that they should carry. It is certainly logically possible to behave as an engineer without accepting the ethical burdens engineers bear. Indeed, engineers themselves struggled for a long time with their ethical responsibilities about safety, sustainability and public welfare, and might instead have arrived at a view of engineering that was purely technical. No doubt there are still engineers who would still like to think of themselves as nothing but technical advisers without ethical responsibilities. Moreover, it must feel very comfortable to place oneself in an unchallenging ethical world where one can assume that the institutions within which one works are justified, be that the market or the state, and so anything one does within those institutions is itself prima facie justified. But, in the post-financial crash era, the prima facie justification for the market as a moral institution is surely in as much doubt as the prima facie justification for the state has been since at least the time of Radbruch. Knowing what we now know about the power of lawyers to do harm as well as to bring benefits, to adopt the guise of engineers without also adopting the ethical standards that apply to them would be opportunistic, callow and self-serving. Lawyers can do better than that.

Bibliography

Abbott, A. 1988 *The System of Professions: An Essay on the Division of Expert Labor* (Chicago: University of Chicago).

Akerlof, G. 1970 'The Market for "Lemons": Quality Uncertainty and the Market Mechanism' 84(3) Quarterly Journal of Economics 488–500.

Anon. 2010 'Who should be Responsible?' 29(4) International Financial Law Review 15.

Arthurs, H.W. 1995 'A Lot of Knowledge is a Dangerous Thing: Will the Legal Profession Survive the Knowledge Explosion?' 18 Dalhousie Law Journal 295–309.

Balkin, J. 1996 Interdisciplinarity as Colonization' 53 Washington Lee Law Review 949–70

Barton, B. 2010 *The Law-Judge Bias in the American Legal Process* (Cambridge: Cambridge U.P.).

Bean, C. 2010 'The Great Moderation, the Great Panic and the Great Contraction' 8 Journal of the European Economic Association 289–325.

Bedau, M. 1997 'Weak Emergence' 11 Philosophical Perspectives 375–99.

Bedau, M. 2001 'Downward Causation and the Autonomy of Weak Emergence' (2002) 6(1) Principia 5–50.

Bell, J. 2000 'What Is the Function of the Conseil d'Etat in the Preparation of Legislation?' 49 International and Comparative Law Quarterly 661–72.

Bellis, M.D. 2001 'Drafting in the US Congress' 22 Statute Law Review 38–44.

Bennett, R. and P. Robson 1999 'The Use of External Business Advice by SMEs in Britain' 11 Entrepreneurship & Regional Development 155–80.

Ben-Shahar, O. and J. Pottow 2006 'On the Stickiness of Default Rules' (2006) 33 Florida State University Law Review 651–82.

Bentham, J. 1808 Letter to James Mackintosh *Works* (J. Bowring ed., Edinburgh, 1838–43).

Berger, K.-P. 2011 'European Private Law, Lex Mercatoria and Globalization' in A. Hartkamp, M. Hesselink, E. Hondius, C. Mak and C. E. du Perron, *Towards A European Civil Code* 4th edition (Alphen aan den Rijn: Kluwer-Ars Aequi Libri).

Bernstein, L. 1995 'The Silicon Valley Lawyer as Transactions Cost Engineer' 74 Oregon Law Review 239–55.

Bickel, A. 1986 *The Least Dangerous Branch* 2nd edition (New Haven, CT: Yale U.P.).

Binmore, K. and P. Klemperer 2002 'The Biggest Auction Ever: the Sale of the British 3G Telecom Licences' 112(478) Economic Journal C74–C96.

Black, D. 1993 *The Social Structure of Right and Wrong* (San Diego, CA: Academic Press).

Bogart, D. 2000 'The Right Way to Teach Transactional Lawyers: Commercial Leasing and the Forgotten "Dirt Lawyer"' 62 University of Pittsburgh Law Review 335–66.

Bond, P. 1916 *The Engineer in War* (New York: Mcgraw-Hill).

Boon, A. 2004 'Cause Lawyering and the Alternative Ethical Paradigm: Ideology and Transgression' 7 Legal Ethics 250–68.

Boorman, S. and P. Levitt 1983 'Blockmodeling Complex Statutes: Mapping Techniques Based on Combinatorial Optimization for Analyzing Economic Legislation and Its Stress Points Over Time' 13 Economics Letters 1–9.

Bradney, B. 2003 *Conversations, Choices and Chances: The Liberal Law School in the Twenty-first Century* (Oxford: Hart).

Brest, P. and L. Hamilton Kreiger 1999 'Lawyers as Problem Solvers' 72 Temple Law Review 811–32.

Brown, L. and E. Dauer 1978 *Planning by Lawyers: Materials on a Nonadversarial Legal Process* (Mineola, NY: Foundation Press).

Brownsword, R. 1992 'Teaching Contract: A Liberal Agenda' in Peter Birks (ed.), *Examining the Law Syllabus: The Core* (Oxford: Oxford U.P.).

Bruce, M., F. Leverick and D. Littler 1995 'Complexities of Collaborative Product Development' 15(9) Technovation 535–52.

Buchanan, R. 2009 'Thinking about Design: An Historical Perspective' in Antonie Meijers (ed.), *Philosophy of Technology and Engineering Science* (Oxford: Elsevier).

Butt, P. and R. Castle 2006 *Modern Legal Drafting: A Guide to Using Clearer Language* 2nd edition (Cambridge: Cambridge U.P.).

Campbell, R. and E. Gaetke 2003 'The Ethical Obligation of Transactional Lawyers to act as Gatekeepers' 56 Rutgers Law Review 9–71.

Caruth, D. 1998 *A Life of Three Strands: A City Lawyer's Memoir* (London: Avon Books).

Chadha, J. and S. Holly (eds) 2012 *Interest Rates, Prices and Liquidity: Lessons from the Financial Crisis* (Cambridge: Cambridge U.P.).

Choi, S. and M. Gulati 2004 'Innovation in Boilerplate Contracts: An Empirical Examination of Sovereign Bonds' 53 Emory Law Journal 929–96.

Choi, S. and Mitu Gulati 2005 'The Evolution of Boilerplate Contracts: Evidence from the Sovereign Debt Market' New York University School of Law, Law and Economics Research Paper Series: Research Paper No. 05-17.

Collini, S. 2012 *What are Universities for?* (London: Penguin).

Cownie, F. 2003 'Alternative Values in Legal Education' 6 Legal Ethics 159–74.

Cownie, F. 2005 'The Academic Stage of Training for Entry into the Legal Profession in England and Wales: Response by the Society of Legal Scholars to a Consultation by the Law Society of England and Wales and the General Council of the Bar of England and Wales with Law Faculties offering Qualifying Law Degrees' http://www.legalscholars.ac.uk/documents/SLS%20Reply%20HoDs.doc.

Cownie, F. 2011 'Exploring Values in Legal Education' (2011) Web Journal of Current Legal Issues.

Cownie, F. and A. Paterson 2004 'Evidence Submitted by the Society of Legal Scholars to the Review of the Regulatory Framework for Legal Services in England and Wales' (http://www1.legalscholars.ac.uk/education/clementi.pdf.

Cragg, W. 1997 'Teaching Business Ethics: The Role of Ethics in Business and in Business Education' 16 Journal of Business Ethics 231–45.

D'Amato, A. 1984 *Jurisprudence: A Descriptive and Normative Analysis of Law* (Dordrecht: Martinus Nijhoff).

Dasgupta, S. 1996 *Technology and Creativity* (Oxford: Oxford U.P.).

Dauer, E. and A. Leff 1977 'The Lawyer as Friend' 86 Yale Law Journal 573–84.

Davis, M. 1998 *Thinking Like an Engineer: Studies in the Ethics of a Profession* (Oxford: Oxford U.P.).

De La Merced, M. and J. Werdigier 2010 'The Origins of Lehman's "Repo 105"' New York Times, 12 March 2010.

De Weck, O., D. Roos and C. Roos 2011 *Engineering Systems* (Cambridge, MA: MIT Press).

Deakin, S. and A. Koukiadaki 2009 'Governance Processes, Labour–Management Partnership and Employee Voice in the Construction of Heathrow Terminal 5' 38 Industrial Law Journal 365–89.

Dennett, L. 1989 *Slaughter and May: A Century in the City* (Cambridge: Granta).

Dennis, R. 1997 'Commentary: The Epistemology of Corporate Securities Lawyering: Beliefs, Biases and Organizational Behavior' 63 Brooklyn Law Review 677–84.

Dent, G. 2008 'Business Lawyers as Enterprise Architects' 64 Business Law 279–314.

Dobbins, R. 2005 'The Layered Dispute Resolution Clause: From Boilerplate to Business Opportunity' 1 Hastings Business Law Journal 161–82.

Dodds, R. and R. Daniels (eds) 2005 *Engineering for Sustainable Development: Guiding Principles* (London: Royal Academy of Engineering).

Domnarski, W. 1987 'Trouble in Paradise: Wall Street Lawyers and the Fiction of Louis Auchincloss' 12 Journal of Contemporary Law 243–59.

Donakey, A. 2005 'It's Who You Know . . . PSLs, Knowledge Brokers and Firm-wide Innovation' 7 Managing Partner 9.

Dorff, M. 2002 Why Welfare Depends on Fairness: A Reply to Kaplow and Shavell' 75 Southern California Law Review 847–99.

Dorst, K. and N. Cross 2001 'Creativity in the Design Process: Co-evolution of Problem–Solution' 22(5) Design Studies 425–37.

Duxbury, N. 1995 *Patterns of American Jurisprudence* (Oxford: Clarendon Press).

Dworkin, R. 1977 *Taking Rights Seriously* (Cambridge, MA: Harvard U.P.).

Dworkin, R. 1986 *Law's Empire* (London: Fontana).

Economides, K. and J. Rogers 2009 *Preparatory Ethics Training for Future Solicitors* (London: Law Society).

Edwards, H. 1992 'The Growing Disjunction Between Legal Education and the Legal Profession' 92 Michigan Law Review 34–78.

Eidson Espenschied, L. 2010 *Contract Drafting: Powerful Prose in Transactional Practice* (Chicago, IL: American Bar Association Publishing).

Ellis, N. 1998 'Emergentism, Connectionism and Language Learning' 48(4) Language Learning 631–64.

Engel, G. 1983 '"Bills are made to Pass as Razors are made to Sell": Practical Constraints in the Preparation of Legislation' 4 Statute Law Review 7–23.

Erlanger, H., B. Garth, J. Larson, E. Mertz, V. Nourse and D. Wilkins 2005 'Is it Time for a New Legal Realism?' [2005] Wisconsin Law Review 335–63.

Evans, D. 2008 'The Conflict of the Faculties and the Knowledge Industry: Kant's Diagnosis, in his Time and Ours' 83 Philosophy 483–95.

Feldman, S. M. 2004 'The Transformation of an Academic Discipline: Law Professors in the Past and Future (or Toy Story Too)' 54 Journal of Legal Education 471–98.

Fenner, R., C. Ainger, H. Cruickshank and P. Guthrie 2005 'Embedding Sustainable Development at Cambridge University Engineering

Department' 6(3) International Journal of Sustainability in Higher Education 229–41.

Feynman, R. 1986 'Personal Observations on Reliability of the Shuttle' Appendix F of vol. 2 of W. Rogers (chair), *Report of the Presidential Commission on the Space Shuttle Challenger Accident* (Washington, DC: NASA, 1986).

Finn, D. 2006 *The Moral Ecology of Markets: Assessing Claims about Markets and Justice* (Cambridge: Cambridge U.P.).

Fish, S. 2008 *Save the World on Your Own Time* (Oxford: Oxford U. P.).

Fleischer, V. 2002 'Deals: Bringing Corporate Transactions into the Law School Classroom' 2 Columbia Business Law Review 475–97.

Fleming, J. 2000 'The Lawyer as Citizen' 70 Fordham Law Review 1699–716.

Flood, J. 1991 'Doing Business: The Management of Uncertainty in Lawyers' Work' 25 Law and Society Review 41–71.

Flood, J. 1996 'Megalawyering in the Global Order: the Cultural, Social and Economic Transformation of Global Legal Practice' 3 International Journal of the Legal Profession 169–214.

Flood, J. 2007 'Resurgent Professionalism? Partnership and Professionalism in Global Law Firms' in D. Muzio and S. Ackroyd, *Redirections in the Study of Expert Labour* (Basingstoke: Palgrave).

Flood, J. and E. Skordaki 2009 'Structuring Transactions: The Case of Real Estate Finance' in V. Gessner (ed.) *Contractual Certainty in International Trade: Empirical Studies and Theoretical Debates on Institutional Support for Global Economic Exchanges* (Oxford: Hart Publishing).

Fournier, E. 2010 'The Reality of Repo 105' 29(3) International Financial Law Review 60.

Fox, R. 1957 'Training for Uncertainty' in Robert Merton et al., *The Student Physician: Introductory Studies in the Sociology of Medical Education* (Cambridge, MA: Harvard U.P.).

Francis, A. 2011 *Law at the Edge: Emergent and Divergent Models of Legal Professionalism* (Farnham: Ashgate).

Franssen, M., G.-J. Lokhorst and I. van de Poel 2010 'Philosophy of Technology' in E. Zalta (ed.), *The Stanford Encyclopedia of Philosophy* (Spring 2010 Edition).

Fuller, L. 1953 'American Legal Philosophy at Mid-Century – A Review of Edwin W. Patterson's Jurisprudence, Men and Ideas of the Law' 6 Journal of Legal Education 457–85.

Fuller, L. 1969 *The Morality of Law* (New Haven, CT: Yale U.P.).

Fuller, L. 1981 'The Lawyer as an Architect of Social Structures' in L. Fuller, *The Principles of Social Order: Selected Essays of Lon L Fuller* (Durham, NC: Duke U.P.).

Fung, Y.C. and P. Tong 2001 *Classical and Computational Solid Mechanics* (Singapore: World Scientific).

Galanter, M. 2006 'In the Winter of Our Discontent: Law, Anti-Law and Social Science' 2 Annual Review of Law and Social Sciences 1–16.

Garnier, E. 2010 'The Law Officers and Legislative Procedure' Speech to ALBA Summer Conference 17 July 2010, (http://www.adminlaw.org.uk/docs/sc%202010%20by%20Edward%20Garnier.pdf).

Garvey, G. 1971 *Constitutional Bricolage* (Princeton, NJ: Princeton U.P.).

Gerstl, J. and L. Cohen 1964 'Dissensus, Situs and Egocentrism in Occupational Ranking' 15(3) British Journal of Sociology 254–61.

Gilmore, G. 1961 'Legal Realism: Its Causes and Cure' 70 Yale Law Journal 1037–48.

Gilson, R. 1984 'Value Creation by Business Lawyers: Legal Skills and Asset Pricing' 94 Yale Law Journal 239–313.

Glanert, S. 2008 'Speaking Language to Law: The Case of Europe' 28 Legal Studies 161–71.

Glegg, G. 1969 *The Design of Design* (Cambridge: Cambridge U.P.).

Goldman, S. and T. Jahnige 1971 'Systems Analysis and Judicial Systems: Potential and Limitations' 3(3) Polity 334–59.

Goodrich, P. 1987 'Of Blackstone's Tower: Metaphors of Distance and Histories of English Law Schools' in P. Birks (ed.), *Pressing Problems in the Law (2): What Are Law Schools For?* (Oxford: Oxford U.P.).

Gordon, R. 1993 'Lawyers, Scholars and the "Middle Ground"' 91 Michigan Law Review 2099–119.

Gordon, R. 2004 'Professors and Policymakers' in Anthony Kronman (ed.), *History of the Yale Law School* (New Haven, CT: Yale U.P.).

Gotterbarn, D. 2001 'Informatics and Professional Responsibility' 7 Science and Engineering Ethics 221–30.

Gotterbarn, D. 2008 '"Once more unto the Breach": Professional Responsibility and Computer Ethics' 14 Science and Engineering Ethics 235–39.

Greenberg, D. 2011 *Laying Down the Law: A Discussion of the People, Processes and Problems that Shape Acts of Parliament* (London: Sweet and Maxwell).

Grote, K.-H. and E. Antonsson 2009 *Springer Handbook of Mechanical Engineering*, Volume 10 (New York: Springer).

Gulati, M. and R. Scott 2011 'The Three and a Half Minute Transaction: Boilerplate and the Limits of Contract Design' Columbia Law and Economics Working Paper No. 407.

Gunn, A. 2010 'Integrity and the Ethical Responsibility of Engineers' in I. van de Poel, D. Goldberg and M. Davis (eds), *Philosophy and Engineering: An Emerging Agenda* (London: Springer).

Hadfield, G. 2006 'Don't Forget the Lawyers: The Role of Lawyers in Promoting the Rule of Law in (Emerging) Market Democracies' 56 DePaul Law Review 401–21.

Haggard, T. and G. Kuney 2007 *Legal Drafting: Process, Techniques, and Exercises* (Eagen, MN: Thomson-West).

House of Lords Select Committee on the Constitution 2009 *Fast-Track Legislation: Constitutional Implications and Safeguards* (London: TSO).

Halliday, S., J. Ilan and C. Scott 2012 'Street-Level Torts: The Bureaucratic Justice of Liability Decision-Making' 75 Modern Law Review 347–67.

Harris, C., M. Pritchard and M.J. Rabins 2009 *Engineering Ethics: Concepts and Cases* (Belmont, CA: Wadsworth Cengage).

Hartkamp, A., M. Hesselink, E. Hondius, C. Mak and C. E. du Perron 2011 *Towards A European Civil Code* 4th edition (Alphen aan den Rijn: Kluwer-Ars Aequi Libri).

Hazard, G. 1992 'Lawyer Liability in Third Party Situations: The Meaning of the Kaye Scholer Case' 26 Akron Law Review 395–406.

Hazard, G. 1997 'The Client Fraud Problem as a Justinian Quartet: An Extended Analysis' 25 Hofstra Law Review 1041–61.

Heinz, J., and E. Laumann 1982 *Chicago Lawyers: The Social Structure of the Bar* (New York: Russell Sage).

Heinz, J., R. Nelson, R. Sandefur and E. Laumann 2005 *Urban Lawyers: The New Social Structure of the Bar* (Chicago, IL: University of Chicago Press).

Hepple, B. 1996 'The Liberal Law Degree' 55 Cambridge Law Journal 470–87.

Herring, J. 2007 *Family Law* (London: Pearson).

Hodges, J. 2010 'Linklaters opinion letter at centre of Lehman funding controversy' legalweek.com 12 Mar 2010.

Hohfeld, W.N. 1919 *Fundamental Legal Conceptions as Applied to Legal Reasoning* (New Haven, CT: Yale U.P.).

Hollander, G. 2010 'Lehman exploited Linklaters opinion to tidy up balance sheet' The Lawyer 12 March 2010.

Hollnagel, E., C. Nemeth and S. Dekker 2008 *Resilience Engineering Perspectives, Volume 1: Remaining Sensitive to the Possibility of Failure* (Aldershot: Ashgate).

Hollnagel, E., D. Woods and N. Leveson (eds) 2006 *Resilience Engineering: Concepts and Precepts* (Aldershot: Ashgate).

Howarth, D. 2004 'Is Law a Humanity (Or Is It More Like Engineering)?' 3(1) Arts and Humanities in Higher Education 9–28.

Huff, C. 2008 'It is Not All Straw, But it Can Catch Fire: In Defense of Impossible Ideals in Computing' 14 Science and Engineering Ethics 241–44.

Huff, T. 1985 'The Temptations of Creon: Philosophical Reflections on the Ethics of the Lawyer's Professional Role' 46 Montana Law Review 47–77.

Hull, N.E.H. 1997 *Roscoe Pound and Karl Llewellyn: Searching for an American Jurisprudence* (Chicago, IL: University of Chicago Press).

Humbach, J. 2009 'Shifting Paradigms of Lawyer Honesty' 76 Tennessee Law Review 993–1037.

Inkeles, A. and P. Rossi 1956 'National Comparisons of Occupational Prestige' 61(4) American Journal of Sociology 329–39.

Iseda, T. 2008 'How should we Foster the Professional Integrity of Engineers in Japan: A Pride-based Approach' 13 Science and Engineering Ethics 165–76.

Jabbari, D. 2006 'Know it All: The New KM Strategy at Allen & Overy' 9 Inside Knowledge 8.

Jackson, S. 2010 *Architecting Resilient Systems: Accident Avoidance and Survival and Recovery from Disruptions* (Hoboken, NJ, London: John Wiley).

Jarrett-Kerr, N. 2011 'Alternative Business Structures – the Long Pregnancy' 11 Legal Information Management 82–85.

Johnson, P. 1983 *A History of the Modern World from 1917 to the 1980s* (London: Weidenfeld and Nicolson).

Jones, R. and K. Joscelyn 1976 'A Systems Approach to the Analysis of Transportation Law' 8 Transportation Law Journal 71–89.

Kalman, L. 1986 *Legal Realism at Yale 1927-1960* (Chapel Hill, NC: University of North Carolina Press).

Kalman, L. 1998 *The Strange Career of Legal Liberalism* (New Haven, CT: Yale U.P.).

Kaplow L., and S. Shavell 2006 *Fairness versus Welfare* (Cambridge, MA: Harvard U.P.).

Kappel, T. and A. Rubenstein 1999 'Creativity in Design: The Contribution of Information Technology' 46(2) IEEE Transactions on Engineering Management 132–43.

Kelman, M. 1990 *A Guide to Critical Legal Studies* (Cambridge, MA: Harvard U.P.).

Kim, S. H. 2010 'Lawyer Exceptionalism in the Gatekeeping Wars' 63 SMU Law Review 73–136.

Kincaid, H. and D. Ross 2009 *The Oxford Handbook of Philosophy of Economics* (Oxford: Oxford U.P.).

Koops, B.-J. 2006 'Should ICT Regulation be Technology-Neutral?' in B.-J. Koops, M. Lips, C. Prins and M. Schellekens, *Starting Points for ICT Regulation: Deconstructing Prevalent Policy One-liners* (The Hague: TMC Asser Press).

Kreitner, R. 2010 'Biographing Realist Jurisprudence' 35 Law & Social Inquiry 765–91.

Kritzer, H. 1999 'The Professions Are Dead, Long Live the Professions: Legal Practice in a Post-professional World' 33 Law & Society Review 713–59.

Kronman, A. 1995 *The Lost Lawyer: Failing Ideals of the Legal Profession* (Cambridge, MA: Harvard U.P.).

Kronman, A. (ed.) 2004 *History of the Yale Law School* (New Haven, CT: Yale U.P.).

Lallement, G. 1818 *Choix de Rapports, Opinions et Discours Prononcés à la Tribune Nationale* vol. 2 (Paris: A. Eymery et Corréard).

Landsman, S. 2010 'The Risk of Risk Management' 78 Fordham Law Review 2315–27.

Laracy, J. 2007 'Addressing System Boundary Issues in Complex Socio-Technical Systems' 2(19) Systems Research Forum 19–26.

Lasswell, H. and M. McDougal 1943 'Legal Education and Public Policy: Professional Training in the Public Interest' 52 Yale Law Journal 203–95.

Lasswell, H. 1946 'The Interrelations of World Organization and Society' 55 Yale Law Journal 870–88.

Lasswell, H. and M. McDougal 1966 'Jurisprudence in Policy-Oriented Perspective' 19 University of Florida Law Review 486–513.

Lasswell, H. and M. McDougal 1992 *Jurisprudence for a Free Society: Studies in Law, Science and Policy* (Dordrecht, London: Nijhoff).

Lawry, R. and others 2001 The Jonathan M. Ault Symposium, 'Professional Responsibility and Multi-Disciplinary Practice' 52 Case Western Reserve Law Review 861–1004.

Laws, S. 2011 'Giving Effect to Policy in Legislation: How to Avoid Missing the Point' 32 Statute Law Review 1–16.

Legrand, P. 1996 'Sens et Non-sens d'un Code Européen' 4 Revue internationale de droit comparé 779–812.

Leiter, B. 1995 'Legal Indeterminacy' 1 Legal Theory 481–92.

Leveson, N. 2011 *Engineering a Safer World: Systems Thinking Applied to Safety* (Cambridge, MA: MIT Press).

Leveson, N. 2011 'The Role of Complexity in Safety Management and How to Manage It' http://tx.technion.ac.il/~gordoncn/05072011/3.Nancy_presentation.ppt.

Levin, C. (Chair) 2011 *Wall Street and the Financial Crisis: Anatomy of a Financial Collapse* United States Senate, Permanent Subcommittee on Investigations of the Committee on Homeland Security and Governmental Affairs.

Lewis, J. with J. Keegan 1997 *Defining Legal Business: Understanding the Work of the Largest Law Firms* (London: Law Society).

Llewellyn, K. 1942 'The Crafts of Law Re-valued' 15 Rocky Mountain Law Review 1–7.

Llewellyn, K. 1943 'McDougal and Lasswell Plan for Legal Education' 43 Columbia Law Review 476–85.

Llewellyn, K. 1947 'The Modern Approach to Counselling and Advocacy – Especially in Commercial Transactions' 46 Columbia Law Review 167–95.

Llewellyn, K. 1960a *The Bramble Bush* (New York: Oceana Publications).

Llewellyn, K. 1960b *The Common Law Tradition: Deciding Appeals* (Boston, MA: Little, Brown).

Llewellyn, K. 1962 *Jurisprudence: Realism in Theory and Practise* (Chicago, IL: University of Chicago Press).

Llewellyn, K. and E.A. Hoebel 1941 *The Cheyenne Way* (Norman, OK: University of Oklahoma Press).

Luban, D. 1988 *Lawyers and Justice: An Ethical Study* (Princeton, NJ: Princeton U.P.).

Luban, D. and M. Milleman 1995 'Good Judgment: Ethics Teaching in Dark Times' 9 Georgetown Journal of Legal Ethics 31–87.

Luegenbiehl, H. 2010 'Ethical Principles for Engineers in a Global Environment' in I. van de Poel, D. Goldberg and M. Davis (eds), *Philosophy and Engineering: An Emerging Agenda* (London: Springer).

Luntz Research Companies 1997 *Language of the 21st Century* (Alexandra VA: Luntz Research Companies).

Luntz, F. *Republican Playbook* http://www.politicalstrategy.org/archives/001205.php.

Madni A. and S. Jackson 2009 'Towards a Conceptual Framework for Resilience Engineering' 3(2) IEEE Systems Journal 181–91.

Maher, M.L. and J. Poon 1996 'Modeling Design Exploration as Co-evolution' 11(3) Microcomputers in Civil Engineering 195–209.

Maki, U. (ed) 2002 *Fact and Fiction in Economics: Models, Realism and Social Construction* (Cambridge: Cambridge U.P.).

Manheim, M. 1966 *Hierarchical Structure: A Model of Design and Planning Processes* (Cambridge, MA: MIT Press).

March, J. and H. Simon 1958 *Organizations* (New York: John Wiley).

Marshall, H., L. McClymont and L. Joyce 2007 *Public Attitudes to and Perceptions of Engineering and Engineers* (London: Royal Academy of Engineering).

Martin, D. 2009 *One Stop Company Secretary* 6th edition (London: ICSA).

Maxeiner, J. 2006 'Legal Indeterminancy Made in America: U.S. Legal Methods and the Rule of Law' 41 Valparaiso University Law Review 517–89.

McCormick, K. 1985 'Prestige versus Practicality – a Dilemma for the Engineering Profession' IMechE Proc B 199 B3 139–44.

McDonagh, E., S. Wermlund and J. Crowther 1959 'Relative Professional Status As Perceived By American And Swedish University Students' 38(1) Social Forces 65–69.

McDougal, M. 1941 'Fuller v. The American Realists' 50 Yale Law Journal 827–40.

McDougal, M. 1956 'Law as a Process of Decision-A Policy-Oriented Approach to Legal Study' 1 Natural Law Forum 53–72.

McDougal, M. 1966 'Jurisprudence for a Free Society' 1 Georgia Law Review 1–19.

McDougal, M. 1979 'The Application of Constitutive Prescriptions: An Addendum to Justice Cardozo' 1 Cardozo Law Review 135–70.

Mindes, M. and A. Acock 1982 'Trickster, Hero, Helper: A Report on the Lawyer Image' 7 Law & Social Inquiry 177–233.

Morsch, T. 2003 'Discovering Transactional Pro Bono' 72 UMKC Law Review 423–31.

Motte, D. 2006 'A Review of the Fundamentals of Systematic Engineering Design Process Models' (International Design Conference, Dubrovnik, Croatia).

Moulton, B. 2010 'Pro Bono in Engineering: Towards a Better Understanding' in M. Iskander, V. Kapil and M. Karim, *Technological Developments in Education and Automation* (Netherlands: Springer).

Murphy, M. and M. Peel 2010 'Linklaters faces fall-out from Repo 105' Financial Times 13 March 2010.

Nagel, T. 1991 'Ruthlessness in Public Life' in *Mortal Questions* (Cambridge: Cambridge U.P., 1991 [1979]).

Nathanson, S. 1997 *What Lawyers Do* (London: Sweet and Maxwell).

Nedjah, N. and L. De Macedo Mourelle 2005 *Real-World Multi-Objective System Engineering* (Hauppauge, NY: Nova).

Nemeth, C. 2009 'The Ability to Adapt' in C. Nemeth, E. Hollnagel and S. Dekker, *Resilience Engineering Perspectives, Volume 2: Preparation and Restoration* (Aldershot: Ashgate).

Nemeth, C., E. Hollnagel and S. Dekker 2009 *Resilience Engineering Perspectives,* Volume 2: *Preparation and Restoration* (Aldershot: Ashgate).

Newmanm J.H. 1907 *The Idea of a University* (London: Longmans).

Oakeshott, M. 1962 *Rationalism in Politics and Other Essays* (London: Methuen).

O' Dair, D.R.F. 1997 'Ethics by the Pervasive Method: the Case of Contract' 17 Legal Studies 305–22.

Office of Parliamentary Counsel 2011a *A Summary of Working with Parliamentary Counsel* (London, Cabinet Office) (http://www.cabinet

office.gov.uk/sites/default/files/resources/wwpc_web_guide_ summary_6_dec_2011.pdf.

Office of Parliamentary Counsel 2011b *Drafting Guidance* (London: Cabinet Office) (http://www.cabinetoffice.gov.uk/sites/default/files/resou rces/Office_of_the_Parliamentary_Counsel_revised_guidance_16_ 12_11.pdf).

Office of Parliamentary Counsel 2011c *Working With Parliamentary Counsel* (London: Cabinet Office) (http://www.cabinetoffice.gov.uk/ sites/default/files/resources/WWPC_6_Dec_2011.pdf).

Olgiati, V. 1998 'Can Legal Ethics Become a Matter of Academic Teaching? Critical Observations from a Late-Modern Perspective' in Kim Economides, *Ethical Challenges to Legal Education and Conduct* (Oxford: Hart).

Ong K. and E. Yeung 2011 'Repos and Securities Lending: the Accounting Arbitrage and their Role in the Global Financial Crisis' 6(1) Capital Markets Law Journal 92–103.

Orozco, D. 2010 'Legal Knowledge as an Intellectual Property Management Resource' 47 American Business Law Journal 687–726.

Ottens, M. 2010 'The Limitations of Systems Engineering' in I. van de Poel, D. Goldberg, M. Davis (eds), *Philosophy and Engineering: An Emerging Agenda* (London: Springer).

Page, E. 2009 'Their Word is Law: Parliamentary Counsel and Creative Policy Analysis' [2009] Public Law 790–811.

Pahl, G., W. Beitz, J. Feldhusen and K.-H. Grote (K. Wallace and L. Blessing, translators) 2007 *Engineering Design: A Systematic Approach* 3rd edition (London: Springer).

Painter, R. 2012 'Transaction Cost Engineers, Loophole Engineers or Gatekeepers: The Role of Business Lawyers after the Financial Meltdown' in Brett McDonnell, *Research Handbook of the Economics of Corporate Law* (Cheltenham: Edward Elgar).

Parnell, G., P. Driscoll and D. Henderson 2010 *Decision Making in Systems Engineering and Management* (Hoboken, NJ, London: John Wiley).

Paulson, S. 2006 'On the Background and Significance of Gustav Radbruch's Post-War Papers' 26 Legal Studies 17–40.

Pinkus, R. 1997 *Engineering Ethics: Balancing Cost, Schedule, and Risk* (Cambridge: Cambridge U.P.).

Pitt, J. 1999 *Thinking about Technology: Foundations of the Philosophy of Technology* (New York: Seven Bridges Press).

Podgórecki, A. 1996 'Sociotechnics: Basic Issues and Concepts' in A. Podgórecki, J. Alexander and R. Shields, *Social Engineering* (Ottawa: Carleton U.P.).

Podgórecki, A., J, Alexander and R. Shields 1996 *Social Engineering* (Ottawa: Carleton U.P.).

Polanyi, M. 1960 *Personal Knowledge: Towards a Post Critical Philosophy* (London: Routledge).

Polanyi, M. 1967 *The Tacit Dimension* (New York: Anchor Books).

Poon, G. 2010 *The Corporate Counsel's Guide to Mediation* (Chicago, IL: ABA Publishing)

Popper, K. 1957 *The Poverty of Historicism* (London: Routledge).

Pound, R. 1922 *An Introduction to the Philosophy of Law* (New Haven, CT: Yale U.P.; London: Oxford U.P.).

Pound, R. 1923 *Interpretations of Legal History* (Cambridge: Cambridge U.P.).

Pound, R. 1942 *Social Control Through Law* (New Haven, CT: Yale U.P. New Brunswick: Transaction Publishers, 1997).

Pound, R. 1953 *The Lawyer from Antiquity to Modern Times* (St Paul, MN: West).

Pound, R. 1958 *The Ideal Element in Law* (Calcutta: University of Calcutta).

Powell, M. 1993 'Professional Innovation: Corporate Lawyers and Private Lawmaking' 18 Law & Social Inquiry 423–52.

Radbruch, G. 1932 *Rechtsphilosophie* (Heidelberg: Müller, 2011 [originally 1932]).

Radbruch, G. 1945 'Fünf Minuten Rechtsphilosophie' Rhein-Neckar Zeitung 12 September 1945, translated by B. Litschewski-Paulson and S. Paulson (2006) 26 Legal Studies 1–15.

Radbruch, G. 1946 'Gesetzliches Unrecht und übergesetzliches Recht' Süddeutsche Juristenzeitung (1946) I 105-8, translated by B. Litschewski-Paulson and S. Paulson (2006) 26 Legal Studies 1–15.

Rasmussen, J. 1997 'Risk Management in a Dynamic Society' 27 Safety Science 183–213.

Rawls, J. 1955 'Two Concepts of Rules' 64(1) Philosophical Review 3–32.

Rayner, J. 2011 'Solicitor wants forum for 'isolated' NHS lawyers' Law Society Gazette, 27 January 2011.

Rendel, M. 1970 *The Administrative Functions of the French Conseil d'Etat* (London: Weidenfeld and Nicolson).

Rhode, D. 1985 'Ethical Perspectives on Legal Practice' 37 Stanford Law Review 589–652.

Ribstein, L. 2010 'The Death of Big Law' [2010] (3) Wisconsin Law Review 749–815.

Ritchie, D. 1980 *James M. Landis: Dean of the Regulators* (Cambridge, MA: Harvard U.P.).

Rittel, H. and M. Webber 1969 'Dilemmas in a General Theory of Planning' 4 Policy Sciences 155–69.
Robson, P. 2006 'Lawyers and the Legal System on TV: the British experience' 2 International Journal of Law in Context 333–62.
Rogers, W. (chair) 1986 *Report of the Presidential Commission on the Space Shuttle Challenger Accident* (Washington, DC: NASA).
Rost, K., E. Inauen, M.Osterloh and B. Frey 2010 'The Corporate Governance of Benedictine Abbeys: What Can Stock Corporations Learn from Monasteries?' 16(1) Journal of Management History 90–115.
Ryan, T. and J. Bisson 2011 'Can Ethics be Taught?' 2 International Journal of Business and Social Science 12–52.
Sage A. and W. Rouse 2011 *Handbook of Systems Engineering and Mangement* (London: John Wiley).
Salvendy, G. (ed.) 2012 *Handbook of Human Factors Engineering and Ergonomics* 4th edition (Hoboken, NJ, London: John Wiley).
Sandel, M. 2012 *What Money Can't Buy: The Moral Limits of Markets* (London: Allen Lane)
Schlag, P. 1989 'Rules and Standards' 33 UCLA Law Review 379–430.
Schwarcz, S. 2007 'Explaining the Value of Transactional Lawyering,' 12 Stanford Journal of Law Business and Finance 486–535.
Shell, D. 2007 *The House of Lords* (Manchester: Manchester U.P.).
Shiller, R. 2012 *Finance and the Good Society* (Princeton, NJ: Princeton U.P.).
Silverman, G. 2012 'Law Games: the Importance of Virtual Worlds and Serious Video Games for the Future of Legal Education' in Edward Rubin, *Legal Education in the Digital Age* (Cambridge: Cambridge U.P.).
Simmonds, N. 1992 'Bluntness and Bricolage' in H. Gross and R. Harrison (eds), *Jurisprudence: Cambridge Essays* (Oxford: Oxford U.P.).
Simmonds, N. 2008 *Law as a Moral Idea* (Oxford: Oxford U.P.).
Simon, H. 1996 *Sciences of the Artificial* (Cambridge, MA: MIT Press).
Skyttner, L. 2001 *General Systems Theory: Ideas and Applications* (Singapore: World Scientific).
Snow, C.P. 1998 *The Two Cultures* (Cambridge: Cambridge U.P., repr. 1998).
Snyder, D. 2002 'Closing the Deal in Contracts – Introducing Transactional Skills in the First Year' 34 University of Toledo Law Review 689–697.
Sorkin, A. 2010 *Too Big to Fail* (London: Penguin).
Spice, B, 2000 'CMU's Simon reflects on how computers will continue to shape the world' Pittsburgh Post-Gazette, 16 October 2000.
Stallybrass, W.T. 1948 'Law in the Universities' [N.S.1] Journal of the Society of the Public Teachers of Law 157–169.

Stapleton, J. 1994 'In Restraint of Tort' in Peter Birks (ed.), The Frontiers of Liability vol. 2 (Oxford: Oxford U.P.).

Stark, T. 2004 'Thinking Like a Deal Lawyer' 54 Journal of Legal Education 223–234.

Stevens, R. 2007 *Torts and Rights* (Oxford: Oxford U.P.).

Stewart, H. 2010 'Lehman's advisers were guard dogs that didn't bark' The Observer 14 March 2010.

Stieb, J. 2008 'A Critique of Positive Responsibility in Computing' 14 Science and Engineering Ethics 219–33.

Stieb, J. 2009 'Response to Commentators of "A Critique of Positive Responsibility"' 15 Science and Engineering Ethics 11–18.

Strokoff, S 1996 'How Our Laws Are Made: A Ghost Writer's View' 59(2) The Philadelphia Lawyer, Philadelphia Bar Association Quarterly Magazine, expanded version available at http://www.house.gov/legcoun/strokoff.shtml#footnote1.

Suchman M. and M. Cahill 1996 'The Hired Gun as Facilitator: Lawyers and the Suppression of Business Disputes in Silicon Valley' 21 Law and Social Inquiry 679–712.

Suchman, M. 2000 'Dealmakers and Counselors: Law Firms as Intermediaries in the Development of Silicon Valley' in Martin Kenney, *Understanding Silicon Valley: the Anatomy of an Entrepreneurial Region* (Palo Alto, CA: Stanford U.P.).

Suh Nam-Pyo 1990 *The Principles of Design* (Oxford: Oxford U.P.).

Susskind, R. 2005 *The Susskind Interviews: Legal Experts in Changing Times* (London: Sweet and Maxwell).

Susskind, R. 2008 *The End of Lawyers? Rethinking the Nature of Legal Services* (Oxford: Oxford U.P.).

Tamanaha, B. 2006 *Law as a Means to an End: A Threat to the Rule of Law* (Cambridge: Cambridge U.P.).

Teichman, D. 2010 'Old Habits are Hard to Change: A Case Study of Israeli Real Estate Contracts' 44 Law and Society Review 299–330.

Teubner, G. (ed.) 1987 *Autopoietic Law: A New Approach to Law and Society* (Berlin/ New York: de Gruyter/ EUI).

Teubner, G. 2011 '"And God Laughed . . .": Indeterminacy, Self-Reference and Paradox in Law' 12 German Law Journal 376–406.

Thompson, D. 1980 'Moral Responsibility of Public Officials: The Problem of Many Hands' 74 American Political Science Review 905–15.

Thring, H. 1874 'The Simplification of the Law' (Jan 1874) 136(271) The Quarterly Review 55–74.

Tradewell, J. 2011 'The Power to do anything . . .' in Mirza Ahmad (ed.), *A Passion for Leadership & Going Beyond Austerity* (ACSeS).

Treverton, G. 2005 *Making Sense of Transnational Threats: Workshop Reports* (Santa Monica, CA: RAND).

Trivers, R. 2011 *Deceit and Self-Deception: Fooling Yourself the Better to Fool Others* (London: Penguin).

Türke, R.-E. 2008 *Governance: Systemic Foundation and Framework* (Heidelberg: Springer Physica Verlag).

Turner, A. 2009 *The Turner Review: A Regulatory Response to the Global Banking Crisis* (London: Financial Services Authority).

Tushnet, M. 1996 'Defending the Indeterminacy Thesis' 16 Quinnipiac Law Review 339–56.

Tversky, A. and D. Kahneman 1981 'The Framing of Decisions and the Psychology of Choice' 211(4481) Science 453–58.

Twining, W. 1967 'Pericles and the Plumber' 83 Law Quarterly Review 396.

Twining, W. 1973 *Karl Llewellyn and the Realist Movement* (London: Weidenfeld and Nicolson).

Twining, W. and D. Miers 2010 *How To Do Things With Rules: A Primer of Interpretation*, 5th edition (Cambridge: Cambridge U.P.).

Tyler, T. 2006 *Why People Obey the Law* 2nd edition (Princeton, NJ: Princeton U.P.).

Utset, M. 1995 'Producing Information: Initial Public Offerings, Production Costs and the Producing Lawyer' 74 Oregon Law Review 275–313.

Utset, M. 2012 'Designing Corporate Governance Regimes' 15 Journal of Applied Economy (http://ssrn.com/abstract=1810148.

Valukas, A. 2010 *Report of the Examiner in Bankruptcy in Re Lehman Brothers Holdings Inc.* (9 vols) US Bankruptcy Court, Southern District of New York.

Vermaas, P., P. Kroes, I. van de Poel, M. Franssen and W. Houkes 2011 *A Philosophy of Technology: From Technical Artefacts to Sociotechnical Systems* (Morgan and Claypool).

Vick, D. 2004 'Interdisciplinarity and the Discipline of Law' 31 Journal of Law and Society 163–93.

Vincenti, W. 1990 *What do Engineers Know and How do they Know It?* (Baltimore, MD: Johns Hopkins U.P.).

Waldron, J. 1999 *The Dignity of Legislation* (Cambridge: Cambridge U.P.).

Weidemaier, M. and M. Gulati, 2012 'How Markets Work: The Lawyer's Version' (http://works.bepress.com/mark_weidemaier/7).

Wendel, W.B. 2005 'Institutional and Individual Justification in Legal Ethics: The Problem of Client Selection' 34 Hofstra Law Review 987–1042.

White, G.E. 1972 'From Sociological Jurisprudence to Realism: Jurisprudence and Social Change in Early Twentieth-Century America' 58 Virginia Law Review 999–1028.

Wiener, M. 2004 English Culture and the Decline of the Industrial Spirit (Cambridge: Cambridge U.P.).

Wikeley, N. 2004 'The Law Degree and the BVC' (2004) The Reporter – The Newsletter of the Society of Legal Scholars 23–24.

Wikstrom, P.-O., D. Oberwittler, K. Treiber and B. Hardie 2012 *Breaking the Rules: The Social and Situational Dynamics of Young People's Urban Crime* (Oxford: Oxford U.P.).

Wood, D. 2006 'The Essential Characteristics of Resilience' in E. Hollnagel, D. Woods and N. Leveson, *Resilience Engineering: Concepts and Precepts* (Aldershot: Ashgate).

Wood, P. 2009 *Life after Lehman: Changes in Market Practice* (London: Allen and Overy).

Woolley, A. and S. Bagg 2007 'Ethics Teaching in Law School' 1 Canadian Legal Education Annual Review 85–114.

Wulf, W. 2004 'Engineering Ethics and Society' 28 Technology in Society 385–90.

Index